UNTHINKING COLLABORATION

UNTHINKING COLLABORATION

American Nisei in Transwar Japan

A. Carly Buxton

University of Hawai'i Press

Honolulu

To Rose

CONTENTS

ACKNOWLEDGMENTS

I extend my deepest gratitude first to the faculty and students of the University of Chicago. As a member of the Department of East Asian Languages and Civilizations, I benefitted from the direction of supportive professors and colleagues, especially my advisory committee, Professors James Ketelaar, Kyeong-Hee Choi, and Hoyt Long. Thank you also to Michael Bourdaghs and Susan Burns, and to the scholars in Japan and beyond who supported my work: Mark Caprio, Kayoko Takeda, Igarashi Akio, Komiya Mayumi, Kadoike Hiroshi, Marlene Mayo, Paul Spickard and the "Hui," Duncan Williams, Art Hansen, Jim Morishima, Puck Brecher, Michael Myers, and Ben Uchiyama. I am grateful to the participants of the Arts and Politics of East Asia Workshop, the Gender and Sexuality Studies Working Group, the Caprio *Zemi,* and the "Kamakura-bu," especially Joshua Solomon, Sonia Gomez, Robert Hegwood, Brian White, David Krolikoski, Alex Murphy, Helina Mazza-Hilway, Aliz Horvath, Paride Stortini, Chris Bovbjerg, Ender Ricart, Bill Feeney, Cameron Penwell, Andy Yamazaki, Katherine Alexander, Lindsey Conklin, Michael Chladek, Susan Menadue-Chen, Nakada Yukimi, Ellie Bae, Che Jung Sook, and Satō Makoto. This book would not have been possible without your thoughtful insights and moral support.

Over the years, I have received generous financial support from the University of Chicago, the Fulbright US Student Program, Toyota Foundation, the Terasaki Center for Japanese Studies at UCLA, University of Chicago's Center for the Study of Gender and Sexuality, the Association for Asian Studies, Columbia University Library's Research Awards Program, and the United States Department of Education. I thank Sarah Arehart, Dawn Brennan, Sarah Tuohey, Tate Brazas, and Jinko Brinkman for their help in securing and making the most of these funds.

I am grateful also to the individuals who have devoted their time and energy to support my research in museums, archives, volunteer groups, classrooms, and in their own homes. Thank you to Amy Wasserstrom and Kana Jenkins at the Gordon W. Prange Collection; the Densho Organization, especially Ruth Hara and Virginia Yamada; Ioka Kazue, Fujino Michiyo, Miyabata Keisuke, and the members of the Heiwa no Katari Be in Shinjuku Ward; Ishioka Yoshiko of the Tokyo Metropolitan Institute of Gerontology; the National Nikkei Museum and Heritage Center; Matsumoto Shōgo and Kuzuhara Kazumi at the Yūshūkan; Kunugihi Hiroyuki of the Okinawa Prefectural Peace Memorial Museum; Morizumi Keita of 1945; Satō Ari and the faculty at the Inter-University Center; Nakatani Tomoki and Kusada Kenji of the Wakayama Civic Library; Fukubayashi Tōru and the POW Research Network; Yamaguchi Takayuki of the Heiwakinen; Araki Seiji of the Hiroshima Prefectural Archives; Hamamura Yoshiko of NPO Meiku Mirakuruzu; Murakami Keiko of the NHK Broadcasting Cultural Research Institute; Aruka Miwako of Tokyo Women's Christian University; and the staff at the Melrose Public Library in Melrose, Massachusetts. Special thanks go to Paula S. Brown, Ellen F. Brown, Stephanie Chun, Marc Miyake, and Masako Ikeda for the valuable editing guidance they provided; Read Brown for archival assistance; and Nobuko Gerth, Iwao Peter Sano, Rose Tsunekawa, Emiko Sawada, and all of my other interview subjects. I am deeply moved by your generosity and your interest in this scholarship.

Finally, I give thanks to my family and to my dear friends for the years of steadfast encouragement that made this book possible. And to my husband Garrett, my unwavering supporter throughout this entire journey: thank you.

Author's Note

The Japanese word *nisei* (二世) means "second generation." Throughout this book, the word is stylized as "Nisei," referring to the generational group of individuals born to Japanese immigrants, predominantly in North and South America and the islands of the Pacific, in the late nineteenth and early twentieth century. This study focuses almost exclusively on the lives of American Nisei, though the transwar experiences of Nisei born in other "new worlds" would certainly make for an interesting project. American-born Nisei were all citizens of the United States due to the US Constitution's birthright citizenship policy. And as a result of the early twentieth-century immigration patterns from Japan to America, this second generation was rather sharply demarcated. Generally speaking, Nisei were born in America from around the turn of the twentieth century through the 1920s. They were youth and young adults during the years of World War II, middle-aged when the occupation era faded into the years of Japan's "Economic Miracle," and senior citizens when sharing their stories in the late twentieth and early twenty-first century. In public discourse both in Japan and America, they were a group—a unit with shared traits and challenges—and many considered themselves as bound by this category of "Nisei" and its ancillary stereotypes and assumptions, much as "Millennials," for example, are bound cognitively today.

A note on naming: public figures in this book—government officials, scholars, politicians, and the like—are referred to by their given names and surnames at first mention, and then subsequently by their surnames. In contrast, the Nisei and Japanese subjects whose individual stories serve as access points to transwar Japan, including those who serve as interlocutors in the book through oral histories, letters, and memoirs, are referred to by their given names alone upon second mention and thereafter. This is by design and is intended to bring the reader nearer to the physical and discursive environment of these individuals in their moment of action and of retelling. The names of Japanese people in this book appear in their original order, with surnames first, with the exception of Japan-born individuals who published in English and Nisei, whose names appear in the order of "Western" names.

All translations provided in this book, except where otherwise noted, are my own.

Introduction

San Francisco, 1949: In a striking illustration of the power of public opinion to sway judgment in a court of law, Los Angeles-born Nisei ("second-generation" Japanese American) Iva Toguri was found guilty of treason and sentenced to ten years in prison. One of several young Nisei women mobilized by the Japanese government to portray the propaganda paramour "Tokyo Rose" on Radio Tokyo's wartime programming, Iva alone was tried and convicted, the scapegoat of anti-Japanese sentiment and victor-vanquished aggression. The San Francisco trial—and the mass media extravaganza accompanying it—would codify in American public opinion an unsavory paradigm of the Nisei Japanese American female: traitor, spy, and scheming seductress.

But what of the other "Roses," the thousands of American Nisei who, like Iva, had remained in Japan either by choice or by unforeseen circumstance throughout the years of conflict with the United States? Although the whims of sensational journalism did not assign these individuals the toxic moniker "Tokyo Rose," they, too, had contributed to the Japanese empire's war effort alongside members of the Japanese populace during the war.

An estimated thirty-five thousand American-born Nisei, or one-third of the entire American Nisei population, were living in Japan as of 1942.[1] And whereas white American citizens in Japan were mostly sent home on repatriation ships or sequestered into government encampments after the attack on Pearl Harbor, American citizens of Japanese descent were expected to carry on their daily lives as Japanese subjects (albeit under the watchful eye of the special police), regardless of whether or not they possessed dual Japanese citizenship. As the fighting continued and living conditions in Japan deteriorated, Nisei students in Japan were mobilized alongside their Japanese classmates to assist with the war effort, building the instruments of war that would be used against their former American neighbors and friends—and, in many instances, their own relatives. Able-bodied Nisei men were conscripted into the Japanese military, and Nisei with advanced English skills like Iva Toguri were called to support the war effort as cryptographers, propagandists, and interpreters.

1

Tens of thousands of American-born Nisei living in Japan participated along-side their Japanese neighbors on the battlefield and on the home front during the years of total war (1941–1945), ever the target of anti-American propaganda and suspicion. When the dust of air raid bombings cleared and the Supreme Commander for the Allied Powers (SCAP) assumed command in Japan, many of these same Nisei transitioned into roles in service of the Allied occupation. As censors, translators, interpreters, and administrative staff, they played integral roles in facilitating American-Japanese interaction, as well as in shaping policies and public opinion in the postwar era. These were the same Nisei who had been on the receiving end of anti-American propaganda campaigns during the war, a time when higher education "coursework" consisted of fire drills, farming, and cryptography work programs more often than reading, writing, and arithmetic.

Most of the scholarly literature on wartime Japanese American history has dealt with the internment struggles of people of Japanese ancestry in the United States. In more recent years, researchers have turned to the contributions made by Nisei to the American military cause as translators, interpreters, and on the battlefield.[2] Nisei journalists Kazumaro "Buddy" Uno and Bill Hosokawa have received peripheral attention through the works of scholars Yuji Ichioka and Greg Robinson, and a growing field of literature examines the symbolic power of Nisei dual identity to promote reconciliation and to deter the spread of communism in the postwar era.[3] But overwhelmingly, the familiarity of English-language publications regarding Nisei *in Japan* during the war stretches only as far as the legend of Tokyo Rose.[4]

The wartime experiences of American Nisei mobilized for the Japanese war effort against the country of their birth remain largely untold. This is perhaps because their stories complicate the dominant narrative of Japanese American loyalty and patriotism in the face of racial prejudice and mistrust—a narrative that served in the postwar era to promote healing and shift the public conversation from the wrongs of mass incarceration. This book shares the stories of these Nisei in transwar Japan—not to suggest that race-based confinement was at all justified, but rather to unpack the complexities of "collaboration" more broadly. A closer look into the everyday lives, education, opportunities, social expectations, and treatment of Nisei in transwar Japan sheds light on the nature of loyalty, the power of propaganda, and the flexibility of cultural identity.

Iva Toguri: The One and Original Tokyo Rose?

Iva Toguri, a California-born American citizen and UCLA graduate, sailed to Japan in July of 1941 to look after a sick aunt, planning tentatively to return home to California the following spring. She moved into her relatives' home in Setagaya, a suburb of Tokyo, and enrolled in Japanese language courses at the Matsumiya Nihongo Bunka Gakkō. As tension mounted between Japan and the United States in the fall of 1941, Iva and her traveling companion (a fellow Californian Nisei named Chieko Ito) attempted to arrange for a passage home, but because they did not hold the proper passport and immigration papers, both Iva and Chieko were unable to return to the United States before the attack on Pearl Harbor halted all passenger traffic. As a result, Iva would face the years of war on Japanese soil, completely severed from all communication with her mother, father, brother, and two sisters on the other side of the Pacific Ocean.[5]

In the early months of war, in response to persistent visits to her relatives' home by the increasingly forceful special police, Iva decided that she could no longer be a burden to her aunt and uncle. She moved into a boarding house and started looking for employment to finance her new situation. With the help of a student friend, Iva found a job in the Monitoring Division of the Domei News Agency at Atago Hill, listening to shortwave radio broadcasts by the Allies and sending reports to the agency's central office. She was the only female among more than 100 applicants for the Domei position, almost all of them Nisei.[6] At Domei, Iva's coworkers included Nisei from various parts of North America, as well as mixed-race individuals like Felipe d'Aquino, a Yokohama-born, part-Japanese Portuguese citizen who would become Iva's husband in the final months of the war.[7]

In the late summer of 1943, Iva saw an ad in the *Nippon Times* calling for English-language typists at Radio Tokyo. She responded by postcard, took an employment exam, and got the job. She reported to work on August 23, 1943, at Radio Tokyo as a typist in the administrative section of the American Division of the Overseas Bureau at Nippon Hōsō Kyōkai (the Japan Broadcasting Corporation, NHK). In time, Iva transitioned into an on-air role as "Orphan Ann," a radio personality on an English-language program called *Zero Hour,* Radio Tokyo's shortwave broadcast created to demoralize English-speaking soldiers stationed in the Pacific. Working alongside Allied prisoners of war, she introduced jazz and classical records, delivered news headlines designed to dishearten soldiers far from home, shared messages from POWs, and lightheartedly taunted her listeners about sweethearts thousands of miles away who had no doubt strayed in their affections.

By late 1945, the Broadcasting Section's Radio Room employed about fifty monitors, including Nisei journalists who worked for Japanese press outlets, such as the Tokyo-based *Nippon Times,* and students who took classes during the day at a government school known as the Heishikan and worked night shifts in the Radio Room.[8] There were at least twenty English-speaking women employed at Radio Tokyo during the war, including several Nisei.[9] Iva was just one of dozens of female workers at NHK who likely assisted in the delivery of *Zero Hour* broadcasts—a group that included California-born Katherine Kei Fujiwara, Katherine Kaoru Morooka, and Miyeko Furuya, as well as half-Japanese women and Japanese women educated abroad.[10] But in late August 1945, when Allied journalists flooded into defeated Japan eager to get "the scoop" on the identity of "Tokyo Rose" whose English-language broadcasts had been a favorite of English-speaking soldiers in the Pacific, the staff at the Overseas Bureau of NHK eventually pointed to Iva as the famous siren. American reporters Clark Lee and Harry Brundidge offered Iva $2,000—an exorbitant sum in war-shattered 1945 Japan—for an exclusive interview for *Cosmopolitan* magazine. Iva was at first reluctant to give an interview, explaining to the reporters that she was only one of many female announcers at Radio Tokyo, but on September 1 in the Imperial Hotel in downtown Tokyo, she signed her name to a document drawn up by Brundidge on behalf of *Cosmopolitan,* declaring herself "the one and original 'Tokyo Rose' who had broadcasted from Radio Tokyo." The fruits of their four-hour interview were splashed on the pages of American newspapers within a few days, and Iva rode a wave of celebrity, responding playfully to rapid-fire questions at a press conference overflowing with international journalists, and mugging for the camera at a staged press shoot recreating her *Zero Hour* news desk for the Eighth Army.

Figure I.1. Correspondents interview "Tokyo Rose" in September 1945. Courtesy National Archives, photo no. 520994.

The tenor of her celebrity took a sour turn in weeks, however, and on October 17, Iva was arrested by officers of the Allied Counter Intelligence Corps on suspicion of wartime treason for her work on the broadcasts. She was transferred to Sugamo Prison in the Ikebukuro district of Tokyo, where she was held until the following October, when the War Department, concluding that they lacked the evidence to prosecute her for treason, cabled for her release. At that point, Iva might have faded into history with no further fanfare, but in August 1947, news of her intention to move back to the United States leaked to the press, and the American public went into uproar. Swayed by public opinion and mounting fears of treason in the delicate climate of the immediate postwar, the Justice Department arranged for Iva's arrest in Tokyo and extradited her to San Francisco where she was convicted of treason against the United States and sentenced to ten years in prison and a fine of $10,000.

Iva—"the one and original 'Tokyo Rose'"—was instead merely the one "Rose" plucked from a garden of thousands. At least three other American Nisei were known to have performed precisely the same work at Radio Tokyo as Iva, and tens of thousands of other American Nisei were mobilized by government programs, inspired by propaganda campaigns, and motivated by economic necessity to participate in the war effort in a host of diverse capacities. Only two other American Nisei gained blips of press attention for wartime acts performed against the United States, and the buzz of their cautionary tales never rivaled that of Tokyo Rose. The first was California-born Tomoya Kawakita, a dual US-Japanese citizen who had worked as an interpreter at a POW camp in Japan. Claiming that his wartime work had been the result of duress, Kawakita was able to return to the United States after the end of the war. In 1946, however, he was spotted in a Los Angeles department store by William L. Bruce, a former prisoner who identified Kawakita as the guard "Meatball," a particularly abusive tyrant from his days as a POW in Japan. Bruce reported Kawakita to the FBI, and in September of 1948, Kawakita was convicted of treason and sentenced to death, but was later paroled and deported to Japan by President John F. Kennedy. One other notorious (though little-remembered) Nisei who was known to have actively supported the Japanese war effort was Kazumaro "Buddy" Uno, an Oakland-born civilian journalist for the Japanese press bureau. In May 1945, he was taken prisoner by Filipino guerrillas and was held by US forces in Manila. Buddy was eventually released and never attempted to return to the US or to reinstate his lost US citizenship. He was never tried for treason.[11]

Two Canadian Nisei also made headlines after Japan's surrender for their contributions to the Japanese war effort. The first, Kanao Inouye, was a British

Columbia-born Nisei who was living in Japan when war broke out. He was conscripted into the Japanese Army, where he served as an interpreter and prison camp guard in the Japanese Army, and later as an officer of the Kempeitai special police. When the war ended, Inouye was tried for treason in Hong Kong, where testimony relayed his brutal torture of POWs and suspected traitors. He was found guilty and was executed by hanging in August of 1947.[12] The second Canadian Nisei, ex-Lance Corporal Toyokazu Hikita originally of Vancouver, Canada, was sentenced to four years in prison for his work questioning POWs as an interpreter for the Japanese Military Police Headquarters in Tokyo, though his demise left almost no trace in the press.[13]

Far eclipsing the fates of these other Nisei in terms of public attention, the sensational downfall of Iva Toguri provided a point of collective catharsis through which anxieties over the cultural ambiguity of American Nisei could be mediated in the postwar era. And yet, absorbed within the dramatization of Iva's public persecution were the stories of thousands of other American Nisei in Japan who had also weathered the years of total war in Japan. Iva Toguri's infamy has overshadowed the tumultuous experiences of these Nisei whose actions contributed to the imperial war effort. Indeed, the storied legacy of Tokyo Rose and her treason trial has cast a moral judgment on all Nisei who lived in Japan during the war—Nisei whose experiences were diverse, ranging from volunteer military service to conscription, from propaganda dissemination to forced labor at munitions factories. It is the stories of those other Nisei that fill the pages of this book.

During the years of World War II, as Iva Toguri was bantering with Allied prisoners of war over the airwaves of the Pacific, the thousands of Nisei living in Japan had little means of discovering what had become of their friends and family members back in the United States. Some were able to receive a rare communication from the Red Cross, and some heard or read reports in Japanese newspapers about the plight of Japanese immigrant families interned in the American heartland. For the most part, however, when the attack on Pearl Harbor halted all passenger ships between Japan and the US, the expansive transnational network of people and ideas that characterized the Japanese diaspora was severed, and Nisei in Japan had no option but to endure the years of war as members of the Japanese populace. They faced the challenges of total war—food and supply shortages, air raid drills, conscription, and labor mobilization—alongside their Japanese neighbors, uncertain if they would ever see their friends and family in America again. The ways in which these Nisei navigated their environment—how they found food and shelter, continued their education, related to their fellow Nisei and to Japanese society, and altered their bodies in order to

Figure I.2. Iva Toguri at Sugamo Prison in Tokyo, March 7, 1946. Courtesy National Archives, photo no. 296677.

survive—shed light on the factors that shaped the behavior and self-representation of Nisei in Japan during and after World War II.

As Iva's trial played out in news media across the globe after Japan's surrender, other Nisei who had supported the Japanese war effort distanced themselves from the image of the famous traitor, many of them transitioning into roles serving the Allied occupation. The striking contrast of the fate of the "one and original 'Tokyo Rose'" with that of other American Nisei in Japan—a veritable garden of "Roses"—inspired this book. At Iva's trial, the defense team painted her as an unwaveringly loyal American who had risked severe punishment by smuggling food, medicine, blankets, and war news to the Allied POWs who shared her broadcast desk. But the Court's ruling stated that these moments of compassion for individual prisoners could not discount or disprove Iva's "general treasonable intent to betray the United States."[14] Meanwhile, individual American courts were processing citizenship reinstatements of thousands of American Nisei men and women who were petitioning to return to the United States. Why were these other American Nisei who had been mobilized for the war effort not similarly maligned for "betraying" the United States? And what were the factors that motivated these Nisei to cooperate so flexibly with the Japanese war effort during the war and with the Allied occupation after Japan's defeat? The answers to these questions—explored throughout this book—hinge on the complexities of bicul-turalism, the power of propaganda, and the war as remembered.

A Transwar, Trans-Disciplinary Rethinking of Collaboration

In the age of decolonization and post-colonialism, significant scholarly attention has been directed to analyzing "collaboration" during World War II, both in Nazi Europe and across the Japan-led Greater East Asia Co-Prosperity Sphere. The specter of "pro-Japanese" collaboration through the years of Japan's colonial expansion continues to haunt in histories of the former colonies and occupied territories of Korea, Hong Kong, Shanghai, Manchukuo, and Taiwan, as scholars wrestle with the complexities of navigating this fraught history and the moral judgment inherently implicated. In South Korea, the issue of pro-Japanese col-laboration remains further complicated by the legacy of the Korean War and American hegemony, as US occupying forces relied on ex-colonialists—who tended to hail from elite ranks—in their efforts to combat the encroaching threat of communism. Those elites scrambled to recast their self-narratives, obfuscat-ing wartime support of the Japanese empire as they clung to power—in many cases only to be satirized or even made pariahs amid the South Korean national-ist movements of the late 1960s and beyond.[15]

Overwhelmingly in studies of pro-Japanese cooperation across Japan's colo-nial empire, collaboration is a dirty word, tagged as a moral failure, an antonym to patriotism, a pejorative shorthand for treason. Bound by the term's inherent moral judgment, historians tend either to malign their collaborators as traitors who found themselves on the wrong side of history, or attempt to exonerate them by seeking evidence of hidden subversion or lack of alternative options. In more recent years, scholars have endeavored to look earnestly at collaboration, to un-derstand the actions of collaborators in a way that suspends judgment and es-chews a moral register. This is a welcome first step in understanding treason and loyalty more deeply. And yet, when historians place inordinate stock in free will, in a historical subject's ability to *choose* the path of supporting the enemy, the subjects become calculating, weighing benefits and losses, making conscious de-cisions to betray their race, betray their nation, or betray their family. Timothy Brook's *Collaboration: Japanese Agents and Local Elites in Wartime China*, for example, is a foundational work that makes bold strides in interrogating the ap-plications and implications of the term "collaboration." Brook evaluates the fac-tors that motivated Chinese local elites to facilitate Japanese occupation in wartime China, and though he implores his readers to suspend judgment on these historical players, his reverberating emphasis on active, conscious choice makes it difficult to do so: his subjects "came forward" to collaborate; they consciously and intentionally "threw their lot in with the invader;" they showed "a willingness to go along with the way things were;" and they made a "decision to *hezuo*, or cooperate, with the powers that be . . . through complex calculation of the benefits and losses that individuals thought they could decipher at the time."[16]

This emphasis on conscious *choice*, on *calculation*—this is not how the human brain works in a moment. In recent years, cognitive neuroscientists have shown the power of the unconscious brain to shape behavior. The way humans act, the way they represent themselves, and the decisions they make: these are manifestations of a brain that processes more than ninety-five percent of perceptions, preferences, and feelings below the threshold of consciousness.[17] That *effort*, that *intention* that we think of as part of collaboration—that's the five percent. We can't understand human actions—much less judge them—by only looking to five percent of a given story. To understand collaboration, we must not only distance the term "collaboration" itself from moral judgment. We must also resist our natural inclination to analyze the actions of collaborators as conscious, rational choices. We must "unthink" collaboration: divorce our understanding of it from direct conflation with conscious thought alone, and unearth the environmental and situational realities that deserve to be considered alongside "decisions" and "choices." In probing for the environmental, situational, and discursive realities that fostered nonresistance and cooperation among a colonized minority, we distance ourselves further still from the flat, morality-saturated understanding of "collaboration," and we pay respect to the power of the subconscious ("unthinking") mind to shape action.

To this end, *Unthinking Collaboration* explores as "collaborators" all Nisei whose efforts (voluntary or not) supported the Japanese war effort during the years of World War II, as well as those whose efforts supported the Allied occupation in the postwar era, in order to emphasize that complicity, nonresistance, and even active support of a colonizing power are manifestations of multiple, fractured behavioral motivations beyond choice alone. In exploring Nisei as "colonized," I interpret colonization as a process more subtle than external colonization (checked against the boundaries of nations on a map), but rather internal, where the minority group is distinguishable from the majority by some other variable, such as race, religion, language, or some other element of culture. The chapters that follow examine the everyday lives of Nisei in transwar Japan, seeking the factors that motivated their support for Japan during the war—as well as their contributions to the Allied occupation after Japan's defeat. In exploring the actions of these Nisei—the conscripts as well as the volunteers, the children as well as the adults—as "collaboration," *Unthinking Collaboration* represents an endeavor to question our understanding of collaboration itself. I have chosen specifically to use the word "collaboration," rather than less contentious terms such as "cooperation" or "nonresistance," precisely to bring back to the table of consideration all those who have written histories that elide collaboration with conscious decision-making and moral weakness. For as David Joel Steinberg reminds us in his study of Philippine collaboration during World War II, "Not everyone can go into exile or join a guerrilla band . . . Allegiance cannot be turned on and off like a spigot . . . somehow it must be reconciled with the need to survive."[18] The key to rethinking collaboration while reconciling it with the need to survive is to deemphasize the role of conscious choice, emphasizing instead the myriad other elements that guide human behavior: ideals and taboos in the physical and discursive environment, threats of discipline and violence, the pull of complicated personal relationships, and the visceral human drive to thrive.

To be clear, rescuing the term "collaboration" from its pejorative connotation is not the primary aim of this book. Nor is it my intention to malign or even call into question the actions of Nisei who, whether by circumstance or of their own volition, contributed to the Japanese war effort. My goals for *Unthinking Collaboration* are twofold: first, to draw attention to the history of American Nisei who lived in Japan in the years before, during, and after World War II. This study traces not only the factors that influenced Nisei behavior in their historical moment, but also the conscious and subconscious acrobatics of self-representation through which Nisei rationalized, represented, and atoned for their alignment with the Japanese war effort and, later, the Allied occupation. Their little-known stories emphasize the heterogeneity of Japanese immigrant experiences, and shed light on broader issues of identity, race, and performance of individuals growing up in a bicultural or multicultural context, providing lessons for America's society today.

The second goal of this book is to achieve a more nuanced understanding of loyalty and treason by approaching Nisei collaboration as deeply imbedded in the context of immigration history, Japan's wartime policies and total war environment, and war memory, as well as by engaging in a historical practice that takes into consideration key principles of how the human brain shapes behavior in a given moment. To that end, *Unthinking Collaboration* is a historical study that incorporates principles from diverse disciplines including anthropology, sociology, and psychology, such as hindsight bias, the power of material culture to shape popular beliefs, and the role of the subconscious in guiding action. As economic historian Marc Bloch wrote in his classic work *The Historian's Craft*,

"The first duty of the historian who would understand and explain [people from another time] will be to return them to their milieu, where they are immersed in the mental climate of their time and faced by problems of conscience rather different from our own."[19] This effort must entail not only reproducing the actions and statements of historical individuals, but also recreating and acknowledging as influential their physical and discursive environment, their visceral anxieties and aspirations, and the ideals and taboos of their time. It is inspiring to imagine what an interdisciplinary approach could do to advance our understanding of human behavior in the field of history, but readers should bear in mind that this is not a data-driven psychological survey, and that its writer is a historian, not a psychologist or sociologist. *Unthinking Collaboration* is not written for sociologists and psychologists, though its emphasis on subconscious impetuses in historiography must rely on their methods and discoveries. This book offers an alternative approach to history, one that presents insights from adjacent subject fields and encourages the reader to consider these principles as a way to add new dimensions to their understanding of individuals navigating a historical environment.

With these two goals in mind, I have designed *Unthinking Collaboration* to attract diverse audiences from multiple fields of interest. It is primarily a work of historical practice, shaped by my personal background as a historian specializing in East Asian studies, specifically Japan's empire-building endeavors. Although I approach the research as a specialist in Japan studies rather than Asian American studies, *Unthinking Collaboration* must begin by tracing the history of Japanese American immigration to the United States as a necessary root for understanding the experiences of Nisei in Japan. This book represents an effort to deemphasize divisions between Asian studies and Asian American studies, to inspire other perspectives on what we might discover as we blur the lines between these two fields. My hope is that this book speaks to readers who are interested in broader questions of race and trust, empire-building, World War II and its legacy on both the Western and Pacific fronts, and to all who consider questions of loyalty, treason, assimilation, and collaboration.

The everyday lives of Nisei in transwar Japan are at the heart of this analysis, but to recreate the cacophony of Japanese society in the tumultuous transwar period, this book incorporates perspectives shared by Nisei on both sides of the Pacific, by their Issei ("first generation") parents, by Japanese citizens, and by non-Japanese Americans. Readers will share the experiences of coping with dual loyalties and with war hardships such as food and clothing shortages, destruction of home and family, the threat of the enemy, and the grief of mourning. In addition to archival resources such as immigration records, photographs, secondary research, and newspaper articles, I rely on personal accounts—oral histories, autobiographies, and essays—as resources for investigating these lived experiences. Most of the oral histories draw from five major collections: the Densho Digital Repository, the Marlene J. Mayo Oral Histories at the Gordan W. Prange Collection, the Occupation of Japan Project at the Columbia University Oral History Collection, Tomi Kaizawa Knaefler's *Our House Divided: Seven Japanese American Families in World War II,* and my own personal interviews with both Japanese and Nisei war survivors, conducted over a period of approximately two years in the US and in Japan.[20] The autobiographies and essays include those written by Nisei as well as by other Americans who lived in transwar Japan; some were written during or immediately after the experiences they describe, and others are separated from their historical moments by decades and are therefore even more complicated by the politics of memory. The fabric of all of these personal impressions reveals the everyday experiences of Nisei in Japan during the 1920s–1940s and provides insight into mid-century changes to Nisei mobility, opportunity, roles in society, and self-perception.

Combining personal histories with archival data, *Unthinking Collaboration* asks: what do we see when we "walk beside" these Nisei in the space of their daily activities? What do we understand about loyalty and identity as we uncover how they reflected on their experiences in the context of the discursive resources available to them? This book pursues the answers to those questions by illustrating the ways Nisei women, men, and children across the Japanese empire negotiated their everyday concerns and demands in the context of the projections of "Nisei," of "Japanese," and of "American" provided to them in their immediate surroundings.

This book pieces together the storylines of American Nisei in Japan as a means to clarify the processes by which politically or socially dominant ("hegemonic") ideals inspire behavior. It probes the stories shared by Nisei, both male and female, seeking the discursive and material elements that shaped racial, gender, and ethnic identity in their lives as schoolchildren and young adults both in the US and in Japan. It highlights the efforts of both the Issei community in America and politicians and intellectuals in Japan to mold the young people of the second generation as model citizens. It investigates how Nisei like Iva Toguri came to serve the Japanese government during the war, and it follows the lives of these Nisei throughout the occupation years during which many utilized their English language skills to earn a living by working for American companies and the American government.

To illuminate collaboration as something more than just shorthand for "treason," but rather as a process of behavior regulation, this book focuses on the self-regulation and self-representation of Nisei in transwar Japan as inspired by the historical realities of their physical and discursive environment. How were Nisei in transwar Japan prompted by their environment to regulate their bodies in movement, appearance, expression, and action? And how did the tenor of social discourse, in turn, shape the ways Nisei reflected upon their actions as indicative of (or divorced from) cultural identity, gender roles, and the direction of their loyalty? Weaving archival data with oral histories, personal narratives, material culture, and fiction, *Unthinking Collaboration* aims to recreate the environment of everyday life in transwar Japan, offering a space in which to reimagine collaboration as a process of assimilation wherein an individual both consciously and subconsciously regulates her behavior, appearance, and expression in order to survive and thrive.

One further methodological note to bear in mind while reading this book is the term "transwar" that appears throughout the chapters. This term is meant to emphasize the importance of prewar elements that laid the foundations for the Nisei community in Japan, and to underscore the parallel nature of Nisei collaboration during and after the war. "Transwar" indicates the seepage of an event (such as a war) beyond the years accepted as binding that event, gesturing thereby to what literary theorist Jonathan Abel describes as "a mode of thinking that works against the rhetorical constraints underlying most uses of periodization."[21] Through the use of this transwar lens, *Unthinking Collaboration* approaches the experiences of American Nisei in Japan as a story of continuity by examining the everyday lives, education, opportunities, social expectations, and treatment of Nisei in Japan throughout the prewar years, the years of war, and the Allied occupation.

Unthinking Collaboration examines the foundations and realities of Nisei collaboration in transwar Japan in three roughly chronological parts. Part One seeks to understand collaboration vis-à-vis ethnic ambiguity by investigating how Nisei living in America and Japan before World War II were cued by their environment to consider their identities as separately Japanese and American, and as inherently problematic in that cultural dualism. Part Two complicates collaboration by evaluating the regulatory impact of propaganda and disciplinary forces in the everyday environment. It probes for cultural performance in the lives of Nisei in wartime Japan, illuminating the economic and physical realities of war as experienced by women and children on the Japanese home front, and by young men serving as soldiers. Part Three questions collaboration in light of changing anxieties and hegemonies in occupied postwar Japan, highlighting the significance of memory and emotion in the public representation of collaboration, tracing the ways Nisei processed and represented their alignment with the war effort. The concluding chapter theorizes more broadly on the value of re-imagining collaboration, of questioning the meaning of "volition" and "coercion" deemed so central to judgments of treason in the years after World War II. As the conclusion suggests, this nuanced unthinking of collaboration not only offers insight into the challenges faced by Nisei in transwar Japan, but also offers lessons for addressing similar issues of treason and loyalty in today's complicated, multicultural world.

Through attention to everyday life, *Unthinking Collaboration* seeks to understand the capacity of hegemonic ideals for behavior and appearance to shape the actions of Nisei as individuals amid the heightened emotional environment of anxiety, grief, uncertainty, and fear during the years of war and occupation. It draws focus to the process of assimilation: the ways in which a minor subject (here, a Nisei) both consciously and subconsciously aligns his behavior, appearance, and speech with those of a hegemon in order to survive and thrive—to achieve positive affect, to quell dissonance.[22] By breaking down the modes through which promulgated ideals cultivate aspirations in individuals to change their behavior and appearance, the chapters that follow bring to life not only the emotional experiences of Nisei in wartime and postwar Japan, but also a clearer picture of the psychological functions of propaganda in encouraging obedience and cultural assimilation.

When we appreciate the immediacy of economic and familial demands, the power of surveillance, and the influence of propaganda on the self-representation of American Nisei in transwar Japan, we begin to understand that "treason" and "loyalty" are labels applied subsequently—and therefore anachronistically—to a historical moment. Collaboration makes manifest the power of the physical and discursive environment to sculpt individuals' emotions, behavior, and cultural performance. Iva Toguri was one of thousands of Nisei collaborators in transwar Japan. Her sensational saga and their forgotten ones underscore that to understand any historical subject, we must layer their words and deeds with the ideals and taboos of their physical environment. We must look to their zeitgeist as a whole, to the social discourse of their moment in time, scanning for that which inspired behavior on the subconscious level. By excavating the everyday lives, education, opportunities, social expectations, and treatment of Nisei in transwar Japan—as lived and remembered—*Unthinking Collaboration* aims to achieve a more nuanced understanding of collaboration, assimilation, and the ambiguities of loyalty and treason.

PART I

Prewar

CHAPTER ONE

Sojourner, Alien, Ambassador

The prewar and wartime experiences of Chiyo Tanaka—"Muriel" to her English-speaking friends—parallel strikingly the experiences of "Tokyo Rose" Iva Toguri. Born in 1921 and raised in Hawai'i, Muriel was an American citizen with Japanese immigrant parents. Like most Nisei children of Japanese descent in her community, she attended extracurricular Japanese language and culture lessons in addition to her American public education. She spoke English at school and Japanese at home, and her mother, who later became principal of the local Japanese school, taught her Japanese-style flower arrangement, sewing, and handicrafts. Muriel might have continued in this bilingual, bicultural lifestyle familiar to the Japanese American community in Hawai'i had it not been for her family's decision in 1939 to send her to Japan for a gall bladder condition requiring special medical attention. After recovering from a brief and successful treatment, Muriel stayed on with relatives in Tokyo, attending classes at Women's Art College and greatly enjoying newfound friendships with her fellow students.

War with the United States, however, intervened. Recommended to the Japanese authorities by her uncle after the attack on Pearl Harbor, Muriel was recruited to work for Japan's secret army division, monitoring and translating English-language broadcasts for the military alongside several other Nisei young men and women. As Muriel explained in a 2010 interview, the army employed Japanese nationals who had graduated from colleges in America to listen to and type the broadcasts, but they relied on native English-speaking Nisei like Muriel to clarify the messages and explain exactly what was happening. "I was the highest paid employee with English monitoring, for eighty-one *yen* a month," Muriel remembered. "We were very lucky because the Japanese government, Japanese soldiers, they went and confiscated whatever food they needed." Muriel weathered the years of war on a relatively comfortable salary, and despite rationing and food shortages in cities across Japan, she was never short on nourishment, thanks to the Japanese army's penchant for requisitioning the yields of local farmers for military use. And as Muriel was rushing off translations to her superiors—"150 fighter planes just left Saipan, and they're headed for Korea or they're headed for Yokohama . . ."—so that they might plan their maneuvers accordingly, her own brother was providing similar intelligence to the opposing side as a Military Intelligence Service recruit in the United States Army.

Only after Japan's defeat do the fates of Iva Toguri and Muriel Tanaka dramatically splinter. When the fighting ended, Muriel recalled, she felt "so happy" to hear the emperor's announcement of surrender on the radio. A few months later, she was delighted to spend time with her brother and his American GI friends who arrived in Japan as part of the occupation forces with whom she shared laughs, meals, and lessons about Japanese culture. She reestablished her American citizenship and was among the American citizens repatriated in 1947 on a US troop ship to Hawai'i. When Muriel saw the Hawaiian Islands in the distance from the deck of the *General Gordon,* she felt "home."[1]

The sharply contrasting fates of Iva Toguri and Muriel Tanaka underscore that the accurate performance of ideals—cultivated by the preferences of a historical moment—would determine the destiny of Nisei in transwar Japan. To consider Nisei behavior during the transwar period as deeply implicated in these preferences is to achieve a more nuanced understanding of "collaboration" itself: as moments of self-representation shaped by ideals and taboos in the physical and discursive environment.

To "unthink" collaboration is to appreciate the power of norms to shape behavior on a subconscious level. As paradigms take shape through public discourse and policy, they have the power to become thickly rooted in the lives of individuals, so much so that they influence emotions, feelings, and behavior, consciously and subconsciously. The term "soft propaganda" used throughout this study draws attention to the process through which individuals absorb and conform to projections of ideals and taboos. Soft propaganda refers to the power of environmental cues to shape popular belief and behavior by coding actions, objects, words, and spaces with positively (ideal) or negatively (taboo) charged meaning. These ideals and taboos have the power to influence behavior both consciously and subconsciously. I have developed the term "soft propaganda" in an effort to emphasize that propaganda is not limited to times of war, nor to blatantly biased, imposing billboards and newsreels disseminated by a centralized government authority. Rather, like "soft power," propaganda functions subtly— softly—throughout the everyday environment as hegemonic institutions and individuals mobilize visual, expressive, and environmental cues to shape popular belief and behavior.

To introduce the norms and ideals that laid the foundation for Nisei behavior in transwar Japan, this chapter focuses on three key paradigms—*dekasegi* (sojourner), alien ineligible to citizenship, and *kakehashi* (a "wedge" or "bridge" between cultures)—that functioned as sites of meaning deeply entrenched in the discourse and environment surrounding Nisei in the early twentieth century. At times, these were words, lexical terms that floated in the discourse surrounding Nisei. But more importantly, these paradigms constitute "soft propaganda" that were internalized and reproduced—consciously and subconsciously—by Nisei in their behavior, their relationships with family and community, and their pursuit of personal goals.[2] Examining the influence of these paradigms—sojourner, alien, ambassador—on the communities, attitudes, and institutions of Japanese communities in twentieth-century America, this chapter explores how the themes of temporality, belonging, and ambassadorship shaped cultural identity for Nisei.

Nisei Cultural Chameleonism

The taboos and ideals for Nisei behavior in prewar America and Japan demanded that Nisei be dexterous at cultural code-switching. In her autobiographical memoir *Nisei Daughter,* Nisei writer Monica Sone paints a vivid picture of the chameleonic flair with which she alternated between performances of Japanese and American behaviors:

> [Seattle's Japanese school] Nihon Gakkō was so different from grammar school I found myself switching my personality back and forth daily like a chameleon. At Bailey Gatzert School I was a jumping, screaming, roustabout Yankee, but at the stroke of three when the school bell rang and doors burst open everywhere, spewing out pupils like jelly beans from a broken bag, I suddenly became a modest, faltering, earnest little Japanese girl with a small, timid voice.[3]

Growing up along the waterfront Skid Row of Seattle, Monica (born Kazuko Monica Itoi) was expected—as were most Nisei growing up in America at the time—to attend Japanese lessons every day after classes at the public grammar school. Monica's life in Seattle is a picture of bicultural code-switching familiar to thousands of Japanese American children in the early twentieth century: she eats "both Western and Oriental dishes," plays jacks with her school friends and *Jan-ken-pon!* with her mother, bounds about Pier Two with her brother and his friends, and frets over the angle of her formal bow in the presence of her Japanese *sensei.*

But while Issei mothers and fathers kept Japanese culture alive in their households, nativist discrimination and anti-immigration movements in early twentieth-century America fashioned a US education system that endeavored to assimilate immigrant children by maligning "Old World" behavior. As a result,

Nisei felt pressure to alternate between Japanese and American ideals for behavior and appearance, depending on the perceived preferences of their audience.

In the years before World War II, Nisei were encouraged by their Japanese American community leaders and by the Japanese Foreign Ministry to envision their cultural identity in double: *both* Japanese *and* American. And yet, the turn of the twentieth century in America marked a period of race-based agitation, especially in the American West, that loudly maligned the "unassimilable" Japanese and their culturally inferior ways. The anti-Japanese movement in America's western states was in many ways a continuation of anti-Chinese agitation in that region, which began in the 1850s and surged amid the post-Civil War economic recession. At the time, major political parties in California and other western states openly campaigned on anti-Chinese, pro-white America platforms. In 1882, Congress passed the Chinese Exclusion Act, which rendered Chinese immigrants ineligible for citizenship. Although the status of Japanese immigrants as aliens ineligible to citizenship was not formalized until the 1922 *Takao Ozawa v. United States* decision, Japanese immigrants—neither white nor of African descent—were excluded from naturalization with very few exceptions. Amid a din of "yellow peril" outcry, particularly on the west coast of the United States, laws and policies on the state and federal levels increasingly limited the rights of Asian immigrants throughout the first two decades of the 1900s. Alien land laws enacted by most western states established a legal basis for discrimination against Japanese immigrants, who could neither purchase nor lease land.

As historian Paul Spickard details in *Japanese Americans: The Formation and Transformations of an Ethnic Group,* public fervor in support of extending the Chinese Exclusion Act grew more generally anti-Asian after the turn of the century. Chinese immigration was ebbing as Japanese immigration was experiencing a swell, and white labor organizations expanded their outcries to subsume Japanese immigrant groups in a sentiment that targeted "Asiatic races" more broadly. Intensifying this shift further, Japan's unexpected trouncing of Russia, a European power, in the Russo-Japanese War (1904–1905) exacerbated the tone of anti-Japanese rhetoric in the media; campaigns of physical violence and outspoken racist harassment seemed designed to ensure that the Japanese immigrants "knew their place" as inferior to whites.[4]

As anti-Asian agitation continued to foment in the early twentieth century, American political and education leaders questioned the assimilability of the Japanese immigrant community. State authorities responded by placing restrictions on the Japanese schools that increasingly dotted the American landscape. In 1921 for example, California's state legislature enacted Section 1534 of the

California Political Code, which regulated the operation, teacher certification, materials, and curricula of private foreign-language schools.[5]

As cultural hybrids, Nisei faced public pressure from their American teachers and politicians to "act American," but their parents and leaders in the Japanese immigrant community expected them to maintain a sense of their Japanese cultural heritage. The roots of Nisei code-switching lie in these pre-Pearl Harbor demands for cultural flexibility placed on the children of the Japanese Diaspora. Nisei in Japan during World War II would later rely on this cultural agility. "Acting Japanese" would, in many ways, be their path to survival. Nisei collaborating in transwar Japan—whether with the Japanese war effort or with the Allied occupation—were engaging in the code-switching that had been a long-established element of Nisei identity. To understand the situation of Nisei living in wartime Japan, it is therefore necessary to begin by looking at the shape of the communities into which these Nisei were born, as well as the soft propaganda surrounding Nisei both in the United States and Japan. That story begins with the earliest Japanese immigrants, those who pioneered Japanese immigration to the United States at the end of the nineteenth century.

A Community Built by Sojourners

The typical narrative of the Japanese newcomer who arrived in Hawai'i or on America's West Coast in the late nineteenth and early twentieth century is of the immigrant who espoused a so-called *dekasegi* ideal: to earn money as a laborer or farmer and then, a few years later, to return to their homeland as wealthy repatriates. This motive was not common to all Japanese immigrants, nor was it unique to the Japanese immigrant community. Indeed most turn-of-the-century immigrants, including those who arrived from Italy, Greece, and the Balkan states, shared a similar target of eventually returning to their home country.[6] And yet, the conceptualization of an immigrant family's time in America as a temporary sojourn had lasting effects on Japanese American community formation overall—and on the cultural performance of American-born Nisei.

The modern era of Japanese emigration began in the second half of the nineteenth century, when Tokugawa *bakufu* authorities began easing travel restrictions that had prevented residents from leaving Japan for two centuries. The first approvals for overseas travel were issued by the *bakufu* in 1867, and sweeping policy changes and social restructuring of the new Meiji government catalyzed a trend of international diffusion and exploration. Most of the earliest Japanese nationals to arrive on American shores were scholars (albeit few in number), encouraged by the government to travel the world and learn from the progress of leading nations. In the late 1880s, however, the paradigm of the Japanese emigrant saw a dramatic shift from scholar to laborer. Through government promotion of *kan'yaku imin* (contract-migrant) work programs designed to alleviate the pressures of overpopulation in Japan, the number of emigrants surged into the tens of thousands. Under such government-sponsored contracts, Japanese applicants committed to three-year stints as laborers in foreign lands such as Hawai'i. From the first wave of recruitment in 1885 until the start of the Sino-Japanese War in 1894 (when the Meiji regime turned their attention to the conflict against China and stopped recruiting contract emigrants), twenty-six Hawai'i contract-migrant recruitments had prompted an exodus of 28,995 Japanese citizens.[7] In addition to these government-sponsored recruitment plans, private contracting companies—as well as networks of friends and countrymen already established in new lands—encouraged Japanese nationals to emigrate by the tens of thousands, not only to Hawai'i, but also to Australia, various islands in the South Pacific, and to continental North and South America.

The palm tree-lined Hawaiian Islands and the sun-kissed Californian shores began to develop an alluring mystique throughout Japan, particularly in areas struggling with poor harvests—and especially in the minds of second (and third, fourth, fifth) sons who would not inherit their family's property. The immigrants, who were predominantly male and also predominantly hailing from the southwestern prefectures of Japan, were drawn to life in America by a broad range of motives. Although some Japanese immigrants planned to stay in America indefinitely, the trope that lingered as the blanket narrative was that of the short-term contract worker who dreamed of *ikkaku senkin* (making a fortune in a single stroke): sailing abroad, quickly earning money through hard work, and returning to their villages as wealthy men. And yet, as the years wore on in America and the money flowed less liberally than expected, even these immigrants began to send to Japan for their families or for arranged marriage partners to join them in America. Into such Issei families were born the Nisei, American citizens by birth.[8]

In these early years, the Japanese American population in the United States burgeoned rapidly. Between 1894 and 1907, eighty thousand Japanese nationals immigrated to America. As anti-Asian agitation continued to rise in the early 1900s, the United States government, anxious to curb Asian immigration, outlined the so-called Gentlemen's Agreement with Japan in 1907–1908. In this informal arrangement, Japan agreed to stop issuing passports to labor immigrants, and immigration was to be restricted to laborers who had already been in America, and to their wives and children. By the time the Gentlemen's Agreement went into effect, approximately 150,000 Japanese immigrants had entered the

United States.[9] As a result of the restrictive policy, Japanese immigration numbers reflect a distinct demographic shift: immigration during this so-called *yobiyose* (literally "called over") period (1908–1923) consisted primarily of family members joining their relatives who were already established in America. During these years, 62,000 Japanese immigrated to the US, of whom 31,000 were women and 5,000 were children.[10]

The Gentlemen's Agreement, far from achieving its ostensible goal of curbing Japanese immigration, instead resulted in a wave of thousands of women and children who sailed across the Pacific to join—or in the cases of arranged-marriage "picture brides," to meet for the first time—their family members in America. As the Japanese population grew in the American West, anti-Japanese agitation along the West Coast continued to intensify, and in 1924 the so-called Asian Exclusion Act (the Immigration Act of 1924) officially barred further Asian immigration. As a result of the tiered narrowing of these immigration policies, the Japanese American community was markedly generational: Issei had established the Japanese presence in America in the late 1800s and early 1900s; they expanded their families with steady births as their wives and children joined them in the *yobiyose* years, during which most Nisei were born; and the 1924 Asian Exclusion Act effectively sealed off the Japanese-American community from further influx.

The contract migration system, although it was only in place as official government policy for nine years, had a significant influence on the shape of Japanese immigrant communities in the United States. As sojourners, many of the earliest Japanese immigrants arrived in the United States with the primary purpose of earning money through a fixed term of work, after which they would be able to enjoy a more leisurely life back in Japan. These pioneering immigrants predominantly treated their time on American soil as temporary, and they established their stateside institutions and settlements according to that intentionality. Large numbers of Japanese immigrants achieved their sojourner goals and returned to Japan after earning enough money in America to improve their circumstances in the cities and villages of their youth. The majority of Japanese immigrants, however, stayed on indefinitely in the United States. Many of those who had intended to repatriate after a few years of work never made the fortune they had been seeking. Others had grown accustomed to their new lives and communities and resolved to stay. Still others had intended from the start to create a new life in America, perhaps never to return.

The sojourner paradigm was not unique to the Japanese immigrant community, nor was it by any means common across all Japanese immigrants. And as anthropologist James Hirabayashi describes, the 1907 Gentlemen's Agreement marked a transition from sojourner mentality to a "settling period" for Japanese immigrant communities in America, as the emphasis shifted to establishing families and community institutions.[11] And yet, even so, the sojourner mentality itself maintained influence upon Japanese families who sought a new life in the United States—whether or not these immigrant families were *dekasegi*—because sojourner consciousness had shaped the early pillars of the Japanese American community (namely, the Japanese-language press, social and religious organizations, and Japanese language schools) with the intentionality attendant a temporary sojourn in a foreign land. The sojourner roots of these institutions kept alive a heightened awareness of transnational connectedness that informed the ways Japanese immigrants and their children positioned themselves in American society, as well as the ways the non-Japanese population interacted with Japanese immigrant families.

Whether contract laborers toiling in the cane fields of Hawaiʻi or scholars embracing the Meiji mission of seeking knowledge in the Western world, many of the earliest Japanese newcomers on American soil considered their stay in America as temporary, and with that approach to life in America came conscious convictions and subconscious inclinations. These immigrants were residents of the United States and her territories, but as they did not renounce their Japanese citizenship—and were indeed ineligible to citizenship due to race-based citizenship laws of the time—most considered themselves to be still under the jurisdiction and laws of Japan. Their primary consciousness as a subject of global politics and world affairs would, therefore, rest with the Japanese empire. Their networks of communication in the form of the growing Japanese language press—such as Los Angeles's *Rafu Shimpo*, first published in 1903, and the *Nichibei Shinbun* in San Francisco, founded in 1899—reflect this sense of transplanted subjecthood. The growing Japanese-language news media fostered a sense of unity and community in which Japanese immigrants imagined themselves as connected to one another through their shared concern for Japanese affairs, expressed through the medium of their shared Japanese language.

The sojourner newcomers who laid the foundations of Japanese American life considered themselves a group apart, particularly in Hawaiʻi and along the West Coast and in smaller pockets of Japanese population centers in the mountain states, such as Denver and Salt Lake City.[12] Most relied on their Japanese brethren for assistance in matriculating into the American employment structure, as well as for social and religious interaction. As aliens ineligible to citizenship, Japanese immigrants had no prospects for expressing their voices in the American political arena, and so their religious and social organizations became the primary vehicles entrusted to improve the prospects of Japanese immigrant life. The immigrants banded together in various networks of place-based fraternity, such as *kenjinkai,* organizations composed of members hailing from the same home prefectures. The broader *Nihonjinkai* served as more general organizations linking Japanese immigrants in the same area of the United States. Not all Japanese immigrants were members of *kenjinkai* or *Nihonjinkai,* and the influence of these bodies varied across the areas of growing Japanese communities in the US and her territories, but their presence was significant in most cities and villages with a Japanese immigrant population. These organizations were originally established as a means to support immigrants during their sojourn in America's territories by providing a network of assistance and trust, as well as by improving their position as immigrants, promoting Japanese commercial ventures and welfare initiatives.

In providing assistance for Japanese immigrants, such as financial support in times of struggle, the *Nihonjinkai* and *kenjinkai* were the first place immigrants would turn in times of need. For example, whereas other residents in the United States might seek out the local police if they were victims of burglary, Japanese immigrants in the early twentieth century would typically reach out first to their *Nihonjinkai.*[13] Rudy Tokiwa, a Nisei born near San Jose in 1925, later reflected on this important function of *kenjinkai* in his own community: "You know, Japanese used to, everybody used to stick real close, because they weren't people that can go out and say, 'Oh, I've got an American friend over there. He'll do anything for me.' They weren't in that position."[14] Trust within the Japanese community was linked directly to the Japanese community itself—more so than beyond it— and the existence of the *Nihonjinkai* affirmed and perpetuated this system.

Religious institutions met similar needs, and like the *Nihonjinkai,* Japanese temple and church organizations in America carved out specific niches for their communities, thereby emphasizing the liminal existence of Japanese in America. As Yoshida Ryō describes in his history of Japanese Christianity in America, Japanese immigrants overwhelmingly kept to themselves in their religious practice. As Yoshida suggests, it is understandable that the Buddhist organizations in which Japanese immigrants participated were exclusively Japanese (due to the lack of established Buddhist religious organizations in the United States at that time), but the fact that even Japanese Christians predominately formed their own exclusively Japanese congregations is striking, given the majority Christian tenor of religious life in America around the turn of the twentieth century.[15] Many of the Japanese Christian organizations had started through relationships with white American missionaries who assisted immigrant bachelors in the early years of Japanese immigration, but in time they turned inward and became support systems run by pillars of the Japanese community. Frank Miyamoto, a Nisei born in Seattle in 1912, shared his thoughts on this transition in an interview with Stephen Fugita of Densho:

> Once these groups were brought together . . . they in turn, they themselves organize in the typical Japanese fashion, they immediately sensed the need for organization and they would organize and they would take over so that the missionaries then, immediately, increasingly take a secondary role and the group itself becomes the organizing entity. So as far as the Japanese Baptist Church was concerned for example, it very quickly brought in a Japanese minister . . . They bring in a Japanese minister who in turn organizes all the Japanese members into this church and it comes to be well supported.[16]

Both Buddhist and Christian Japanese religious organizations served as social hubs and centers for education, assisting the immigrants with their needs in the United States, including language education, youth organizations, women's clubs, and athletic teams. On this point, Frank Miyamoto continued, "Christian churches didn't flourish in Japan, so the members of this new church were not so much people who came with a Christian background, but people who found that this Christian church . . . offered advantages which they had not appreciated or had not required in Japan."[17]

As with the *Nihonjinkai* and *kenjinkai,* religious congregations directed the consciousness of Japanese immigrants "homeward" (i.e., Japanward), providing a forum through which immigrants and their families could connect to one another through common interest in Japan and her causes. For example, after the outbreak of war with Russia in 1904 (and indeed, throughout the continued years of conflict as imperial Japan expanded her empire in Asia), *Nihonjinkai* and religious congregation members in the United States supported the Japanese army by raising funds and sending care packages. Through *Nihonjinkai, kenjinkai,* and religious organizations, Japanese immigrants relied predominately on their fellow Japanese for trust networks, spiritual support, friendship, business groups, and social life, and it was into this type of separateness and self-reliance that the Nisei were born.

Another element of the lives of sojourners that left its mark on the shape of Japanese American communities is the practice of continued transnational movement. While maintaining the bicontinental families so common to the Japanese immigrant experience, Japanese immigrants endeavored to stay connected to Japan through correspondence with family members "back home" in Japan. Families pursued on a relatively large scale the option of sending one or more of their children to Japan to stay with relatives permanently or to experience the country of their forefathers on a long visit. Steamship fares were cheap, and relatives willing to host their American-born brethren were numerous. Thus, the movement of Japanese and Japanese Americans in the first half of the twentieth century was for many a story of back-and-forth, of consciousness that only gradually turned to rootedness, with the United States as the country just as likely to be shrinking in the distance beyond the ship's rail as the islands of the imperial homeland.

Residing in America with the ever-present possibility of sending their children to Japan, either for a short time or as a long-term goal, the majority of Japanese immigrant families made certain to provide their children with some Japanese language education, as well as some interaction with the Japanese community through religious organizations and social gatherings. As Issei immigrants expanded their families on American soil, the Japanese American community established Japanese language schools to provide education for children whose families either intended to return to Japan, to send their children to Japan for economic reasons or expanded career opportunities, or who simply wanted to instill in their children a knowledge of their ancestral tongue. After the establishment of the first Japanese language school in the continental United States in 1902 in Seattle, similar institutions were founded in Japanese immigrant communities across the West Coast and in the Midwest, with the financial support of Issei donations and generous grants from visiting Japanese dignitaries, such as ministers, diplomats, and members of the aristocracy. Students were trained in Japanese language, ethics, history, geography, and language.[18]

The sojourner consciousness of temporality and separateness thus shaped the early pillars of the Japanese American community: the Japanese-language press, *Nihonjinkai*, religious organizations, steady transnational movement, and the Japanese school. And for all its positive emphasis across Japanese American communities, this connectedness to Japan was posited as urgently problematic, too, particularly in the second generation as families grew and true sojourner practices faded into memory. Although many Japanese schools, for example, were originally established to instill strong ties to Japanese culture in Nisei children, as Japanese families established roots in America, these schools made concerted efforts to support Americanization. This tension is evident in the resolutions adopted at the 1912 Japanese Association of America conference, where representatives from Japanese schools from across California discussed ways "to inspire the spirit of permanent settlement among children in America and help them contribute to this land."[19] This drive to foster Japanese schools that were supportive of Americanization continued after World War I, as seen for example in the textbook compilation project undertaken by Seattle's

Figure 1.1. Members of the Green Lake Seinenkai (Young People's Club), an organization for young adult Nisei in the Green Lake area of Seattle that organized athletic, cultural, and social activities such as the formal dance depicted here. Courtesy of the Tanagi Family Collection, Densho Digital Library.

Nihonjinkai in 1920. Seattle's Nisei students had previously learned directly from readers developed by the Japanese Department of Education, but in an effort to meet the shifting needs and abilities of Nisei, the *Nihonjinkai* composed its own textbook series that aimed to promote a comfortable intermingling of Japanese and American culture. The textbooks integrated virtue tales from Aesop, showed illustrations of phenotypically white children with Japanese names, and replaced the Japanese version of a family in *kimono* practicing calligraphy at a low table with a family sitting on chairs at a round table, complete with a lace tablecloth.[20] As the Nisei population in America grew, Japanese schools strove to undo the image entrenched in broader America of the sojourner Japanese, unassimilable and disconnected.

Because it had informed the earliest development of the main institutions of the Japanese communities in America, sojourner consciousness continued to have sway in the lives of Japanese immigrants, even in families never intending to return to Japan. To be sure, some Japanese immigrant families espoused no such sojourner ideal; they intended to stay in the United States indefinitely and to raise their children in Americanized households. But even these families were shaped by the social perception that Japanese immigrants in America in the early twentieth century existed as a community apart, placing trust in one another, seeking help from one another, maintaining mental connections to (and physical families in) Japan, and visiting often or hearing updates from recently returned friends. To Issei in Japanese American communities, events and rituals such as New Year's festivities, *kenjinkai* picnics, and festivals such as *O-Bon* were not expressions of nostalgia, but rather exercises in active cultural identity. This dynamic maintenance of transnational ties took root in Japanese immigrant communities across Hawai'i and the West Coast and would shape the environments in which Nisei were encouraged by their Issei elders to be distinctly aware of and connected to their Japanese heritage.

Transnationally minded institutions such as Japanese American newspapers, region-based groups, religious organizations, and schools instilled in Nisei a cross-cultural consciousness—a sense of being thoroughly rooted in neither culture. Sojourner community formations established and reiterated that Nisei were cultural hybrids, liminal offspring existing in the contradictory and ambiguous third space, manifesting alternately Japanese and American cultural forms. Nisei inherited a community structure and community institutions built for and by a generation with markedly different goals, experiences, and affiliations. They navigated the inherent contradictions of such a cultural existence by honing an ability to act Japanese when embedded in the community structures built by Issei and to act American in spaces outside that community demarcation.[21]

Aliens and Ambassadors

The paradigm of Japanese immigrants as "aliens ineligible to citizenship" also left its mark on Japanese life and self-representation in early twentieth-century America. The Supreme Court case that sealed the fate of Issei as forever excluded from American citizenship was that of Takao Ozawa. Ozawa had filed for naturalization in 1914, six years after the US Attorney General had attempted to eliminate any gray area about Japanese naturalization by ordering federal courts to cease issuing papers to Japanese petitioners.[22] By the time *Takao Ozawa v. United States* was heard by the Supreme Court in 1922, state legislatures had long been exercising exclusionary policies to restrict the rights of Japanese immigrants. In its decision, the Supreme Court interpreted the US Naturalization Act of 1906 as limiting naturalization to white persons and persons of African descent, of which Asians were neither. Thus, the judgment officially rendered Japanese immigrants aliens ineligible to citizenship. As state and federal legislation and court judgments increasingly constricted Japanese immigration throughout the 1910s and 1920s, many Issei parents—themselves aliens ineligible to citizenship—pinned their hopes for a better future on their Nisei children. The resulting pressure had lasting effects on Nisei identity.

Takao Ozawa v. United States represents a culmination of anti-Japanese discrimination through various legislative and judicial measures throughout the first half of the twentieth century. The restrictions placed on Issei in terms of citizenship, voting rights, and land ownership influenced the lives of Nisei as well. In the wake of the legislation, Japanese American communities reverberated with bitterness at the discriminatory system, uncertainty about the future of the Japanese population in the US, and increased resistance on the part of the Issei to embrace American life fully and indefinitely. Furthermore, the Court's decision placed added pressure on the second generation to improve the reputation of the Japanese American community and advance Japanese immigrant rights. Nisei themselves were forced to consider their own citizenship as tenuous. Rumors abounded that the next restriction on the Japanese immigrant population would be to stop granting citizenship for children of Japanese immigrants born in the United States, or perhaps even to disavow the citizenship of Nisei who had claimed it since birth.[23]

The result of the court's decision sheds light on the struggles of second generation Japanese Americans in the shadow of their parents' alien status. The non-Japanese population typically failed to differentiate Nisei from Issei, and Nisei faced social discrimination despite their status as American citizens. And while other immigrant groups in the United States faced degrees of discrimination as they matriculated into American society, anti-Japanese discrimination had the backing of the federal government. The more than thirty million immigrants who came from Europe to the United States between the end of the Civil War and 1924 faced hardships and discrimination, to be sure, but their whiteness rendered them eligible to achieve citizenship, and therefore gave them access to political activity, to lobbying for change, and to bettering their situations through civic activity. By contrast, Japanese immigrants—who numbered less than 300,000—had no such political recourse.[24]

Nisei raised in a climate antagonistic to their race shouldered the burden of serving as ambassadors of the Japanese community to American society. Issei, who had no voting rights, hoped to raise a generation of upstanding citizens who might represent the concerns of the Japanese American community in civic life.

Similarly, Issei who faced workplace discrimination in unfair hiring practices, promotion tracks, pay scales, and available careers emphasized the importance of education to their American-born children. The importance of education as a weapon in the struggles of racism is manifest, for example, in the recollections of Rose Ito Tsunekawa, a Nisei born in 1930 in Salinas, California, who recalls that her father and his generation would often tell her generation: "You're never going to win over the *hakujins*[25] with your strength, with your body, physically, but do it with your brains. Study hard . . . that's the only way you're gonna get ahead."[26] Issei in America hoped that their children would distinguish themselves through their intellect, so that they might achieve white-collar careers rather than the hard hours of manual labor and blue-collar positions predominant among Japanese immigrants.

Socially as well as intellectually, Issei encouraged their children to be model members of society, so that they might reflect positively on the race they represented. The pressure placed on Nisei to behave with proper decorum echoed Issei leaders' efforts throughout the early 1900s to reshape the American perception of Japanese as civilized, rather than as an unsavory "coolie" culture.[27] Temples and churches with Japanese congregations sponsored clubs (such as the Boy Scouts or the "Busy Bees") to encourage the virtues of civic engagement among the second generation. Aiko Herzig-Yoshinaga, a Nisei raised in Los Angeles, explained that while her father was eager to see high marks in all subjects on his children's report cards, he was particularly strict about her marks in the category of "citizenship." "All the Japanese Americans almost always had A's," she recalled, "because they toed the line. We were taught instinctively to respect authority, which meant teachers, doctors, policemen . . . especially teachers."[28] As their citizenship consciousness took shape, Nisei absorbed an impression of what it meant to be a citizen of the United States in the early twentieth century—and the stakes of performing that role accurately. To Nisei in America, citizenship meant the pressures of serving as positive ambassadors of the Japanese race, of developing a sense of political responsibility, and of excelling in school.

Issei community leaders began to discuss ways to prove to their non-Japanese neighbors that they were trying to foster a generation of virtuous, responsible, engaged American citizens. In the mid-1920s, Japanese immigrant newspapers began publishing select sections in English, with content that focused on social and religious events, Nisei sports teams, accomplishments of local Nisei star students and athletes, and the importance of racial solidarity.[29] Japanese language schools, too, displayed shifts in community relations in the ever-encroaching shadow of anti-Asian racial prejudice. Associations of educators such as the Japanese Association of America organized regular conferences, discussing the importance of raising upstanding Americans who could also be well-versed in Japanese language and ways of life. In short, as a result of the discrimination against the Japanese community and the "alien" status of Issei in early twentieth-century America, the second generation assumed the burden of ambassadorship in an environment of challenges and contradictions. They were expected to devote themselves to education, to be familiar with both Japanese and American culture, and to be virtuous and engaged citizens, yet they were facing those demands in communities shaped by sojourner insularity and Japan-oriented consciousness, in a climate plagued by prejudice and by uncertainty regarding their own future as US citizens.

Ignorant of—or perhaps just optimistic about—the impediments snarling the prospect of Nisei ambassadorship, many Japanese American leaders held out hope for a "both-and" approach to ethnicity as their community grew in the 1900s–1920s. They believed that the second generation could be particularly effective ambassadors of the Japanese race, because unlike the Issei, Nisei belonged to *both* American *and* Japanese society. Leaders in the Japanese American community—and indeed, the Japanese government on the other side of the globe—therefore began to emphasize the very ethnic ambiguity of Nisei as an advantage: a means to secure equal treatment, racial tolerance, and amity.

In 1924, Kyūtarō Abiko, the publisher of the prominent San Francisco-based immigrant newspaper *Nichibei Shinbun,* began to use his paper's wide influence on the US West Coast to stress the important role of Nisei as *kusabi* or *kake-hashi*: "wedges" or "bridges" of understanding between the United States and Japan. Abiko believed that the American population's ignorance about Japan and the Japanese people was the source of anti-Japanese discrimination, and the Nisei, by virtue of their US citizenship, would have the power to counteract this ignorance through informed engagement which would reflect positively on the Japanese community. This rhetoric was echoed by Issei, non-Japanese, and Nisei themselves. For example, Clarence Arai, the president of a Nisei organization called the Seattle Progressive Citizens' League, touted the duty of his fellow Nisei "to bring about a better understanding between the East and the West, thereby eradicating the evil of prejudice from the minds of the people . . . The second generation should consecrate their lives to this special task so that the Pacific Era will be an era characterized with everlasting peace."[30] Nisei, faced with the mission of bridging the gap between American and Japanese cultures, would need to have an understanding of both cultures so that they could serve in this important capacity as they came of age. The emphasis on this unique role of Nisei became even stronger as hostilities between the US and Japan rose throughout the 1930s.

Institutions within the Japanese American community increasingly reflected the aim of shaping the Nisei as civic-minded, engaged "bridges of understanding" as the Nisei generation matured in the 1910s and 1920s. The vision that students could, through a combination of American public school and Japanese supplementary school, cultivate the best attributes of Japanese and American spirits emphasized to Nisei that Americanness and Japaneseness were separate—and in many ways opposite—entities. Amid persistent public complaints and state legislative pressures to curb the Japanese school's influence in immigrant communities, the schools shifted their format.[31] No longer would they serve to counteract Americanization, but rather to promote dual heritage in a way that would effect positive changes for Japanese Americans in the United States, ease tension in Japanese homes, and instill in Japanese students the cultural pride that could combat discrimination and inferiority complexes.[32] And yet, although Japanese educators may have thought it possible to be good US citizens while also honoring and sustaining Japanese culture in the US, the American education system positioned immigrant culture and American patriotism as contradictory.

While Japanese American communities were trying to raise their second generation to be well-informed, positive representatives of Japanese culture in the United States, various associations and officials on the other side of the Pacific were also eyeing Nisei ethnic ambiguity as a potential instrument to promote Japan's interests in America—and as an avenue to forestalling war between these two nations. The impulse to quell tension was particularly palpable in the aftermath of the so-called Manchurian Incident, in which a group of junior Japanese officers staged a sabotage of a length of Japan's South Manchuria Railway line as a pretext for Japanese invasion of Manchuria in 1931. As global public opinion of Japanese expansionism and growing militarism turned increasingly sour in the wake of this event, Japanese officials deemed it necessary to repair Japan's reputation among leading international players lest hostility lead to war.

Japanese leaders targeted Nisei as a promising segment through which to maintain friendly relations, by virtue of Nisei dualism as both Japanese and American. In the spring of 1934, the *Japan Times and Mail,* the oldest English-language newspaper in Japan, reported on several measures "under contemplation" by Japan's Foreign Ministry to promote harmony between Japan and America. Alongside plans for lectures, press coordination, international sports, and invitations of influential Americans to Japan, the plan for amity also included "Utilisation of the second generation Japanese in America for the sake of international friendship."[33] Japan's Foreign Ministry ordered its consulates in the United States to conduct a survey of the Nisei generation in November of that same year, the results of which prompted the consuls to agree that Nisei must be educated about Japan so that they might (in the words of prominent Japanese scholar Nitobe Inazō) "assume a proper pride in their citizenship as well as in the high heritage of their race and transform what they believe to be their handicap into an advantage," for the Nisei were "in a special position to interpret the East to the West and the West to the East . . . so that they may meet on common grounds to effect the principles of peace and mutual welfare."[34]

In many ways, the efforts of the Foreign Ministry to promote exposure to Japan among the Nisei were met with success. These efforts, combined with increased interest in the Japanese empire in the aftermath of the Manchurian Incident, and with the unexpected success of Japan's athletes at the Olympics in Los Angeles in the summer of 1932, resulted in a surge of young adult Nisei who moved to Japan for education or employment.[35] Before 1931, nearly all Nisei living in Japan were school-aged children, babies, and toddlers who had been taken or sent to Japan by their parents. Young adult Nisei living in Japan at the time numbered fewer than 100, but by 1932–1933, their number had increased fourfold, and by 1934–1935, there were approximately 1,700 young adult Nisei in Japan.[36]

A finger on the pulse of the *Japan Times and Mail* throughout the 1930s tracks growing public interest in Nisei, who were referred to in its pages as "Nisei," "Americans of Nippon descent," "Japanese Americans," "American-born Japanese" and "second generation boys and girls." Articles emphasizing Nisei as a point of connection between the US and Japan grew more numerous as Japan's conflict with China wore on. The second half of the 1930s, for example, saw stories informing the English-speaking population in Japan about visits to Japan by Japanese-Hawaiian boy scouts, of the unexpected English language assistance "U.S.-born Japanese boys" give to visiting delegates at the Pan Pacific Education Conference, and of the activities of Japan-America Societies on the Pacific Coast.[37]

With Japan's entry into total war against China in 1937, the Japanese government increased its pro-Japanese propaganda towards its English-speaking audience both in Japan and abroad, and ramped up its efforts to convince American Nisei to visit their parents' imperial homeland, circulating propaganda and offering cheap tourist rates. "We cannot urge too strongly," wrote consular agent Yuki Sato, "the advisability of as many as possible of the young people of the second generation to study first-hand the Japanese conditions, traditions, culture and institutions."[38] This diplomatic thrust to inspire affinity for Japan in American Nisei reflects a shift in the significance of citizenship in 1930s Japan—a Japan growing ever clamorous with claims of Japanese racial ascendancy and with calls to fortify the Japanese empire in breadth, in body, and in spirit on the quest for Japanese supremacy in the Pacific.

In 1939, the Japanese Foreign Office circulated a traveling photo exhibit throughout thirty-six American cities in order "to give a better understanding of this country to the second generation Japanese in the United States as well as to promote friendly relations between the two nations through them."[39] This collection of approximately three hundred photographs depicted famous Japanese places (both urban and rural), traditional dress throughout the year, home life, and Japanese cultural arts such as flower arrangement, music, and drama. Both in the United States and in Japan, the Nisei were being shaped as repositories of the most admirable aspects of Japanese culture, with the design that they would be able to promote Japanese interests by performing this culture throughout the English-speaking social sphere.

In Japanese American communities, the foundational paradigm of *kusabi* or *kakehashi* ("wedges" or "bridges") inspired a genre of Nisei cultural education in the 1920s and 1930s that represented the Japanese American community's hopes of raising a generation that could promote Japanese interests and a favorable impression of Japan in the American political sphere. Such an ideal *kakehashi* Nisei is engaged in his community. He is politically active and vocal in expressing his opinions (which presents a problem for female Nisei aspiring to be both forthcoming *kakehashi* and reserved *ojōsan* daughter). He is connected to—and appreciative of—both Japanese and American ways of life. He is also likely to be landowning and white-collar. The ideal Nisei as posited by the Japanese Foreign Ministry is appreciative of Japanese culture, speaks Japanese, is familiar with Japanese ways of life, and is vocal in his support of the Japanese mission of expansion in the Pacific region.

Japanese in Japan and Issei in the United States had high expectations of the second generation. Nisei were looked to as ambassadors who could serve as cultural bridges between two governments facing mounting hostilities. Issei and Nisei alike were depicted in Japan as "overseas Japanese," an extension of the Japanese empire. And amid the anti-Asian prejudice of early twentieth-century America, Nisei lived a problematic biculturalism—expected at one moment to be an ideal American citizen, and at the next to be a model for the very best that Japanese culture had to offer. Born into communities built for sojourners, Nisei were raised to consider themselves both Japanese and American—but not simultaneously Japanese and American. As Nisei came of age in America, they developed a cultural flexibility that enabled them to oscillate between performances as "American" and "Japanese"—from "roustabout Yankee" to "earnest" Japanese.

Soft propaganda in America in the early twentieth century stimulated Nisei to internalize mannerisms, speech, material culture, and attitudes as "Japanese" or "American"—and to code-switch between these two categories according to the demands of their environment. As a result, Nisei approached Japaneseness and Americanness as opposite, incongruent, separate entities. To be "Japanese," Nisei were told, was not inherent to Nisei. It was, rather, the result of heritage education and practice. To American Nisei, therefore, Japanese identity was a role to play. And yet, the performance was not always a conscious one. As they reproduced their internalized norms of "American" or "Japanese" behavior, Nisei were assimilating in alternation, shaping themselves consciously and subconsciously to share common characteristics with a hegemonic ideal that was, variably, American or Japanese. This understanding of cultural identity as flexible would shape the ability of Nisei in transwar Japan to adapt their behavior and appearance according to the demands and expectations of their environment. This chameleonism would prove fundamental to their survival during the years of World War II and the occupation.

CHAPTER TWO

Nisei Child, Problem Child

According to immigrant community leaders in the United States and Japanese politicians and intellectuals in Japan, Nisei in America had a natural ability to understand both Japanese culture and American culture, and to serve as ambassadors and cultural interpreters between the two increasingly unfriendly nations. There were, however, significant snags in this ideal. First, the insular structure of daily life in Japanese American communities and the prejudice with which many Americans approached Japanese Americans made it difficult for Nisei to embrace and express both Japanese and American cultures simultaneously. Another significant obstacle that made it challenging for Nisei to serve as cultural ambassadors was the persistent social conceptualization of Nisei existence itself as difficult and ambiguous. Japanese, Issei, non-Japanese Americans, and even Nisei themselves spoke of Nisei existence as contradictory and troubled. This discourse cued Nisei not only to think of themselves as bearing the responsibility of connecting East and West, but also to think of themselves as maladjusted, culturally stunted, inferior, and inherently vexed by the challenges of growing up as Nisei. The catchphrase *"dai nisei mondai"* ("Second Generation Problem") goaded Nisei in everyday parlance both in Japan and in America, and although those using the term understood the "problem" differently, they seemed to agree on one thing: Nisei life was fraught with turmoil.

The social and physical development of Nisei transpired in an environment in which Japanese and Issei community leaders crafted the role of Nisei as cultural ambassadors, as capable of linking two peoples of disparate historical and moral backgrounds. And yet, just as these leaders were elaborating upon the "both-and" cultural belonging of the second generation, American public opinion widely espoused an "either-or" definition of cultural identity for its immigrant population. The Second Generation Problem as imagined by the non-Japanese American public is indicative of this sort of anti-Old World tenor that dominated the early twentieth century. The "problem" of the second generation Japanese, to the non-Japanese public, was therefore a perceived incongruence: namely, that children of Japanese extraction intended to stay in America without assimilating properly into American society. In early twentieth-century America, the ebbing nationalistic urge to brew the cultural melting pot of America into a united, patriotic populace meant that the exercise of one's "old country" culture invited scorn from many members of the public, which perceived the maintenance of immigrant cultural traditions with suspicion. This fervor for assimilation by the shedding of ancestral customs became even more vigorous in post-World War I society.

In 1934, Stanford University psychologist Edward K. Strong, Jr. published *The Second Generation Japanese Problem,* a sociological study of the Japanese American population in California, with the support of leaders in the Japanese Association of America and the Japanese American Citizens League. The "problem," as he presents it, is that "the Japanese . . . feel they are better situated [in America] than in Japan and intend to stay here in spite of what America may do to discourage them and their culture, at the same time refusing to admit any superiority of American culture to theirs."[1] In short, American-born children of Japanese parentage possess a right to stay in the country of their birth—a right they overwhelmingly intend to exercise—and yet, they will not be cowed into forfeiting their Japanese ways.

Across America, Japanese immigrant families maintained their Japanese cultural habits. This aroused the mistrust of some members of the non-Japanese public, who saw such behavior as unpatriotic and potentially dangerous. A 1908 article in the *Seattle Times* paints a vivid picture of the suspicion with which Japanese immigrants and their children were perceived in early twentieth-century America:

> That there are more Japanese in Seattle and vicinity than is apparent to most people was forcibly illustrated to the citizens of South Park last Sunday, when 2,000 subjects of the Mikado assembled on the Cavanaugh tract in the suburb and held a picnic. A few of the suburban residents are still of the opinion that the Japanese have had some motive in holding the meeting other than mere innocent amusement, but leading Japanese of the city say that the only object of their countrymen was to have a good time, as is the custom in Japan in the spring of each year.[2]

This article, entitled "Picnic Shows There Are Many Japanese: South Park Residents Wonder Where All of the 2,000 Brown Men Who Met There Sunday Came From," demonstrates the misgivings of the non-Japanese community at the rapid growth of the Japanese population in Seattle. The tone of the article, too, indicates the mistrust with which many Japanese families were greeted in American society; readers are prompted to doubt that these scores of "subjects of the

Mikado" have merely gathered to "have a good time." In light of this, it is little wonder that Nisei Rose Ito Tsunekawa recalled of the Japanese association picnics held in California during her girlhood, "if the *hakujins* came around, then we would all hide our food. We were ashamed to be eating with chopsticks. That I remember very vividly, we would always hide our food."[3] To be regarded as loyal American citizens by white Americans in early twentieth-century America, many Nisei felt compelled to conceal elements of their Japanese culture.

Nisei experiences of being called "un-American" by their teachers and classmates were not uncommon. Marion Tsutakawa Kanemoto had her mouth taped shut by a kindergarten teacher when she used Japanese to ask a fellow student to clarify some English she had not understood, and John Aiso, a Nisei in Burbank who later served in the US Army, was reprimanded by one of his teachers who said that his studying Japanese was "un-American."[4] Indeed, in this xenophobic climate, maintenance of Japanese customs and language was perceived by many as *anti*-American, and in the face of suspicion, many Nisei reacted by striving to be as American as possible. Aiko Herzig-Yoshinaga shared of her life in pre-World War II Los Angeles that "during those days, you open your mouth and you spoke Japanese, you got dirty looks . . . So we tried to be so 'American,' 200 percent American, . . . and resistance to learn Japanese was a detriment to my development, especially my relationship with my parents."[5]

So-called flag-waving Americanism as a reaction to accusations of non-assimilation and doubted loyalty would grow increasingly dominant in the Nisei community during World War II (largely because the leadership of the Japanese American Citizens League espoused such an approach). Indeed, flag-waving Americanism has become the blanket story of early- and mid-twentieth century Nisei—a trope that obfuscates the multi-layered attitudes within the Japanese American community regarding assimilation and wartime loyalty. In the prewar years, these accusations of non-assimilation—and responses of shame felt by Nisei for practicing Japanese culture—resulted in an awareness of cultural practice as coded "right" (American cultural practices) or "wrong" (Japanese cultural practices) by the Nisei themselves.

Issei immigrants, Japanese government officials in America, and even Japanese in Japan also recognized a Nisei "problem," albeit from a different angle than that of the non-Japanese public. As most Issei perceived it, the non-Japanese public discriminated against the Japanese population because they misunderstood Japanese cultural practices as anti-American. In Issei eyes, the problem with Nisei was that Nisei, too, misunderstood Japanese culture, and many Nisei seemed resistant to it and even contemptuous of it. As a result, Nisei were proving unable to serve as cultural ambassadors, because they lacked a proper appreciation for the language and traditions of their parents' country. Instead, Nisei looked upon their Japanese heritage as something of which to be ashamed, resulting in a generation of "spiritual half-breeds," (as they were described by San Francisco Consul General Morizo Ida at the 1928 Pacific State Consuls' Conference), neither fully American nor fully Japanese.[6]

Yamada Tatsumi, writing in 1930s Japan about the "problems of the second generation abroad" describes the problem as actually the culmination of several complexities in the lives of the second generation abroad, including problems of education, marriage, ideology, employment, and several other far-reaching areas of life as a minority in an antagonistic host society. Yamada's work suggests that Nisei are plagued by malaise resulting from an insufficiently supportive home life. Without proper cultural and language education in the home—which, Yamada emphasizes, is the ultimate role of the mother—Nisei are stunted in their moral growth, and they are unable to become well-adjusted human beings.[7] Yamada's analysis reflects many of the biases of the Japanese in Japan toward immigrant families, such as the notion that they were lacking in education and did not properly nurture their children. The result of this extrapolation on the "Second Generation Problem" is that Nisei were cued to understand themselves as culturally ignorant—Japanese by blood, perhaps, but not fully worthy of that affiliation due to their lack of appropriate heritage education.

Nisei also talked about their own generation as problematic, though to them, the problem took a different shape than as discussed by the non-Japanese American public. In Nisei discourse, the Second Generation Problem is, in general, that Nisei are misunderstood—by their parents, by non-Japanese, and by Japanese in Japan as well. They are under pressure to serve as bridges—as civic leaders expressing the voices of the Japanese community—but they are discriminated against in everyday society, where they face the same challenges as their parents, despite their difference of citizenship. How are they to become leaders in a society that discriminates against them in the workplace, socially, and politically? How are they to represent the concerns of a Japanese community that works against them by catering exclusively to the goals and needs of the first generation?

A pamphlet produced in 1926 by the Japanese Students' Christian Association of North America (JSCA) reflects these concerns in a discussion of the multiple dimensions of the Second Generation Problem as perceived by these engaged Nisei. The pamphlet disseminated the results of a conference held to discuss the problem and how to solve it. Its author, Roy Hidemichi Akagi, described the crux of the issue as one of misperception: the sixty thousand Nisei in Hawai'i and the fifty thousand Nisei in the continental United States are US citizens who (like most US citizens) know little about Japan, and this makes it difficult for them to be part of the Japanese community in America. On the other hand, these same US citizens *look* fully Japanese, and so the average American classifies them as Japanese rather than American. The problem, therefore, arises from the dilemma that, "If the second generation of Japanese are by nature incapable of being absorbed by the Japanese community and if they are not accepted as Americans by American society, where should they belong? Thus, they are truly men and women without a country."

The JSCA pamphlet goes on to describe a number of additional problems stemming from this basic contradiction within the lives of Nisei. Those problems: first, intergenerational conflict between overbearing Issei and their Nisei children, who differ from their parents in language, customs, ideals, modes of thinking, religious beliefs, and national loyalty. Second: the struggles of anyone with Japanese physical features to be accepted into the fold of American society, regardless of citizenship, language, or attitude. Third: lack of vocational guidance for a generation eager to achieve higher-paid, better-respected occupations than those held by their parents. Fourth: instability in social life because of the conflict between Japanese values taught at home and the norms reinforced in American society. And finally: the concern that they are "unprovided for" in a religious environment that caters—both in Buddhist and Christian congregations—to the Issei almost exclusively. The second generation, asserts Akagi, should be able to "take pride in their Japanese heritage, both outward and inward," so that they might "weave this heritage into the fabric of American citizenship," but they are unable to do so, because neither the Issei audience nor the non-Japanese audience is receptive to hearing their concerns and recognizing their unique struggles.

The JSCA conference that produced this pamphlet was held in response to the 1924 immigration legislation and the gossip that Nikkei (people of Japanese ancestry) born in the United States might also be excluded from citizenship. In other words, doubts about the future of Nisei in the US rendered the solution of the Nisei problem a matter of pressing concern. The conference reflected on the legislation with an eye to its silver lining, namely that, "it has conclusively demonstrated that there is small hope for the solution of the Japanese question except in the future development, nobly conceived and carefully conducted, of the so-called second generation Japanese." The JSCA urged that Nisei, misunderstood by both Japanese and American society and therefore completely comfortable in neither, must make society aware of their struggles. They must educate the public through writing, speaking, and interracial conferences, organizations, and friendships so that they might prove themselves worthy of their American citizenship by sharing the assets of Japanese culture with American society.[8]

The only people who seemed to understand the Nisei—their opportunities, their struggles, and their obstacles—were Nisei themselves. Nisei grew up amid vociferous discussions on the topics of Nisei identity, loyalty, cultural knowledge, and inherent struggles. They were raised in an environment that attached significant weight to the roles Nisei could (and should) play, resulting in heightened awareness of social expectations and limitations. Nisei shouldered the burden of cultural ambassadorship, and yet they also considered their potential as stunted by the uncertainty of a tenuous future. Nisei were challenged by their community leaders to bridge two cultures—two worlds repeatedly described as utterly opposite and yet, somehow, as embodied simultaneously in the body of the Nisei.

Individuals whose cultures are perceived as particularly contrasting or conflicting—so opposite, for example, that they give rise to a "Second Generation Problem"—tend to be highly aware of the discrepancies between their two cultures, and they cope with this by keeping the two cultures dissociated.[9] Because of the conflicting demands for behavior, expression, appearance, and attitude placed on Nisei by their Issei parents, their Japanese brethren in Japan, and their non-Japanese American audiences, Nisei oscillated between two dissociated cultural performances. These demands persisted, and as a result, Nisei remained well-rehearsed in these two roles. They did not "assimilate" in the sense of adopting one culture at the cost of forever rejecting the other. Instead, their assimilation was the oscillation itself—the practiced maintenance of cultural flexibility, of identity as code-switchable.

The Scripts and Costumes of Nisei Performance

As the Nisei began to come of age in America, their Issei parents and teachers—excluded from citizenship and land ownership—emphasized the importance of cultivating an engaged second generation who would represent Japanese interests in the political sphere. The racial discrimination and prejudice faced by the Japanese community in America, they insisted, resulted from a lack of understanding of Japanese history and customs among Nisei as well as the general American population. Problematized as maladjusted, ungrateful, spineless, and misunderstood, Nisei were characterized in Japan and in America as deficient in Japanese cultural knowledge.

Only a comprehensive heritage education, therefore, could provide the foundation upon which to raise an ideal, informed Nisei citizenry. If the Nisei better understood their Japanese roots, proponents of cultural education urged, they would be better equipped to serve as cultural bridges and so be more effective US citizens. Furthermore, insisted Issei, heritage education would help diffuse tensions between Nisei and Issei and would thereby foster harmony in Japanese households. With skills in Japanese language and culture, Nisei could increase their job prospects; their self-esteem would soar; and they could deftly navigate the transnational network so fundamental to Issei existence in America.

Cultural ignorance, insisted Issei and Japanese leaders, was the root of the problems of the second generation, and so cultural education—especially physical exposure to life in Japan—seemed the natural solution. Japanese cultural education in America took the form of the Japanese school, which provided Japanese American pupils with basic speaking and writing ability in *hyōjungo* (standard Japanese language) as opposed to the regional dialects widely spoken in their households. Immigrant families typically communicated at home in the dialect of their ancestral prefecture, and these dialects constituted the "Japanese" known and spoken by Nisei, as opposed to the *hyōjungo* education they received in Japanese school.

Most Nisei students growing up in cities and towns in Hawai'i and on the West Coast with even modest Japanese populations had access to such schools, which were often affiliated with religious institutions. Pupils attended these extracurricular classes after their regular school day, typically for an hour or so each weekday or for a few hours on Saturday mornings. In addition to drills in speaking, reading, and writing (usually accessing the standard textbooks provided by the Ministry of Education for primary school pupils in Japan), many students in Japanese school in the US were also exposed to teachings in Japanese *shūshin* (ethics) as well as basic etiquette, Japanese geography, and stories of Japanese folk legends and historical heroes. Many schools also offered avenues for students to be exposed to Japanese culture beyond the Japanese language, providing Nisei with a chance to learn martial arts such as *kendō* and *jūdō,* as well as Japanese dance, calligraphy, and flower arrangement.

Thousands of Nisei also learned about the nation of their ancestors through first-hand experience in Japan. In 1924, four young Nisei women from Seattle visited Japan with the Japanese Women's Christian Temperance Union, and upon their return, they delivered speeches about their experiences, which were published in the Seattle Japanese-language newspapers *Hokubei Jiki* and *Taihoku Nippō.*[10] The Japanese Association of America (headquartered in San Francisco) learned of these young women's stories and invited the women to California, where their tales of Japan inspired community leader Kyūtarō Abiko to develop a contest by which his paper, the *Nichibei Shinbun,* would sponsor a Japan *kengakudan* (excursion study group) of its own for Nisei readers. Eleven young adult

Nisei (six girls and five boys) were selected by votes from the newspaper's sub-scribers, and in the spring of 1925, they traveled with Abiko's wife throughout Japan, visiting high-ranking officials and touring the Diet legislature buildings, important banks, and the imperial palace. Their tour included stops in Tokyo, Yokohama, Kamakura, Nikko, Sendai, Nagoya, Nara, Osaka, Okayama, Hiro-shima, and Kyushu. The purpose of the study tour, as described in *Nichibei Shin-bun,* was that the Nisei participants would, "become conscious of their own *minzoku* (ethnicity) and gain confidence in themselves. Individually, they will be blessed with self-assurance; they will become essential links in fostering Japanese-American amity, each in their own personal way; and they will natu-rally realize what they must do as Americans for America."[11]

After the students' return, the *Nichibei Shinbun* published further rhetoric touting first-hand experience in Japan as fostering Nisei potential to thrive as cultural bridges:

> Born in America, educated in American schools, and raised in an Ameri-can environment, the Nisei are American citizens who fully understand the United States. At the same time, they have the potential of under-standing Japan because they possess an "Oriental sensibility" rooted in their racial background. There is no question that the Nisei can promote understanding of the Orient among Americans and that they have the enormous potential of becoming a great bridge between Japan and the United States. If the returning *kengakudan* members do something in the near future towards the realization of this enormous potential, the main goal of our newspaper will have been attained.[12]

Abiko's account demonstrates an interesting turn of logic regarding Nisei ra-cial identity: Nisei, he considers, are susceptible to learning Japanese culture due to their Japanese race, but they are not born into that understanding. Rather, their race provides them with the potential to understand Japanese culture, and to speak on Japan's behalf, but they must first be trained in Japa-nese ways of life and language in order to "promote understanding" of Japan in American society. Eager to participate in the mission of training Nisei as cultural representatives, other Japanese immigrant newspapers and associa-tions followed the lead of the *Nichibei Shinbun* and the Japanese Women's Christian Temperance Union, developing their own study tours of Japan for young Nisei men and women.

In Japanese language schools across the United States, Nisei children were ex-posed to Japanese culture that included language, Japanese ethics, geography, and history. The rise of the study tour trend further demonstrates an understanding of "culture" as inclusive of physical experience—of a body moving through Japanese space, experiencing first-hand the sights, smells, sounds, and tastes of Japan. As the Japanese empire expanded, so did the route of the tours; by the late 1930s, these tours included, for example, stops in Japanese-colonized Korea and Manchuria. Thus, the ideal Nisei cultural "bridge" would access Japanese culture not just through language education, but also by experiencing Japan with all five senses. The benefits of this first-hand experience included improvement in Japanese language skills—including the complexities of *keigo* (polite speech)—as well as a physical experience of the vastness of Japan's expanding empire, her renowned cities, and her traditional arts.

In addition to the institution of the Japanese school in America and the practice of the study tour, the option of a *ryūgaku taiken* (study abroad experience) became increasingly popular throughout the 1920s and 1930s. The surge in the number of Nisei pupils studying in Japan throughout those decades was the result of a variety of causes, including an increase in passenger routes of transoceanic steamship liners, which offered passengers a journey from the West Coast to Yokohama in less than two weeks at a reasonable rate. Other factors that stimulated more and more Nisei to spend extended time in Japan throughout the 1920s and 1930s included the increasingly oppressive anti-Japanese climate throughout those decades (particularly on the West Coast); a rising interest in Japan's expanding empire after the Manchurian Incident in 1931; and a surge of pride among many Nisei after Japanese athletes performed better than expected in the 1932 Los Angeles Olympic Games. And perhaps most importantly, the Japanese government's decision to take Japan off the gold standard in December 1931 resulted in a plunge in yen to dollar value, making the dollar stretch much farther in Japan.

Study abroad options for heritage education increased as interest in such programs strengthened. In the earlier decades of the 1900s, Nisei studying in Japan typically either studied under a private tutor or entered regular Japanese schools alongside Japan-born peers (though they were often held behind several years due to inadequate language preparation in Japanese schools in America). Beginning in the late 1920s, though, many Japanese educational institutions began to admit larger numbers of Nisei students, and some schools in Japan even developed special "foreign student" study divisions that catered specifically to international residents in Japan, including Nisei. For example, the Japanese Foreign Ministry established the Overseas Japanese Educational Association Foundation (Kaigai Kyōiku Kyōkai) in 1932, which offered a school and a dormitory called Mizuho Gakuen in Kawasaki, Kanagawa Prefecture (just outside Tokyo). At Mizuho Gakuen, the students (ages 13–26, at first mostly North American Nisei but increasingly from South America as well) studied 30 hours each week, broken down as follows:

Japanese language 9 hours
Translation 4 hours
Japanese history 2 hours
Japanese geography 2 hours
Mathematics 2 hours
Civics/Politics 1 hour
Ethics 1 hour
Martial arts 2–6 hours each[13]

The martial arts courses included instruction in traditional swordsmanship, hand-to-hand combat, and archery, all of which were designed to train students in *Nihon seishin* (the Japanese spirit). Regarding the military training at Mizuhō Gakuen, the Overseas Education Association boasted that "by means of this sort of training in the Japanese spirit, the way of the samurai—of which imperial Japan may boast to the world—will boil up the blood of the Nisei and cause their hearts to leap without regret."[14]

Another government-funded institution developed specifically for Nisei was the Heishikan. Cognizant of the unfavorable press Japan was receiving in American news outlets, Japanese officials identified several Nisei who demonstrated sympathies to Japan and brought these Nisei to Japan on scholarships to be groomed as press staffers who would provide favorable representations of Japan in the English-language papers and radio programs. The Heishikan was established by the Foreign Ministry in 1939 with its first class of sixteen Nisei invited from Hawai'i, the continental United States, and Canada. At the Heishikan, the students underwent a two-year program on Japanese language and law, history, economics, and politics. Their program also included excursions to historical sites of cultural importance and to Japan's colonies, including Hokkaido and the northernmost island Sakhalin.[15] Yoshio Shimogaki, a member of one of the earliest classes, shared his perspective on life as a Nisei at the Heishikan with interviewers in 2007. Recalled Yoshio, "They supplied us rooming, board, everything . . . plus spending money." And the purpose of the Nisei pupils there, explained Yoshio, was made abundantly clear: "We were supposed to be the goodwill ambassadors between Japan and the U.S."[16]

Many of the schools attended by Nisei were affiliated with religious organizations. For example, Nichibei Home began as a dormitory in Tokyo, the brainchild of Buddhist educator Tsunemitsu Kōnen. Tsunemitsu represented the Hompa Hongwanji Buddhist mission, the largest religious group among the Japanese immigrant population in the United States. He had traveled to the US and Hawai'i in 1928–1929, and in his conversations with members of the Japanese American community, he identified a need for heritage education in Japan and returned to Tokyo to found a facility for such a purpose. Sizable funds offered by Issei and Japanese contributors enabled him to build a program at his dormitory designed to teach the essence of Japan to Nisei youths, positing heritage education as a means to combat low self-esteem among Nisei. Similar to the offerings at Mizuho Gakuen, the program of study at Nichibei Home included language (reading, composition, conversation, calligraphy, and writing); morality, etiquette, and customs; Japanese history and geography; and mathematics. Courses were offered, additionally, in Japanese music and martial arts.[17]

Christian organizations also began to develop opportunities for Nisei study abroad experiences. In 1931, the Tokyo YMCA established Nichigo Bunka Gakkō, a special program that taught Japanese and Japanese culture to foreigners. According to a 1933 curriculum document, the YMCA program's course in Japanese cultural history covered the origins of the Japanese empire, the establishment of *kokutai* (the national polity), and the "roots of modern life traceable to the culture of the ancient and medieval areas." In Geography of Japanese Civilization, students learned the districts of the Japanese empire—their geographical conditions, culture, industries, and customs. In Japanese Customs and Etiquette, Ishikawa Shizuko-*sensei* taught everyday etiquette as well as customs for important ceremonial occasions, manners, appropriate gift-giving, national holidays, and the tea ceremony. And finally, in Japanese Drama, Tamura Hiroko-*sensei* instructed students on Japanese dramatic arts, such as *kabuki,* its history, music, and dance forms. This course included a field trip to a *kabuki* performance at a major Tokyo theatre.[18]

Additional Christian schools in Japan that designed programs specifically for visiting Nisei included Aoyama Gakuin, which was founded as a Methodist school with a special division for foreign pupils. The Surugadai Jogakuin was a YWCA-sponsored school with a special division for foreign female students. And in 1935 the Christian organization Rikkōkai established a school and dormitory specifically for Nisei students and Manchurians.[19]

Kawai Michi, secretary of the Young Women's Christian Association of Japan, had established Keisen School for Young Women in the suburbs of Tokyo in 1929 with a mission to cultivate cosmopolitan Japanese women. In 1935, she received special funds from the Japanese Foreign Office to open a new, special department for Nisei, a place where North American-born Nisei young women could learn from and interact with Japanese young women. For years, Nisei had been coming (sometimes unannounced) to attend Kawai-*sensei*'s school for a year or two after finishing high school in the United States. With the funding from the Foreign Office, Kawai formalized her school's role in facilitating this "Japanese finishing school"-style of education for Nisei.[20] Her mission was not to "Japanify" these Nisei women, but rather to develop in them an appreciation for Japan—and, as an added benefit, to cultivate a worldly élan for the Japanese student population at Keisen. Subjects at the Keisen program included: Japanese language, cooking, sewing, tea ceremony, flower arrangement, Japanese dance, Japanese dyeing techniques, and basic etiquette. Students enjoyed regular field trips so that they might experience the famous sites of Japan first-hand. The education designed for Nisei pupils at Keisen provides a prime example of the rhetoric of cultivating Nisei to be "cultural bridges." In an essay (written in Japanese) entitled "What I Learned from Kawai Michi Sensei," one Canadian Nisei pupil wrote the following:

> When I first arrived to Japan, I did not quite understand our [Nisei] situation, but since I started my studies here [at Keisen Girls' School], [Kawai] Sensei clarified it for us. That is: "You Nisei are the bridges that link the nations of Japan and America. Your mission is to learn the fine points of Eastern culture for two years, return to your hometowns, and through the cultures of both East and West, introduce that knowledge to foreigners, so that they may know the true Japan and her splendid people.[21]

The Keisen Girls' School is often cited as an example of Nisei study abroad education in Japan, due to the records provided by the students themselves, who published the results of a student-led survey on the condition of Nisei in Japan, conducted in the Tokyo area in 1939.

Waseda University, one of the most renowned universities in Japan, began to admit Nisei in 1935 in a special international division, Waseda Kokusai Gakuin (Waseda International School), located in the vibrant Tokyo district of Takadanobaba. Waseda Kokusai Gakuin stands out among other study abroad options for Nisei students in Japan due to its diverse, international flavor. Admission was limited to pupils who had graduated from high school abroad, resulting in a student body comprised of foreigners from across the globe, from American-born Nisei to the sons and daughters of diplomats, missionaries, and businessmen from around the world. Mary Kimoto, a Nisei pupil at Waseda Kokusai Gakuin whose experiences in prewar, wartime, and postwar Japan are preserved in her collection of letters (published as *Dear Miye*), described her female classmates to her Nisei friend Miye Yamasaki back in the US thus:

One is from Deutsch and talks like it. Another is about forty years old and a Korean and she's been in America about ten years, graduated from Oberlin and Michigan and was in Hawaii nine years and she is a physical ed teacher. She is kind of funny but rather boring because she takes a long time to say anything and she always tells us to speak in Japanese. One is a Canadian and something else like Elsie Noguchi—so dainty. The others are Nisei from Idaho and another from I forgot where . . . There is also a girl from Siam and one from Java.[22]

Waseda Kokusai Gakuin also stands out for its co-educational class composition, still rare in 1930s Japan; female students made up about one-third of the student body.[23] Mary Kimoto's letters to Miye and to another friend Kay Oka describe a lively social life in which she pals around prewar Tokyo with male and female students, speaking mostly English with Nisei friends from all over the world, as well as with European friends. The three-year curriculum at Waseda Kokusai included courses in Japanese language, translation, morality, Japanese history, Japanese geography, classical Chinese (*kanbun*), and mathematics. The course of study was designed to prepare students for higher education in Japanese institutions as well as employment in jobs with an international flair. Students went on to employment in the Japanese Foreign Ministry, Japan's Manchurian Rail Company, communications companies, broadcasting, newspapers, and conglomerate corporations. Others proceeded to higher education programs in competitive Japanese institutions.

Students trained in specialized study abroad programs often aimed to test into the Japanese higher education system, taking challenging entrance examinations alongside their Japan-born peers. Women's institutions, such as Japan Women's College, Tokyo Women's College, and Tsuda College, saw increasing numbers of Nisei students. In addition to Nisei who tested into such institutions after preparation in study abroad programs, there were also thousands of Nisei who entered schools in the Japanese education system without such specialized preparation. These were mostly Nisei whose *dekasegi* families had either moved back to Japan after a stint abroad, or Nisei who had been sent to Japan to be raised by relatives there.

As historian Eiichiro Azuma describes, there were three types of Nisei living in Japan in the prewar years: about four thousand *ryūgakusei* (study abroad students) to whom short-term study programs catered, mostly in Tokyo and Osaka; a few hundred professionals (usually college-educated) who had come to seek opportunity and escape racial exclusion; and the largest group, children of immigrant families who had either returned to Japan or had entrusted their children to relatives there. Azuma estimates that the number of this third group of Nisei in Japan, who were "'assimilated' enough to pass as ordinary Japanese," was between 10,000 and 35,000 in the 1930s.[24] These students—pupils at primary schools and higher normal schools—underwent the education designed for the youth of the Japanese empire. Alongside their Japan-born classmates, they bowed to the emperor, sang the *kimigayo* national anthem, memorized the Imperial Rescript on Education, and participated in military training exercises common in prewar Japanese schools.

It was for the first group—the *ryūgakusei*—and for Nisei in the "new world" that Japanese American community leaders so carefully packaged Japanese culture through supplementary education programs and study tours. The imagined ideal Japanese culture that emerges illustrates the ways in which Issei and Japanese in Japan believed that Nisei must—and could—be taught how to be Japanese in order to solve the Second Generation Problem. This education in Japanese identity included a precise, accurate, nuanced understanding of the standard Japanese language; an awareness of Japanese geography and the necessity of her stake in the colonies of Korea, Taiwan, China, and Manchuria; an appreciation for the Japanese imperial institution and its ceremonies; and exposure to Japanese culture and arts. In American Japanese schools as well as in Japan, Nisei were encouraged to appreciate the aesthetics of Japanese cultural arts as time-honored, and as expressing a unique "Japanese spirit." Yamashita Sōen, a Japanese researcher who had lived in Hawai'i and wrote widely on the situation of Nisei in Japan and abroad in the prewar years, recorded a conversation with a Nisei resident of the Tsukikage Dormitory that encapsulates this concept of a pure Japanese spirit. When asked what she wants to learn during her time in Japan, this student (a graduate of the Women's Vocational Art School) replied, "Flowers, tea, *koto*—the pursuits of pure Japan—etiquette, and home handicrafts."[25] Exposure to—and training in—the intricacies of the Japanese spirit would impress upon Nisei that their Japanese heritage should be not a source of shame but rather a point of pride, an advantage over non-Japanese.

Nisei could be proud, as well, of the power of the Japanese empire that was extending its reach across the greater East Asian region. Those students undergoing cultural education in Japan experienced first-hand the strength and breadth of Japan's illustrious empire through field trips to famous places. For example, Mary Kimoto's letters describe a lengthy trek with the Waseda International School by train and ferry to Shimonoseki, Moji, Fukuoka, and Osaka, as well as a field trip to Yokosuka to admire the battleship *Mikasa,* Admiral Togo's flagship during the Russo-Japanese War.[26] Miyazaki Tayako, a student from the Hawaiian Island of Kauai attending of Musashino Girls' High School wrote in the autumn of 1933: "In summer, I traveled from Mount Fuji to Kyushu; in fall I went on a school trip to Matsushima. I passed in Japan the many changes of eight

Figure 2.1. Nisei students at Musashino Girls' High School learned Japanese traditional arts such as calligraphy and the tea ceremony, as depicted here in Yamashita Sōen's *Nikkei shimin no ryūgaku jijō* [Circumstances of Japanese Citizens Studying Abroad], 1935. Courtesy National Diet Library, Japan.

months. Japan—so little on a map—seemed vast when I came and saw it for myself."[27] Through exposure to the geography of the Japanese empire, ever expanding and long celebrated in art and poetry, Nisei could build confidence in Japan's strength, worth, and mission in East Asia.

Also impressed upon Nisei students in Japan (both those in Japanese heritage education programs and those attending community schools) was the sacred power of the emperor and the illustrious history of Japan's imperial line. Although Nisei undergoing Japanese education Stateside were made aware of the figure of the emperor, it was the Nisei living in Japan—in particular, those attending normal Japanese schools—who felt the full influence of the Japanese state-designed indoctrination of emperor reverence. Archie Miyatake, for example, born in Los Angeles in 1924, underwent such imperial education during his three years as a grammar school student in Shikoku, Japan in the 1930s. Of his time as a student in Japan, Archie recalled to interviewer Martha Nakagawa:

> AM: They were . . . trying to teach students to be very patriotic, so . . . in the morning at the school, the whole school would gather in one place and then the principal of the school would tell you to face towards the [capital], Tokyo, which would mean northeast from where Zentsuji was, and then we would always bow our head towards the *tennoheika* (His Majesty the Emperor), every morning before we all went to our own class. And . . . they tried to teach us patriotism that way.

MN: Did you have to memorize the *kyoiku chokugo* (The Imperial Rescript on Education)?[28]

AM: Oh yeah, very much.

MN: When did you recite that?

AM: We recited that in our class, when it came to that period where we talked about how to be patriotic to Japan.[29]

Similarly, Shigenobu Imai, originally of Dee, Oregon, shared of his stint as a grammar school student in late 1920s Okayama, "they were always saying that they believed in the emperor more than God . . . And then they were always saying you do things for the country by sacrificing yourself."[30] As these reflections show, the flavor of imperial propaganda associated with the expanding Japanese empire was influencing Japanese schoolchildren to consider their daily activities through the frame of benevolence to the emperor well before Japan's attack on Pearl Harbor.

An additional facet of Nisei learning to "act Japanese" involved internalizing the strict gender-bound proscriptions for feminine and masculine behavior in Japanese society. Japanese attitudes toward male supremacy, while not a topic of instruction in schools, were emphasized through behavioral assumptions in Japanese houses in both America and Japan. For example, Sumiko M. Yamamoto, a Nisei from California who later worked at the American occupation military headquarters in Fukuoka, remembered the evening ritual of the Japanese-style bath at her home in Gilroy, California, in the 1930s: "Well, it's the menfolks who takes the bath first. And we, the females, they go in last. My mother was the last to take the bath . . . My father, of course, he's the king of the house. He was the first, and my brothers. That's Japanese style."[31] Although Sumiko was not verbally instructed in the superiority of men, this hierarchy was reinforced subconsciously for her every night as she took her bath.

Similarly, Marion Tsutakawa Kanemoto, a Nisei who "repatriated" to Japan during the war on an exchange ship and later worked for the occupation, also recalled an instance of unspoken—albeit evident—reinforcement of the secondary place of Japanese women. Her mother wanted to register Marion's December 30th birth as a January birth so that Marion would not be two years old according to the Japanese tradition of counting age when she was actually only three days old. Yet, instead of registering with a date of January 1, Marion's mother recorded the birth as January 3. Of this, Marion mused, "I'm sure if it was a boy, it would have been January 1st. That would have been okay . . . The girls were always one or two steps behind the men. The men were always taking the front, front seat and it was something that was very accepted."[32]

Thus, although it was not part of the formal "cultural education" in Japanese schools and on study tours, Nisei girls absorbed an impression of women as subordinate in Japanese society. Children were encouraged to measure their behavior against the ideal standards of respectful behavior which, for Japanese girls, was predominantly the image of the *ojōsan,* the demure "young lady" admired for her restrained behavior. Nisei girls who aspired to thrive reproduced the norms of refined behavior that permeated their environment.

When Nisei arrived in Japan for employment, education, marriage opportunities, study visits, or in returned *dekasegi* families, they experienced in mainstream culture the "Japanese" style of female subordination. Many Nisei women who spent time in Japan later recalled their internal conflict regarding this ideal image, for in the United States, they enjoyed relative freedom to run around with their playmates, participate in sports, be outspoken, and attend co-ed schools. Under watchful Japanese eyes, however, they were expected to be unobtrusive, softspoken, and not to mingle with boys. In a letter to her friend Miye, Mary Kimoto relates a nightmare that her time in Japan might be altering her tomboyish ways:

> O, Miye—I had a terrible dream that I came back to America and all those church women were saying how "*ojohin*" (refined) and quiet and demure and Japanese maidenly I had become! O—it got me! They said my movements were so slow and graceful! It makes me laugh now because it is so impossible and ridiculous. I'm just as stubborn and pig-headed as ever and Japan will never take it out of me—I hope.[33]

Mary's dream reflects the importance that her Japanese caretakers and the Issei in her Japanese American community placed on the behavior of young women as a positive reflection on the family. And her hesitance—". . . I hope"—demonstrates that even the most resolute-minded tomboys wondered if the social demands for behavior of women in Japan could become so oppressive that they could no longer be bucked.

The experiences of Yayoi Cooke (née Koyabashi) also illustrate the particular social stresses placed on young women in Japan to be prim in their behavior, and to remember their place as secondary. Yayoi had attended Japanese school on Saturdays in California to learn reading and writing as well as Japanese history and calligraphy. She moved to Japan at the age of sixteen with her family when her mother, a widow, married an Issei who wanted to return to Japan. In Japan, Yayoi attended a school in Kofu operated by Canadian missionaries along with a handful of other Nisei students. Her brothers, also American-born, were held back in school, because they had to undergo the normal examinations taken by native Japanese students, but Yayoi and the other females could "get special treatment when they go to school because it doesn't matter." In Japan, Yayoi did not even dare to walk alongside her brothers in public, for fear that nosy neighbors would report her to the school principal for interacting with males.[34]

In America, Nisei girls—at least when they were beyond the surveillance of their Issei parents and Japanese school teachers—had the freedom to "act American," socializing with boys, playing athletic games, and moving about through their neighborhoods with friends. In Japan, however, mainstream Japanese ideals of restrained femininity regulated Nisei women's behavior. Hiroko Nakashima remembered, "Actually we didn't even know any boys [in Japan]. When you go to a girls' high school, you weren't allowed to mingle with boys. So the only boys I knew were my cousins."[35] Indeed, in their publication of a survey of Nisei living in the Tokyo-Yokohama metropolitan area, members of the Keisen Girls' School observed that, "According to the survey, the greatest difficulty faced by Nisei women in this problem of adjustment is the change in the mode of living . . . because of the fact that women are expected to live up to the strict standards of social etiquette for Japanese women."[36] Yamashita Sōen, too, remarked on the stress of this social reality at a conference held in 1938 on the topic of "The Second Generation Problem in Japan," musing, "Over there [in America], it's 'ladies first,' but here, the attitude toward males and females is completely different. And the boys feel glad about it and really ride it out—excessively so, even—but the girls feel cramped and slighted. They sour over it."[37]

Kazuko Uno, who moved from Seattle to Okayama for six months in 1939, remembered that her frustration over this issue made her quite certain that she could never make Japan her permanent home:

I immediately felt prejudice towards girls . . . They always favored the boys. It got me upset because I was a good student, and I felt like they were looking down on me. Even though I had to go to a Japanese school, I think I did very well. In fact, I did better in, like, math, arithmetic or whatever it was, than the Japanese students. But I still felt like, okay, they promote the boys and they kind of look down on the girls. On the other hand, my brother, who was not very studious, got a lot of attention because he was a boy . . . From the teachers, from the relatives, they kind of played up to him, and he loved it. So when the time came for my father to leave and come back to the United States, I said, "I'm not going to stay here; I'm coming back with you."[38]

Gender conventions in Japan dictated how girls and boys were treated by their relatives, their teachers, and their playmates. In everyday life, girls had to decide if they would conform to standards of ideal Japanese femininity—or whether they would buck the system. Monica Sone, for example, grew up as a self-proclaimed "tomboy" in Seattle, and when she visited her extended family in Tochigi, she insisted on romping around with her brother Henry and the local Japanese boys in their roughhousing play. The boys, she wrote, "never invited me nor spoke to me, but I tagged along anyway. The boys tried to ignore me as all girls deserved to be ignored, but I noticed that they sneaked many side glances, puzzled and bewildered, for in their books girls did not behave as I did."[39]

Passing as Japanese

Nisei—born into Japanese families and with Japanese physical features—were inextricably implicated in American prejudices toward the Japanese people as a nation of emperor worshippers and warriors, where the women were painted dolls trained to walk behind their husbands, and where modernization was proceeding on a distinct time lag. In the hyperpatriotic climate of post-World War I America, Japanese immigrants and their children faced discrimination that emphasized their difference from the rest of the American population. In addition to official anti-Japanese policies, social practices drew a distinct categorical line between Japanese and white Americans. Many schools on the West Coast, for example, had separate athletic teams for Nisei. Japanese (including Nisei) were routinely denied lodging at hotels and service at restaurants, and many cinemas required that Japanese patrons sit at the back of the theatre. These discriminatory practices reinforced that Nisei were to be socially differentiated, categorized racially alongside their Issei parents despite their American citizenship.

Such social discrimination communicated to Nisei not only that they were different, but also that they were inferior to other Americans and had fewer opportunities to succeed. Nisei Bruce T. Kaji, for example, recalled of his youth in Los Angeles that Japanese were not allowed to swim in the public pools until the day before the pool water was to be changed, when the water was cloudy and dirty.[40] Countless clever Nisei were discouraged from continuing their education, told repeatedly by teachers and guidance counselors that a college education would go to a waste on a "Jap," who would probably only be able to find work as a gardener or housekeeper even with a college degree. Aiko Herzig-Yoshinaga, born in Sacramento in 1924, dreamed of becoming a famous dancer or singer, but she dropped out of dance lessons in high school, explaining, "I faced reality. It ain't gonna happen in my time . . . Just because of what we look like. Even if I changed my name to 'Johnson' or 'Smith,' it wouldn't have done any good because of the way I look."[41] No matter how "American" Nisei in the United States dressed, moved, and spoke, their racial features marked them as unmistakably Japanese.

Nisei who went to Japan to seek opportunities for education and employment were hopeful that, because they were racially indistinguishable from the native population, they might at last be free from such discrimination. And yet, many quickly found that in Japan, too, Nisei were marked as different. Monica Sone's memoir *Nisei Daughter,* for example, captures this reality in the character of Jack Okada, who scorns a fellow Nisei's decision to seek work in Japan sneering, "Dick's a fool. He thinks he's going to be kingpin out there with an American education. Those big companies can make use of fellows like him all right, but Dick's going to find himself on a social island. The Japanese hate us Nisei. They despise our crude American manners."[42]

The stereotype of Nisei in pre-World War II Japan was that they were lazy, ill-mannered, ignorant and unsupportive of the motivations for Japanese expansion in the Pacific, and excessively "American"—liberal in behavior and expression. In an effort to prepare their fellow Nisei for this discriminatory attitude in Japanese society, the young Nisei women of Keisen Girls' School in Tokyo advised in their 1939 report that because of the negative reputation of Nisei in Japan, their employment opportunities in Japan may be limited. Would-be employers, they cautioned, are often reticent to hire Nisei, for, as one respondent related, "the Japanese employer resents the individualistic, wanting-to-learn everything attitude of the Nisei." Added another survey respondent, "The Japanese cannot understand the Nisei—they could not understand my expressions and mannerisms and sometimes thought I was queer or abnormal."[43]

Miya Sannomiya, one of the Nisei who had participated in the *Nichibei Shinbun*-sponsored Japan study tour group in 1925, experienced this contempt first-hand when she moved to Japan for employment. Working as a secretary for the Kokusai Bunka Shinkōkai (International Society for Cultural Relations), Miya witnessed the following exchange at a meeting:

Sometime during 1936–37 our Society held a round table discussion for leaders of organizations connected with the care and education of the young Niseis studying in Japan. There were about 14–15 people representing various Buddhist groups, private schools, YWCA, YMCA, Japanese language school for foreigners, etc. For some reason, I had been asked to sit in at the discussions and to take notes. No one there, except one prominent Christian woman educator, knew I was a Nisei. The whole discussion failed because not one constructive idea was taken up seriously. The participants spent the whole afternoon in derisive laughter and critical remarks about the "outlandish ways of these Niseis," their "horrible, low class, boorish, country style Japanese speech" . . . They all nodded solemnly as one speaker said, "The Nisei are children of low class, peasant emigrants, so what could we expect of them?" In other words, they were saying that the Niseis were hopeless cases and they wanted to have nothing to do with them.[44]

Racial features marked Nisei as different in the United States, and in Japan, Nisei could only "blend in" once they had mastered mimicry of Japanese physical traits and movement, as Miya had. Many Nisei, particularly those who entered standard Japanese schools, struggled as they underwent—or resisted—this process of Japanization. They were teased for being *imin no ko* (children of emigrants) and faced discrimination for the fact that their parents had once abandoned Japan. Some Nisei living in Japan as schoolchildren got into scuffles with classmates who threw rocks through the *shōji* screens of their homes, spat at them, and called them "American" (*Amerikajin*), "Korean" (*Chōsenjin*), or even "African" (*Afurikajin*). Despite their racial similarities to Japanese citizens, Nisei in Japan faced discrimination for displaying "Western" features and behaviors, such as longer hair (for males) or a permanent curl (for females), colorful clothing, inability to speak native-level Japanese, outspokenness, and even for their energetic gait.

Facing this frigid social reception, Nisei living in the more heavily Nisei-populated districts of Japan formed their own separate social institutions so that they might feel comfortable and connected. As the Nisei student population in Japan grew, so too did Nisei social organizations. Nisei were often active in the YMCA and YWCA, which offered social gathering opportunities in addition to educational programs and courses in typing and stenography. A group in Tokyo called the Association of Nikkei Shimin held events such as picnics, New Year parties, and field trips to famous Japanese places. The Ria Club for Nisei girls in Tokyo took its name from the acronym for "Raised-in-America."[45] Organizations in Tokyo with Nisei membership, as listed in the Keisen Girls' School Survey (printed in 1939), included: a group of Tokyo Union Church worship singers called the Aeolian Singers, the American Boy Scout Society in Japan, Hui Hawaii (for Hawaiian girls over age sixteen), the Japan-America Young People's Federation, the Keisen Fellowship (a friendship program for Nisei at Keisen), the Little Club (young women who have lived abroad), the Little N's (English practice club), the Nikkei Bussei Society of Tokyo (for foreign-born Buddhists, age seventeen to thirty), the Pacific Club, Sigma Kappa Theta (a religious organization), Sigma Nu Kappa (a fraternity for Nisei at Meiji university), Tokyo Union Church Second-Generation Committee, the Waseda American Society, and the Yokohama Society of Second-Generation Japanese.[46] Such organizations were most plentiful in the Tokyo area, where the majority of young adult study abroad students flocked for their education, but similar organizations also existed in Kyoto, Osaka, Wakayama, and Hiroshima. These organizations offered Nisei spaces to vent about common experiences of discrimination or the at-times oppressive demands of Japanese culture, but such spaces were not available to Nisei living as "ordinary Japanese" in *dekasegi* families or with relatives in rural areas.

Yamashita Sōen, who wrote widely about the lives of Nisei in early twentieth century Japan, painted a lively picture of the social environment of Nisei in large cities such as Tokyo, which he described as markedly different from the lifestyle of young Japanese men and women. According to Yamashita's various interviews with Nisei study abroad students in Japan, foreign-born Nisei communicated with one another predominantly in English, read American magazines, listened to American records, and wrote letters home to Nisei friends in English (although letters home to parents were mostly in Japanese). Some of the study abroad students also counted Japanese friends in their social sphere, although they noted that such Japanese friends tended to be interested in international events, English, and life abroad. In Yamashita's interaction with Nisei study abroad pupils, he observed that Nisei generally spent their free time much as they might have done in the United States, enjoying music (ukulele, steel guitar, singing), chatting over ping-pong or board games, playing sports (catch, volleyball, basketball, tennis, baseball, swimming, American football, skiing, ice skating, track, and wrestling), taking walks, visiting friends, watching sport events, going to films, and shopping with other Nisei. Traditionally Japanese pastimes, such as the musical instrument *koto,* tea ceremony, flower arranging, and Japanese martial arts of *jūdō* and *kendō,* were also popular among Nisei living in Japan, as exercises of Japanese cultural learning—as "Japanese" pursuits.[47]

When Nisei were interacting with one another, they could "act American," that is, they could speak English and engage in the pastimes they enjoyed in America. As a student at Waseda International School, Mary Kimoto wrote to her friend Miye, describing the comfortable feeling of sharing space with fellow Nisei in Japan: "Last night we went to song practice at a girl's place. She lives in an international house. It felt almost like America in her room, with furniture and *Life* magazines and popular music the kids played on the piano."[48] As Mary's letter and Yamashita's interviews with Nisei suggest, "America" was alive in everyday pre-World War II Japan through material culture—magazines, musical instruments, and furniture—as well as through hobbies and behaviors familiar to Nisei from their lives back in America. The experiences of Nisei adapting to life in Japan during this period demonstrate a keen awareness of differentiation between Japanese and American objects and practices. Just as they had done in the United States, Nisei in rural and urban Japan were territorializing behaviors and aspects of their physical environment as "Japanese" or "American," honing their ability to code-switch between those two territories based on their conscious and subconscious readings of their surroundings.

The stakes of Nisei code-switching in Japan, however, were different from the stakes of code-switching in America. In both America and Japan, race functioned as a dominant silo of social categorization in the lives of Nisei. The hegemonic racial profile in early twentieth century America was that of the *hakujin,* the white American. Nisei in the United States could mimic white American behaviors to gain privilege in social settings, to receive high marks from teachers, and to advance in their careers, but their phenotypical features denied them access to unquestioned Americanness. In Japan, however, these phenotypically Japanese features provided an opportunity for American-born Nisei to claim affiliation with the Japanese race. Only when they manifested subtler "tells" of their American background—differences in speech patterns, movement, and dress that signified "foreign" or "American"—would they be classified as not wholly Japanese.

The code-switching demonstrated by Nisei in both America and Japan represents their attempt to control the process of categorical signification itself. In race studies, "passing" refers to the attempt to render invisible one or more categories of one's group membership. That aim to erase or conceal is often intimately connected with a moral judgment of denial, and as such, the experience of passing can involve both risk and pleasure, both shame and pride.[49] In Japan, many Nisei made an effort to quell anxiety and to advance in society by "acting Japanese" when surrounded by mainstream Japanese culture, and by "acting American" when surrounded by other Nisei or non-Japanese friends. In this sense, Nisei in prewar Japan were chameleons, editing their mannerisms and appearance through mimicry of those around them. Whereas Nisei chameleons "acting American" in America might sense an audience dubious of Japanese features and overcompensate to prove group membership as American, Nisei chameleons in Japan could potentially pass as Japanese—if they mastered the cultural performance of Japaneseness.

As Nisei in Japan confronted the social coding practices demarcating "Japanese" from "American" or "Western," they interpreted their own appearance and behavior in terms of the expectations and social values held by those around them. The normalizing gaze of society confronted Nisei and influenced the ways they adjusted to their social climate. Received by their host Japanese society as foreigners, many Nisei living in Japan found themselves regular targets of strangers' interest, attention, and suspicion. This attention, it should be noted, was not necessarily malicious. Oregon-born Frances Ota, for example, recalled of her reception in 1930s' Japan:

> In fact, we were looked upon sort of in awe, you know. My older sister . . . would often say, "Oh, these people are staring at us," and such. And she was tall for her age, so she was called a beanpole or whatever, and she makes that remark, but we weren't discriminated. They seemed to treat us like in awe.[50]

San Jose-born Peggy Furukawa, too, was an object of curiosity when she arrived as an eleven- year-old schoolgirl to Okayama in 1939. She explained:

> We're like museum people. Because it was kind of new. Nobody came from America or something. So they all want to sit down and stare at us . . . We looked different, we walked different . . . See, they were more smaller. And we walked different, and we talked different, see, so they liked to sit down and listen to my sister and I, but we talk English.[51]

As a result of this social reception, Nisei were cued to consider themselves as different from their Japanese relatives and neighbors—and to be continually aware of these differences. Under these circumstances, performing as Japanese offered a means for Nisei to ease anxiety, especially for Nisei children living in rural Japanese communities who lacked access to Nisei networks and social groups.

The personal experiences of many Nisei who moved to Japan in the 1920s and 1930s illustrate the power of society's normalizing gaze to codify behavior according to social ideals. Mitsue May Yamada, for example, was actually born in Japan (her mother, still rattled from a particularly difficult childbirth the previous year in Seattle, insisted on giving birth in Japan), but Mitsue was nevertheless considered "American" by her community in Japan. "You know," she explained in a 2002 interview, "the Japanese people were very vocal about how different [Americans are], they call you *Amerika no ojōsan* (American daughter), and they comment on your clothes, and they comment on your speech, and they comment on your age . . . on your appearance and so forth. So you were always constantly aware."[52] Yoneko Dozono of Portland, Oregon, recalled a similar experience of standing out as a foreigner in Gifu, where she moved in 1931 to receive "bride school" training in womanly arts:

> Where I lived, this was the first time that any Japanese American had gone there, . . . I was a great novelty, and I was written up in the papers quite frequently . . . whenever I walked through the streets to go to school, the children of the village would follow me . . . And so my aunt and uncle said,

"No, you can't do this because you draw too much attention." And so they made me wear Japanese clothes. And life was very strict, but I remember my aunt said, "You can choose your own *zōri*," the footwear. And she took me to this shop, and I chose a pair of black *zōri,* and she laughed, and she said, "Those are for older people. You have to wear something red." And I thought, wow, she tells me I can choose something, but I really can't choose things. I have to be very rigid, and I have to conform. And so in order not to draw attention . . . I had curly hair at that time. It was natural, and she would comb my hair in the morning to make it straight. And being sixteen, seventeen in America, I started polishing my nails, and she said, "You can't polish your nails." I had sterling silver bracelets that were given to me when I left, and she said, "That makes noise, you can't use those." You can't wear lipstick, and everything was conformity, conformity . . .[53]

Ever conscious of their difference from the Japanese population, many Nisei felt that if they altered their American behavioral and physical markings, they would be able to blend into Japanese society, and would thereby alleviate some of this social pressure. Mitsue May Yamada shared a story about such an urge:

I told Mom, "Everybody thinks I'm *Amerika no ojōsan,* so it must be my clothes that I'm wearing." . . . And so Mom took me to the store and then, and bought me a pair of shoes, because they had different . . . kind of clunky-looking shoes that they had. And so they dressed me completely in Japanese-bought, Japanese-bought Western clothes. And then they, and then they still called me *Amerika no ojōsan.* So I remember asking my cousin, "What's so different?" And then she said, "Oh, Mitsu-san, it's because of the way you walk . . . you have to walk in little steps. And you walk like this." . . . [my walk] was one thing that Mom was always criticizing me for . . .[54]

Marked as foreign in their new neighborhoods, many Nisei felt pressure to conform to Japanese ways of life by reflecting Japanese preferences for clothing, hairstyles, forms of expression, and movement.

For many Nisei in Japan, the judging eyes of society were felt sharply not only through the hovering shadow of curious glances but also through ridicule and even violence. Frank Hironobu Hirata, for example, who moved at the age of nine from Spokane to Okayama, recalled one particular occasion when his teacher derided him for his American appearance. Frank was standing in front of the class working math problems on the blackboard, wearing wool pants sent from his mother in Spokane. As Frank struggled to complete the equation on the board, the teacher exclaimed, "'Hey, look at this guy, this *Amerikan kabure* (pro-American),' you know, 'He thinks that he's half American. See what he's wearing? No wonder he cannot do his homework.' Because in those days, the only thing that the students were supposed to wear was made by cotton, no wool."[55] Frank Fukuhara of Hawai'i likewise learned the importance of assimilating into Japanese society one afternoon at his family's new home in Hiroshima when a fifth-grade student at his school physically attacked him for wearing a blue shirt instead of the white one required by the uniform code at their school.[56] The forces shaping Nisei cultural performance demonstrate that various factors in the environment—including motivations and deterrents posited by social preferences and by real threats of punishment—condition individuals consciously and subconsciously to mimic hegemonic behavior and appearance. In a subtle process of mimicry, Nisei assimilated alternately to Japanese ideals and to American ideals, dependent upon the hegemonic preferences of their environment in a given moment. This interplay of voluntary self-regulation and involuntary (subconscious) self-regulation will be echoed in Part Three of this book, in Nisei postwar narratives of coerced collaboration.

Awareness of social judgment and the threat of ridicule and violence inspired many Nisei in Japan to mitigate the pressures of societal scrutiny by mimicking behaviors and features coded as "Japanese" as opposed to "American." Kazue Murakami Tanimoto of Hilo, Hawai'i, for example, shared her method for coping with the social awkwardness she felt as a high school pupil living at a Tsurumi dormitory in the 1930s:

> The high school that I went to, the girls laughed at me because my Japanese was mixed slang. So I thought, "Oh, well, I'm going to shut up." [Laughs] I'm not going to talk, I'm going to listen to what they're saying to learn their Japanese. So, okay, that's what I did. I didn't talk to them. But when they offered me to go to their house, I went, to see how they operate and how they talk. That's how I pick up my Japanese. I pick it up faster.[57]

Kazue's response to the teasing of her classmates was to suppress her imperfect, Hawaiian Japanese until she could properly imitate standard Japanese as spoken by her Japanese classmates.

Iwao Peter Sano of Brawley, California, also described mimicry of Japanese behavior as his coping mechanism. Peter, who was adopted by relatives in Yamanashi in 1939 and later served in the Japanese army, described that he "*enryo*-ed," meaning that he kept his behavior in check when he arrived in Japan:

If I was in the United States, I was not 100 percent American. And when something like comparing would come up, I would be a foreigner . . . I guess I felt like an outsider in Japan, or that I should try harder to be more like a Japanese. And I think I, maybe that was the most thing that came up more often, like I'm not treated like a Japanese, what can I do? I should try harder to be more [Japanese] . . . and I think in a way, maybe not even realized that I was feeling that way. I think I did finally act that way, too.[58]

Peter's thought process, reflected in this expression of his struggles as a Nisei, demonstrates the psychological process through which social discourse posits standards for appearance and behavior. In times of stress, surveillance, or struggle, Nisei in Japan tried to pass as Japanese, altering their behavior and appearance to ease the pressure of their own difference from such ideals.

In large cities such as Tokyo and Kyoto with concentrated numbers of study abroad pupils, Nisei could find escape from the pressures of conforming to Japanese life in their specialized social organizations, separate study divisions, and dormitories. Nisei who moved to their ancestral hometowns, however, had relatively little opportunity to engage in "American" hobbies and behaviors. These Nisei, many of whom never intended to return to the United States, gradually transitioned into Japanese life, answering to their Japanese names rather than the American names many had been given or had chosen in the US, improving their Japanese language skills through supplementary tutoring, and altering their physical appearance. The reflections of Grant Hirabayashi, born in Thomas, Washington, in 1919, demonstrate this delicate transition into Japanese ways of life. As a schoolboy in the hometown of his aunt and uncle, he recalled:

My teacher was very sympathetic, I wore my hair [long] for a good six months, and he let me wear my shoes. Like only teachers were allowed to wear shoes in class, but I did have permission. But I, when the shoes wore out, I went native and had my hair cut . . . as time went on, I was able to communicate, and by then, my hair was short, shoes was gone, and I was wearing slippers.[59]

Grant's relatives and teachers were patient with his transition from "American" appearance and behavior into "Japanese" ways of life. But his experience emphasizes that a heightened awareness of Japanese versus Western objects and practices caused stress for Nisei, regardless of their living situation. Nisei in Japan internalized the differences between Japanese and American behaviors and features, and under a normalizing gaze that coded Japanese features as positive and American/Nisei features as negative, Nisei honed their ability to suppress Americanness and mimic Japaneseness when the setting called for it. Similarly, they could exercise their Americanness and suppress their Japaneseness when surrounded by fellow Nisei or fellow foreigners.

Nisei living in Japan navigated an environment rife with specific classifications that signified Japanese behaviors and objects as directly opposed to American behaviors and objects. Nisei internalized these discursive codes, assigning positive and negative values to physical objects as well as to mannerisms. Nisei adjusted their own behavior and appearance—consciously and subliminally—in conversation with these codes. In this way, mainstream Japanese culture exerted its power to "Japanize" Nisei not hierarchically with a master plan but rather dynamically—rhizomically, like plant roots growing in horizontal webs underground—through a broad network of internalized and mimicked signifiers of hegemony. Through this rhizomic process, ideals for Japanese behavior and appearance wielded the power to shape Nisei self-representation as Japanese.

Contributing further to this process of self-regulation, Nisei in Japan confronted an environment that was generally more rule-bound than that which they had known as children in the United States. Issei parents in the United States typically worked long hours, leaving Nisei relatively free from adult supervision for several hours of the day, explained Minoru ("Min") Tonai, who moved from Terminal Island, Los Angeles, to Wakayama as a young boy. In Japan, however, most Nisei were faced with increased adult supervision and regulation. Min described that he and his younger siblings "were left in the country and I hated it. I used to fight with my grandmother all the time." And when Min and his grandmother got into their frequent arguments, she would "tell me that, 'You shouldn't talk to your grandmother like that. I am a descendant,' . . . of this famous Japanese family . . . back in the year 1040 or something like that." The more rebelliously Min acted, the more authoritatively his grandmother attempted to rein him in. One day, insisting that she saw the remains of lice eggs in Min's hair, she forcibly shaved his head into the Japanese schoolboy style as "a way of disciplining me."[60] Alongside self-regulation, such disciplinary forces from guardians, neighbors, and schoolmates also propelled Nisei in 1920s–1940s' Japan toward assimilation into the Japanese populace.

Despite being free from the watchful eye of their parents or other relatives, Nisei living in dormitories in Japan still could not escape the more regulated atmosphere of Japanese society. They faced rigid schedules with mandatory prayer hours, study halls, curfews, and requirements for special permission to go out in the evenings. Dormitory heads assumed the role of supervisor of all aspects of the residents' lives, from their progress in study to their changing behaviors and their absorption of Japanese ways of life. For example, Kawasaki Shizuko, proprietress of a Buddhist-affiliated girls' dormitory in Musashino, wrote of her residents, "In addition to their studies in flower arranging, tea ceremony, and *koto,* they have gotten skillful in their manners, from how to wear Japanese clothing to how to spread *futon* bedding, even bowing."[61] As Kawasaki's letter reflects, Nisei living in dormitories and in relatives' homes were lauded for displaying "Japanese" behaviors and physical traits.

Many Nisei experienced a daily reminder of this more stringent emphasis on conformity as they donned their Japanese school uniforms. Hiroko Nakashima, for example, recalled that when she and her family moved to Yamaguchi in 1939 to attend school, she and her sister often looked out the window and remarked about the Japanese children on their way to school, "We thought, gee, [that's] really different 'cause in America you just wear any clothes, but in Japan all the students were uniformed from kindergarten up to high school."[62] In time, both sisters were wearing the navy blue, sailor-style tops and pleated skirts of their Japanese classmates. Jack Dairiki, who sailed from California on the *Tatsuta Maru* just before World War II broke out in 1941, described the strict daily ritual of uniform check at his new school in Hiroshima:

> First we go, get all assembled by class group, and then there'd be a leader of the group who'd call attention to everybody, and then bow to the principal, and then we also had inspection of our fingernails, make sure the fingernails clipped and clean, and there's an inspection of your pocket to take out a handkerchief, make sure it was a clean handkerchief in your pocket and no, no ornaments on yourself. And see, I remember the girls used to have, they don't have a pocket, so they used to pin their handkerchief on their clothes. Boys had a pocket, so they had handkerchief in the pocket. And then we'll, after a simple exercise and maybe announcement of the day, each one will go to their classroom. We'd take our footgear off, put it in the box, shelf that we had outside and then go to each classroom, some upstairs, some downstairs. It's a two-floor building. We open the glass sliding door, move in—and an assigned seat, and then wait for the teacher to come in, and the teacher will come in by themselves. When the teacher come in, close the door, the leader of the class would say, "Attention," everybody would stand up and bow. We'd all bow to the teacher, and Teacher said sit down and everybody'd sit down together.[63]

This exhausting routine at Jack's school was a typical experience for many Nisei assimilating into Japanese culture at the time, especially for those living with family and attending local schools. In Japan, Nisei bodies were regulated as Japanese by uniform wearing as well as through rituals of regulated movement.

By blending in with the general Japanese population, Nisei in Japan could minimize the stresses of social discrimination against second generation Japanese Americans. And by performing ideals for Japanese femininity and reining in "unfeminine" behaviors, women in Japan could earn praise and social advantages. Nisei in Japan—for whom "American" versus "Japanese" traits and "feminine" versus "unfeminine" traits had been so clearly differentiated—adapted to their new surroundings by honing their ability to mimic these ideal or undesirable behaviors and characteristics.

As the reflections of Nisei shared in this chapter express, Nisei living in Japan wrestled with decisions of how (and whether) to regulate their behavior in Japan. Some Nisei living in Japan before the start of World War II were resistant to the demands of Japanese life and rebelled against Japanese customs and rigid social expectations by refusing to take off their shoes on *tatami* bamboo flooring, or by disobeying the rules put into place by overbearing guardians. Though these Nisei were resolute not to change their appearance and behavior despite scornful, surveying eyes, they were nevertheless aware that their behavior was antithetical to the ideals of their host society in Japan. This ability to identify and categorize behaviors as "Japanese" or "American" would be central to Nisei life in Japan after the start of the war, when resolute resistance to performance as Japanese was no longer a viable option for those who hoped to survive.

Other Nisei felt that they could rein in their "American" behaviors around audiences unappreciative of such behaviors, waiting until they were in the company of other Nisei to play American music, interact with members of the opposite sex, and chat in English. These Nisei were adept at code-switching between Japanese and "Western" behaviors. They recognized that they would be rewarded and praised for performing Japanese characteristics when they deemed the audience appreciative of such performances; and, likewise, that they would in certain company be scorned, chastised, and even humiliated or abused for displaying behaviors or physical traits antithetical to Japanese ideals.

As Nisei adjusted to Japanese society by performing as Japanese, many felt dissonance between their actions of mimicry and the American behaviors with which they were more comfortable. Yoneko Dozono, for example, who was sent from Portland to Gifu in 1931 at the age of sixteen, remembered that when she began attending school in Japan, she felt extremely awkward about Japanese customs of emperor reverence:

> When you walk into the [school] gate, the first thing you do is you bow and show respect to the school and to the emperor's emblem. Well, being American, I thought, "What in the dickens am I doing bowing to somebody or

something that I didn't even know anything about?" But my aunt kept on saying, "This is something you have to do because in Japan you show honor and respect to the emperor." And so the first day when she took me, I had on my hat and I had on my gloves like the proper Japanese American girl would do, and she said, "Take your hat off, take your gloves off." And I said, "What is going on?" But I was very obedient. So every day that I would go to school which I did go every day for five days a week in the morning, first thing, I would go into the school and I would bow, and I would be so embarrassed, thinking who's watching me.[64]

Under the scrutiny of watchful neighbors, foreign-born Nisei living in Japan were constantly reminded that the imitation of Japanese behaviors and adoption of Japanese physical traits were of utmost importance for their advancement, praiseworthiness, and to reflect well on their family's reputation. It was of little importance whether these behaviors felt authentic to the Nisei herself. This dissonance is reminiscent of the Nisei experiences in American society discussed in the previous chapter; marked as socially different in America, Nisei were received by the non-Japanese public as falling short of authentic Americanness, despite how American they acted, dressed, or spoke.

In both America and in Japan, education in "Japaneseness" (in the home, in schools, and in society) instructed Nisei to appreciate the content of Japanese culture, including the importance of standard language ability, demure femininity, the unique Japanese spirit expressed in Japanese traditional arts, and the might of an empire rooted in an illustrious imperial line and a time-honored warrior culture. Japanese education thus presented "Japaneseness" as ideal, learnable units of culture and history—a culture about which Nisei, without proper instruction, would be ignorant. Heritage education and exposure to Japanese culture and glory, hoped Issei and Japanese alike, would help to alleviate the woes of the Second Generation Problem by raising Nisei to be proud of their culture and adept at demonstrating its gendered ideals.

As much as they learned about Japanese culture, however, American Nisei would not "turn Japanese" as a result of their Japanese education. Rather, school curriculum, environment, and social reception of Nisei both in America and in Japan prompted Nisei to code certain mannerisms and physical attributes as "Japanese" or "un-Japanese" (i.e., "Western" or "American" in their parlance). They learned which behaviors were expected of them in which settings, and they could pick and choose the attributes to express. This aspiration to assimilate—to perform as alternately Japanese or American—was cultivated in Nisei by the power of ideals reverberating in their physical and discursive environment, and by the promises these ideals held of alleviating the stresses of a "problematic" existence.

In Japan as well, as discussed in this chapter, Nisei were looked down upon and faced ridicule. Nisei learned that they could make themselves more comfortable in their environment by mimicking behavior coded as Japanese and suppressing behavior coded as foreign. Thus, in spite of the public rhetoric of Nisei as "bridges" between two cultures, and in spite of the calculated methods of educating Nisei to fulfill such a role of being "both Japanese and American," the social realities they faced in both America and in Japan conflicted with this Nisei paradigm, particularly in terms of gender roles. Despite being trained in America to take an active role in the promotion of Japanese culture, Nisei women were also cued to consider themselves as inferior to their male counterparts. In Japan, they faced double discrimination, as women and as objects of social disdain—the "children of emigrants."

When American Nisei moved to Japan in the prewar decades for schooling, job opportunities, or with sojourner parents who were returning to Japan indefinitely, their ability to appear Japanese in dress, movement, speech, and social interaction was suddenly much more important than it had been back in America. Surveillance by schoolmasters, dorm supervisors, strangers, and relatives kept Nisei ever aware that Japanese behavior would be rewarded, and resistance to assimilation into Japanese culture could result in feelings of awkwardness or humiliation, and perhaps even in violence. Nisei living in Japan, therefore, learned that to succeed in Japanese society, they would need to conform by reflecting behaviors coded as Japanese and by suppressing behaviors coded as "American," "Western," and even "Nisei." It mattered not to their audience how authentic Nisei felt about "acting Japanese." As long as they donned the costumes, pronounced the lines, and memorized the choreography lauded by their Japanese host society, daily life would be smoother, and opportunities for praise and social advancement would be more abundant.

In considering the influence of social discourse and the physical environment on self-representation, one refrain echoes throughout the personal accounts of Nisei who came of age in the early twentieth century. This is the refrain of cultural identity as equivalent to cultural performance. Nisei in America and those transitioning into life in Japan expressed their own cultural identity as indoctrinated, as problematic, and as a separate entity not inherently or authentically their own—but rather a role to play. As bicultural individuals growing up in increasingly antagonistic environments both in America and in Japan, Nisei envisioned "Americanness" and "Japaneseness" as separate roles between which they could oscillate, based on their assessments of the preferences of their audience.

Nisei positioned American and Japanese identity as opposite—as two distinct mantles that could be assumed as occasion demanded, but as costumes nonetheless. As Nisei engaged in behaviors socially coded as distinctly Japanese or distinctly American, they faced resistance from societies that received them as neither authentically Japanese nor authentically American. Nisei, therefore, were trained through their everyday experiences to perceive both "Japaneseness" and "Americanness" as exercises of cultural performance rather than innate, authentic aspects of an individual self.

Flexibility of cultural representation, advised Nisei who knew life in Japan, is the key to functioning successfully in Japanese society. "If the Nisei can overcome their egoism and resolve to observe the adage 'When in Rome do as the Romans do,'" urged the Nisei Survey board of the Keisen Girls' School, "they will be welcome in Japanese society."[65] The question of cultural identity for Nisei in the 1920s through the 1940s represented a struggle of conflicting paradigms, rendering identity itself an abstraction—a process of self-representation that would likely never feel entirely authentic. For those Nisei who remained in Japan throughout World War II, this perception of identity would frame individual experiences of war propaganda, interaction with Japanese relatives, and the impressions they projected as they collaborated with Japanese or occupation authorities.

Nisei perception of cultural identity as a fundamentally inauthentic performance would be critical to the ways these Nisei managed to survive in Japan during the years of total war. The sensory experience of cultural norms and ideals in the everyday environment informed Nisei performances of Japaneseness and Americanness, and cultivated in Nisei the aspiration to assimilate in order to achieve personal goals. The ability to oscillate between cultural performances would enable Nisei living in Japan throughout the war—who had been drilled in spearing the heart of American invaders, and who had carried cyanide in their pockets to commit suicide should they see an American soldier—to transition so quickly into postwar life, sharing offices with these same American soldiers as typists, translators, and censors during the occupation.

PART II

Wartime

CHAPTER THREE

Liminal, Subliminal, Sublime

On December 2, 1941, the Nippon Yūsen ocean liner *Tatsuta Maru* set sail for San Francisco from the port of Yokohama. Among its many American passengers hastening to return home to the United States was Mary Kimoto, a young Nisei woman born and raised in California's Central Valley. Mary had been living as a study abroad student in Tokyo since June of 1939, and she was eager to return to her friends and family in Ceres, California. Mary's wartime narrative, composed in 1947 as letters to her friend and fellow Nisei Kay Oka, reflects relief as she begins the journey back to California: "Now that I finally made the boat I can relax and get rested. There are over one hundred Nisei on board here. Most of them are Nisei girls like me who are returning. There are a few white American teachers and missionaries." Mary's respite, however, would be short-lived. On December 8, the *Tatsuta Maru* abruptly shifted course and turned back to the islands of Japan. Amid confusion and flying rumors, Mary penned another letter to Kay: "Dear Kay, I am coming back to you. Our ship has turned back, and we are heading toward Japan. I have no idea why." In an update dated December 20, 1941, Mary describes the fate of the Nisei who had been aboard the ship.

> Dear Kay,
>
> Now I am facing reality. Those fantastic tales [about Japan's attack on Pearl Harbor] that I heard while on the ship have all turned out to be true. When we landed in Yokohama, the police questioned us. We had to give them the time we would leave Yokohama, our destination, and our future plans. They say that all the white Americans were interned. Since we look Japanese, I guess they thought it would be safe to turn us loose.[1]

Like thousands of American-born Nisei who had not returned to the United States by the time Japanese bombs fell on Pearl Harbor, Mary Kimoto would face the years of World War II on Japanese soil—not as an imprisoned suspect of espionage, not as an interned enemy alien, but as a member of the imperial Japanese populace.

Mary's wartime struggles, preserved in her "Dear Kay" epistolary memoirs, provide a window to the everyday concerns, environment, and activities of Nisei on the Japanese home front during World War II. The fabric of Mary Kimoto's experiences, combined with archival materials and personal accounts of other Nisei, of non-Japanese foreigners, and of Japanese citizens provide access to the ways in which the Japanese government's policies and propaganda campaigns—and their reverberations in the physical and discursive environment—influenced the assimilation of American Nisei in Japan during the years of Japan's conflict with the United States. These wartime experiences of Nisei in Japan during World War II complicate the concept of collaboration by highlighting the capacity of social discourse, ritual, disciplinary methods, and the physical environment to mold the behavior and self-representation of Nisei during the years of total war.

Soft Propaganda in Wartime Japan

In recreating the environment of Nisei living in total war Japan, Part Two of this book continues to build on the layered consideration of propaganda raised in Part One—as something subtler than the one-sided visual or verbal material disseminated by hegemonic institutions. Propaganda extends far beyond clear-cut representations of positive and negative attributes in public media. Institutions, individuals, and even objects reiterate and enforce norms for ideal behavior in society. Functioning through administrative policies, community organization systems, and modes of information distribution, the messages trumpeted by "hard propaganda" (explicit directives for behavior established by hegemonic institutions or individuals) leach into the environment itself. As human beings absorb and reflect these ideals and taboos, the messages of propaganda echo throughout social discourse—in conversations with neighbors, at the workplace, at the dinner table, and beyond. In the physical environment, too, propaganda messages are woven into practices of design and consumption (of clothing, food, modes of transportation, and even the physical layouts of cities and homes, for example).[2] Through this more subtle "soft propaganda," hard propaganda wields its influence, molding minds and shaping behaviors in everyday life by coding social discourse and the physical environment with the positive and negative charges established by hard propaganda.

To study wartime soft propaganda in practice, Part Two looks to the rituals and material culture of the historical moment of total war Japan in the context of the government's hard propaganda campaigns and policies. This analysis seeks not only the values and evils posited by propaganda, but also the efficacy of those representations—by probing for evidence of the power of institutions, material culture, and discourse to influence the behavior of individuals on an everyday level.

A note here about the dubious light that has been cast on questions of propaganda efficacy in wartime Japan, largely as a response to John Dower's sweeping study of racially charged propaganda promulgated by both the Japanese and their Western adversaries during World War II: yes, the architects of propaganda in wartime Japan disseminated rhetoric that vilified Westerners and glorified self-sacrifice, but did the general populace actually *believe* the propaganda? As Historian W. Puck Brecher has pointed out, ubiquity of propaganda does not constitute evidence of an indoctrinated public. However high the din of government-sponsored propaganda in Japan during the years of total war, it cannot be assumed that the general populace blindly swallowed these messages and committed to the rhetoric. Indeed, writes Brecher in *Honored and Dishonored Guests: Westerners in Wartime Japan,* the omnipresence of state control and government propaganda rather served to distance the general public and foster apathy.[3] And yet, as developments in neuroscience have shown, human behavior stems from perceptions (visual, auditory, memory imprints, and other elements of sensory input) that proceed along pathways not associated with intention, awareness, or conscious effort.[4] In short, human behavior depends very little on what people *think*. Instead, it depends almost entirely on the constant stream of sensory and social cues provided to humans by their environment, which their brains perpetually process, negotiate, and distill. Whether or not human subjects "believed" propaganda, both hard and soft, becomes of little consequence. They could not help but absorb its paradigms and scripts and shape a great deal of their behavior accordingly—whether consciously (out of fear of social distain or even punishment) or subconsciously (due to the reptilian brain's drive to survive and thrive).

Central to this study's emphasis on the power of soft propaganda is an understanding of the human body as governed by its entanglement in material life, by quotidian elements in the physical environment such as clothing, food, educational materials, magazines, and newspapers. A glimpse into the "everyday" as a site of praxis—actors engaged in their time and place—provides a means to delve into the complex processes of individuals making sense of the world. The wartime actions of Nisei in Japan were both consciously and subliminally shaped by soft propaganda-infused discourse, by value-coded material culture and ritual, by methods of psychological and bodily discipline, and by economic and familial considerations. The wartime behavior of American-born Nisei must be considered as embedded in these realities of the historical moment, without anticipation of the accusations of treason that would follow in the wake of Allied victory.

The Bridge Crumbles

Mary Kimoto's life in Japan began in June of 1939. A twenty-year-old graduate of Modesto Junior College, Mary had worked as a housekeeper in the suburbs of San Francisco for one year to save money for her passage to Japan, where—as her siblings had done before her—she would be able to meet her extended family, study Japanese, and have broader job opportunities than she could hope for as a Nisei in California. Mary followed in her older brother George's footsteps, registering as a student at Waseda Kokusai Gakuin and settling into a Japanese household (the Nagata family) in the Tokyo area. As a young student in Tokyo, Mary seems to have paid little attention to the news about Japan's battle successes in its war against China, much less to the progress of Hitler's expansion in Europe. In a letter from Tokyo dated October 13, 1939, Mary wrote to her friend Miye Yamasaki in California: "Have any American ships been submarined? Do you really hear a lot about the war? . . . Over here I'm hardly aware that a war is going on. No one talks about it. Or if they do, I can't understand them." As the months of 1939 and 1940 passed, Mary's letters to Miye remained buoyant—full of details about her leisure activities with friends and classmates, her exasperation with the self-effacing behavior of Japanese women, her yearning for romance, and her classes and examinations at school. In late 1940 and early 1941, however, shadows of Japan's war began to darken Mary's typically lighthearted letters; she remarked, for example, on food scarcity in Tokyo and on the growing Japanese military.

Uncertain about whether to continue her education in Japan or to return to the United States, Mary at last decided to sail home to America on the *Asama Maru*, which was scheduled to leave Yokohama in early July 1941. However, just a few days before her planned date of departure, Mary received a cablegram from her parents in California instructing her to remain in Tokyo. Encouraged by news of ongoing diplomatic negotiations between Japan and America, Mary's parents had decided that she should remain in Japan as long as possible to continue her education at the special foreign division of Tokyo Women's University (Tōkyō Joshi Daigaku, now called Tokyo Women's Christian University), where she had recently been accepted as a pupil.[5]

Even as Mary warily stayed on in Tokyo, hundreds of Nisei and other foreign citizens were flooding out of Japan in anticipation of war. The US State Department reached out as early as October 1940 to encourage Americans in Japan to consider returning to America, but evidently not everyone received word. Mary herself recalled that, "Before I had left Japan, I had never been contacted by the American Consul with any warnings that the situation was becoming so dangerous that I should return home."[6] Although it seemed increasingly possible that tensions would culminate in war, many Britons, Americans, Canadians, and other foreign nationals living in Japan believed that the fighting might not start for quite some time, if ever. Americans in particular were holding out hope that Ambassador Kichisaburō Nomura's negotiations in Washington would be successful. And as these negotiations continued, the US government endeavored to keep its warnings to Americans in Japan low-key so as not to spark any sensational implications that might hinder diplomatic progress. Instead of an unequivocal warning, the State Department "quietly" suggested to Americans in Asia that they consider returning to the United States. Nisei and other foreign nationals who stayed in Japan as winter approached in 1941 either never received these official government warnings, failed to understand their urgency, or ignored them, intending to remain in Japan indefinitely.

John Morris, a British citizen who arrived in Yokohama in October 1938 with the dual posts of English lecturer at a university in Tokyo and advisor to the Japanese Foreign Office, wrote that in October 1941:

Although the situation was getting worse it was apparently not yet critical. A certain number of British people, whose presence in the country was not absolutely necessary, had already been evacuated, but, while all of us were advised to go, it was thought that a few of the teachers who held key positions might still do useful work for the British cause by remaining a few more months. I decided to stay. I was extremely interested to see how the situation was going to develop, and I wanted to see things through to the end.[7]

In addition to the optimism that war might be avoided, financial and familial considerations prohibited many foreign citizens from exiting Japanese territory despite subtle warnings to leave. The United States and the British Empire had frozen Japanese assets in their territories in July of 1941. In response, the Japanese government promptly froze American and British assets in its territories, and Americans attempting to leave areas under Japanese control faced restrictive regulations.[8]

Additionally, many foreigners—including Nisei—had married and started families with Japanese citizens, and to such residents, uprooting the entire family on the suspicion of war seemed either impossible or at least overly hasty. Nisei had situational reasons for staying, too. Taz Iwata, a Nisei who had been sent to live with relatives in Japan in 1936 at the age of eleven, did recall receiving a letter from the consulate advising her to return to the United States with haste. "My sister was visiting me at that time," shared Taz in a 2007 documentary interview, "and she packed up and left right away, but I wasn't gonna go, go back, because I wanted to finish my schooling."[9]

As demonstrated by the example of Mary Kimoto, some Nisei either did not receive an official warning about returning to the United States, or their language skills were not yet sharp enough to comprehend fully the volatility of the situation between the two countries. For example, in the official statement for her treason trial in 1949, California-born propagandist "Tokyo Rose" Iva Toguri recalled that when the news of Pearl Harbor was announced on Japanese radio, she simply did not have enough knowledge of Japanese to understand what was happening. "I could understand the word 'war,' but I could not believe that war had really broken out, and I could not understand enough Japanese to get the full story."[10] Iva was unable at that time to read Japanese newspapers, and although English newspapers were available, she had been warned by her uncle not to be seen reading a paper written in English. Mary, like Iva, had not fully grasped the magnitude of the threat of war and had therefore waited until December before boarding a ship home to the States. She—and thousands of other Americans—had waited too long.

The Roots of Anti-West Stigmatization

When war against the United States broke out in early December 1941, Nisei living in Japan faced a stark reality that to some had seemed impossible: war between their two nations. In the years before the outbreak of war with the United States, Nisei living in Japan had been socially marked as different from the average Japanese population. Differences in mannerisms, language skills, and physical appearance belied Nisei as non-Japanese, and as such, many Nisei faced social discrimination as excessively boisterous, independent-minded "children of emigrants" worthy of distain. The physical, linguistic, and behavioral differences associated with Nisei in Japan stigmatized Nisei who fell short of the requirements for in-group membership in Japanese society. Whereas before December 8, 1941, a Nisei stigmatized as "American" might be rendered socially discredited, after the declaration of war between Japan and the United States, the stigma of association with the enemy could endanger the Nisei.

It is important to note the jarring contrast between the anti-West stigmatization that characterized the years of total war and the attitudes toward foreign culture that had preceded the outbreak of war in Japan. Indeed, Nisei living in urban Japan between the end of World War I and the start of the full-scale Pacific War in 1937 navigated a social environment that was in many ways receptive to internationalism. In the decades following the mid-nineteenth century opening of Japanese ports to foreign trade, increasing numbers of foreign missionaries, teachers, merchants, entrepreneurs, and artists—and their families—had flocked to Japanese shores. Port cities such as Yokohama and Kobe saw particularly large numbers of foreign settlers, who predominantly lived in new, Western-style homes in segregated settlements. While World War I preoccupied many of the top Western global powers, Japanese heavy and light industries grew stronger; cities burgeoned, and international trade expanded. By the 1920s, new trends in consumerism and consumption—such as the demand for foreign goods, the rising popularity of dance halls and coffee shops, the pop-culture fantasy of the *modan gāru* (modern girl) and the building of Western-inspired *bunka jūtaku* (culture houses)—cultivated in Japanese cities an atmosphere of cosmopolitan modernity in which foreign language ability, foreign styles of dress, and modern sensibilities were cause for fascination and even admiration. Nisei may have been stigmatized as "American" amid this historical milieu, but the perceived ability of Nisei to straddle Western and Japanese culture was imagined by many (especially in Japan's urban centers) as an asset.

A broad social and administrative turn away from internationalism and Western modernism in the late 1930s, however, aggressively curbed this fascination with Western-style *bunka seikatsu* (cultural living). By 1937, as Japan entered full-scale war with China, the pleasures of consumer culture seemed increasingly inharmonious with administrative austerity measures and propaganda campaigns maligning self-indulgence. The discourse on modern life turned away from the glamorous and worldly and toward the practical aspects of everyday work and home life. Western material culture, Western media, and association with Western ideas were characterized by intellectuals, politicians, and in print media as something to be "overcome"—through strength of focus on a Japanese spirit, Japanese historical consciousness, and Japanese ways of life.[11]

Playing upon the anxieties of a nation on the brink of war, anti-West propaganda in Japan instilled contempt in the populace of Western thought and speech by coding the English language, Christianity, and liberal expressions as threats to Japanese national morality. As fighting intensified in China in the late 1930s, leading Japanese intellectuals and politicians insisted that Japan must purge itself not only of Western people and Western words, but also of indulgent, individualistic Western culture entirely. This nationalistic mood was further bolstered by the National Mobilization Law (1938) and the National Spiritual Mobilization Law (1939), which established government control over civilian organizations, rationing, the news media, and many industries. By the late 1930s, various agencies of the government had tapped into the channels that would enable the government to permeate the social environment with its key messages of

Japan's mission to lead the Pacific region in the face of Western aggression, and of self-sacrifice as patriotic duty. As war tensions mounted, and as nationalistic sentiment swelled, a propaganda-orchestrated wave of negative energy regarding elements of Western culture likewise intensified.

Christianity, for example, was a Western extraction that came under fire as incompatible with the official tenet of the emperor's divinity. Christians who would not confirm belief in the emperor's divinity—such as Mary Kimoto's family friend Reverend Kaoru Itō—faced imprisonment. Many Christian schools altered their mission statements to emphasize imperial devotion over—or instead of—Christian beliefs. Tokyo's Rikkyō University, for example, which was founded by a missionary of the Episcopal Church in 1874, edited its creed in September of 1942, erasing the clause "to provide an education in accordance with Christian principles" (基督教主義ニヨル教育ヲ行フ) and replacing it with "to provide an education in accordance with the imperial Way" (皇國ノ道ニヨル教育ヲ行フ).[12] A significant number of Nisei were Christians or were at least familiar with Christian culture from their time spent in the States, and the antagonism shown Christianity was a significant message communicating the fundamental importance of distancing themselves from American culture.

The growing anti-Western mood in Japan targeted the English language as well. On March 4, 1942, the *Japan Times* reported that, "because it is spoken by Japan's enemy nations, the English language has fallen into discredit and there is even an outcry for its abolition." Appearing in Japan's oldest English-language newspaper, this message of self-loathing was, of course, delivered in the odious medium of the enemy language itself. All irony aside, the statement represents a level of hostility in Japan toward the English language—and English speakers—that continued to rise throughout the years of total war. This anti-English antagonism had been brewing for several years before the start of World War II, not as a vilification of English as an enemy language but rather as a nationalistic movement underscoring the importance of promoting the Japanese language. For example, the 1916 *Eigo kyōiku fuyōron* (English Education is Unnecessary Thesis), promulgated by the lawyer and politician Ooka Ikuzō, pushed for the liberation of education in Japan by means of abolishing English as a required subject in schools.[13] Although this debate was limited in scope (its participants were mostly academics and politicians), it represents the patriotic sentiment that had been spreading across the nation in the years before the declaration of war, stigmatizing English while championing the Japanese language as a means to sustain and encourage the Japanese nation and the Japanese people.

After Japan entered a state of war against the United States, various government agencies (such as the Ministry of Education, the War Department, and the

Interior Ministry) pushed for formal anti-English policies to strengthen the nation by distancing the Japanese populace from the "enemy language." For example, prior to 1942, English had been an officially required subject in girls' schools across the nation, and according to the *Asahi Shinbun*, approximately 700 of the nation's 900 girls' schools had followed that stipulation.[14] In July of that year, however, the Ministry of Education formally established English as an elective subject rather than a required subject in girls' schools, and the weekly hourly allotment decreased from five to three hours.[15] In justifying this change, the Ministry of Education stated that in a time of war, a woman's education should focus primarily on running the home, especially on raising healthy children. To remove the demand of English study from their lives would be to remove a "suffering" that hinders their ability to serve, foremost, as mothers.[16]

The Ministry of Education also made English voluntary for all middle school pupils in grades three and above in 1943.[17] Many Nisei members of the school population across Japan were alert to the discussions regarding the role English should play in Japanese education. As Jack Dairiki remembered of his time as a student in wartime Sunabashi, "there was an argument that they shouldn't study an enemy language, but again, there's a philosophy that came out, you have to know the enemy and doing so you got to learn their language, so there was an argument there, and the junior high school I attended I had an English class available."[18] Regardless of the policies their schools adopted, Nisei could sense that their English ability was a stigmatized element of their identity; affiliation with the enemy language could put a target on one's back.

Japan's Ministry of Education also targeted schools affiliated with foreign sponsors regarding the English flavor of their school names. As Yayoi Cooke remembered of her time at Tōyō Eiwa Jogakuin, which had been established by Canadian Methodist missionaries, "the government's eye was on our school to see if our school was trying to cooperate with the government in winning the war . . . What the students were doing was very important. We had to make more effort than the other people to show that we were, you know, cooperating with the government."[19] The names of many such schools that had been established through contact with English-speaking nations contained foreign words rendered in *katakana* or the character *"ei"* (英) for "English." Under government pressure, however, many well-known schools with *katakana* names such as the Wilmina Jogakuin, Palmore Joshi Eigakuin, and Ferris Waei Jogakkō adopted fully *kanji* names in the early 1940s.[20] Schools with names containing the character *"ei"* for "English" either dropped the character completely or substituted with a homonym such as *"ei"* for eternity (永) or prosperity (栄). Yayoi Cooke recalled that these measures affected not only her high school but her college as well: Tsuda Eigaku Juku was renamed "Tsuda Juku Senmon Gakkō," because, as she explained, "The *'ei'* wasn't proper anymore."[21] The government did not require these name alterations by any sort of official policy. Rather, the Ministry of Education strongly encouraged the offending schools to adopt revamped names as a patriotic gesture, as suggested in the following example of correspondence from the Ministry of Education to Yamanashi Eiwa Gakkō: "The Ministry of Education desires the alteration of school appellations containing foreign names or phrases such as 'Eiwa gakkō.' And so, although we understand that you might experience some inconveniences in your renaming, we would like you to consider it part of your contribution to the new order."[22]

Schools with foreign ties, Christian affiliations, or particularly strong English programs often undertook extreme measures to overcompensate for their foreignness, shuttering English departments, rephrasing school creeds, and even burning English books. According to Marion Tsutakawa Kanemoto, a Nisei who entered Doshisha University in Kyoto immediately after the war, the English department there had burned all of their English material, and so her English education at Doshisha during the occupation consisted primarily of translating Shakespeare into Japanese.[23] Japanese national Nobuko Gerth, an English major at Tokyo Women's University (the same school Mary Kimoto attended during the war), recalled that one of her classmates on the train was slapped in the face for studying English. "Well," she explains, "at least we learned not to open English books on the train." Nobuko and her friends could not wait to get to campus where they would be able to speak and read English in peace, and once their classes were disbanded in the final months of total war, they practiced English in secret, establishing a makeshift journal called *Kagaribi* ("Bonfire") which they circulated among themselves as regularly as possible, as long as they could find paper.[24]

In addition to government policies, social discourse—fed by conversations in newspapers, journals, and other mass media—further contributed to the anti-English climate of wartime Japan. Spirited calls for the complete abolishment of English in Japan arose soon after the start of World War II, amid the victory mood that accompanied the fall of Singapore and Manila in early 1942. Journal articles, newspapers, and speeches by well-known politicians and journalists encouraged Japanese subjects to consider the ways in which the enemy had infiltrated their daily lives and their consciousness via the poison of the English language. "We must reject the enemy language of English no matter what it takes," writes military commentator Mutō Teiichi in an essay published in the March 7, 1942 evening edition of the *Hōchi News*. His essay, "The Source of the Enemy Stain Is English," urges readers to consider the ways in which the enemy haunts their daily lives through the words they use and the items they consume every day. "Coffee," "whisky," "radio," "news," and other loan words peppering daily Japanese conversation had become so commonplace, he argues, that they are regarded as part of Japanese life. Only by rejecting these loan words will Japanese minds free themselves from the enemy. The journalist-politician Akagi Kakudō expresses a similar opinion in 1943 in the journal *Nippon to Nipponjin*. In his article "We Must Completely Abolish English Education," Akagi declares that the dominating presence of the West in the world of education had governed the ways in which Japan framed and considered its own history and culture; as a point of pride, Japan must distance itself from the West by all means possible, particularly in education. Later that same year, Murakawa Kengo, a professor at Tokyo University, published an article in *Nihon Hyōron* acknowledging the contributions of the West since the Meiji era, insisting that through this exchange with the West, English had slowly but surely "without our even realizing it" infiltrated the Japanese psyche, making them forget the unique nature of the Japanese national polity. English, demonized in social discourse, was the subversive force that poisoned Japanese minds and weakened Japanese resolve. Its venom was often invisible, seeping into Japanese conversations as loan words, slinking before Japanese eyes on English or *katakana* signboards, and spilling down Japanese throats as "whisky" or "coffee." By rooting out this evil presence of English, urged ideologues such as Mutō, Akagi, and Murakawa, Japanese subjects could triumph over the Western enemies who had endeavored to dominate them for the past hundred years.[25]

Riding the tide of this social movement to overcome the English language in 1940s Japan, celebrities, singing groups, companies, sports teams, shops, magazines, and news outlets rebranded themselves with *kanji* names. In baseball, for example, the Senators became the 翼 (*Tsubasa*), the Lions were renamed the 朝日 (*Asahi*), the Eagles became the 黒鷲 (*Kurowashi*), and the Osaka Tigers were renamed 阪神 (*Hanshin*). The entire vocabulary of the game, too, was completely overhauled, with Japanese equivalents substituted for baseball's loan word expressions. Thus, as the scenery across Japan grew increasingly *kanji*-heavy, the anti-English movement also influenced the way individuals spoke—the very words they used. In *Unwilling Patriot*, Takaaki Aikawa describes the sometimes farcical anti-English atmosphere in Japan:

> Even the names of things which came from foreign countries and had no Japanese name were given new Japanese names with the classical flavor. For instance, glass, for which we had no word, was called *usutoshi-gami* ... [which] literally means "thin transparent paper." To call glass

that was really ridiculous, but this is how they invented and forced us to use many odd Japanese words for foreign sports, food and customs.[26]

Leading up to World War II and throughout the years of war, the actions of government agencies—coupled with stinging anti-English rhetoric in popular discourse—kindled a social environment that equated English with "enemy" and cast suspicion on anyone who possessed interest or ability in the English language. Through soft propaganda that permeated the environment, anti-English sentiment constricted the everyday lives of English-speaking residents of Japan, such as American Nisei. This social climate reshaped the very means through which Nisei could express themselves.

And yet, for Nisei in wartime Japan, English ability was a double-edged sword. While Nisei in Japan negotiated anti-English antagonism, many Nisei nevertheless relied on their English ability to make ends meet during the war. In January of 1942, Mary Kimoto reenrolled at Tokyo Women's University and began attending classes while living as a "school girl" (domestic servant) at the home of a strict, demanding physician, Mrs. Sakai. After two arduous months of strenuous housework for Mrs. Sakai, Mary was noticeably altered; a teacher at her college observed Mary's distress and helped her procure a spot at the school's dormitory. There, Mary was able to capitalize on her English skills, tutoring Japanese students in English conversation and translating a Japanese history textbook for a professor from Waseda Kokusai.[27] In this way, Mary's English ability served as her lifeline, enabling her survival during the war, but Mary undoubtedly felt the suffocating antagonism toward English speakers and the English language that permeated the environment of wartime Japan. She wrote to Kay of this hostility in her wartime memoirs, relating a story of a mutual acquaintance:

> Did you hear about Toshi? The other day she was reading an English book on the way to school when an ultra-nationalist Japanese man slapped her face and berated her with "How dare you read an English book! Don't you know we are fighting a war and we are going to exterminate America and England?" . . . These small-minded Japs! Reports are that in America they are studying Japanese as never before, and look at them here—taking English out of the schools and abusing those who read the "language of the enemy."[28]

As English words and English speakers were increasingly vilified throughout the late 1930s and 1940s, many Nisei keenly felt the impact. Reading, writing, and conversing in English had served as refreshing points of connection to many Nisei who were nostalgic for their American friends, family, and home. But as nationalism and anti-Western sentiment escalated, the role of English in the daily lives of Nisei saw striking constriction. English ability—which had served as a point of opportunity for many Nisei in Japan—became taboo, a suffocating marker for suspicion.

Peggy Furukawa, who moved with her sister from San Jose to Okayama in 1939, remembered of those wartime years that although she had always spoken English with her sister even in Japan, after the war started, they were too frightened to be overheard speaking English, and so "we couldn't talk."[29] Government policies and propaganda, and their reverberations in social discourse, thereby sustained an environment in which Nisei were directed to consider English itself as an enemy. Nisei like Mary and Peggy living in wartime Japan were further cut off from America as English magazines and movies, English songs, and English loanwords in *katakana* evaporated from the streets of Japan. Anti-English propaganda and discourse altered the physical environment of Nisei on the home front—what they saw, heard, and said everyday—thereby further emphasizing the importance of cleaving themselves from their former American lives. During wartime, social pressures prompted Nisei to refrain from speaking English in public, and to attempt to erase English from their lives. Thus, as a result of the anti-English movement in wartime Japan, the environment through which Nisei moved grew increasingly distant from the American culture they knew, and the very voices of Nisei were altered.

Most businesses, teams, and individuals framed their participation in the anti-English movement as voluntary expressions of patriotism, but in reality, the forces of government and social intimidation, including public humiliation, played major roles in this swelling tide of anti-English, *kanji* pride. The Cabinet Intelligence Office, for example, ran an article in the weekly photo magazine *Shashin Shūhō* in February of 1943, shaming those remaining businesses with English words on signs outside their doors. "No, these are not the streets of New York or London," reads the description accompanying fourteen photos of English language signage. "These are the streets of Japan, and what's more, we are fighting with the United States and England at this very moment." In the face of such intimidation and public shame, Japanese shopkeepers redesigned their decor, restaurateurs revamped their menus, parks (such as the Kyoto Botanical Garden) replaced *katakana* flower and plant names with *kanji* substitutes, and transportation systems across Japan removed down signs for "W.C." or "Station Master" in favor of signage with *kanji* terminology. The anti-English movement therefore was influencing the everyday, physical environment of all Japanese subjects, emphasizing to the entire populace the importance of eschewing English.[30]

The fervor of anti-West sentiment also seeped into the material environment of wartime Japan via attacks on objects and trends associated with "the enemy," such as toys, instruments, and artistic media. American and British cinema had played a significant role in the popular culture of prewar Japan, but when war in the Pacific broke out, cinemas were ordered to stop showing American and British films. Just a few weeks after the attack on Pearl Harbor, the Information Bureau officially banned all "enemy music."[31] In Okayama, Michiko Usui Kornhauser was instructed by her music teacher not to be seen carrying her violin in public, because it was a Western instrument.[32] Nisei musicians whose jazz and Hawaiian sounds had made a splash on the airwaves of pre-war Japan rebranded themselves: Hawaiian-born Katsuhiko Haida formerly of the "Moana Glee Club" began touring with "His Southern Melodeers,"[33] and trumpeter Hisashi Moriyama of San Francisco (who toured the South Pacific in a government-sanctioned "musical consolation corps" during the war), switched from *jazu* (jazz) to *kei ongaku* ("light music").[34]

The oft-cited example of the "blue-eyed sleeping dolls," provides a further illustration of public wariness toward all things Western as a popular form of patriotism during the war. These thousands of dolls, which had been presented to Japanese schools by American charities in 1927, were targeted as Western infiltrations into Japanese life, which must be purged from the Japanese environment as a point of national pride. The February 19, 1943, *Mainichi Shinbun* evening edition provides the results of a survey, given to children above the fifth grade at Ajigasawa National School, an elementary school in Aomori prefecture. To the question of what to do with the blue-eyed dolls, the pupils responded as follows:

Dispose of them—89 respondents
Burn them—133 respondents
Send them back—44 respondents
Put them someplace prominent and ridicule them everyday—31 respondents
Throw them into the ocean—33 respondents
Make them hold white flags—5 respondents
Think of them as American spies and be on our guard—1 respondent.[35]

In the end, the Ministry of Education decreed that all schools in Japan remove or destroy the American dolls in their possession.

From material culture to Christianity to English words, the distaste for all things Western—and in particular, all things Caucasian—permeated the everyday lives of Japanese citizens throughout the years of war. In "Girls on the Home

Front," Hiromi Dollase explores material changes in the content of *Shōjo no tomo* (*Girl's Friend*), a popular magazine for girls in early twentieth-century Japan (and one of only two girls' magazines that survived throughout World War II). As Dollase explains, the magazine's editor Uchiyama Motoi had previously been an avid supporter of illustrator Nakahara Jun'ichi, whose ethereal, stylized sketches of whimsical, wide-eyed girls with perms and sailor middies often graced the pages of the magazine. In July of 1940, however, Uchiyama began to censor the images, and throughout the war, the sketches in the magazine were of girls who were unmistakably Japanese—in clothing, hairstyle, and facial features.[36]

Whether or not anti-West propaganda was "believed" by the general populace, anti-West anxieties severely constricted the lives of Nisei after the United States and Japan entered a state of war on December 8, 1941. Government policies and social campaigns emphasized that the residents living in imperial Japan—whether in the *naichi* (mainland) or in Japan's peripheral colonies—should embrace Japanese customs and stifle "foreign" mannerisms in order to survive and thrive in the new world order of a Japan-led Greater East Asia Co-Prosperity Sphere. The messages of propaganda diffused throughout the physical and discursive environment, and by manipulating Nisei goals rhizomically, this soft propaganda inspired Nisei consciously and subconsciously to alter their behavior and appearance to mimic Japaneseness and conceal Americanness. The tenuous bridge between the United States and Japan had crumbled, and the American Nisei who had endeavored to straddle that bridge—and even to *be* that bridge—found themselves marooned on one side, trying to survive.

No Gray Zone in a War Zone

Nisei in total war Japan faced a climate antagonistic toward Western culture in its many forms—from speech to aesthetics, from religion to material culture. In this environment, American Nisei were squeezed dry of their American culture—outwardly at least. If performing as American in the wartime climate welcomed distain, suspicion, and even danger, what were Nisei to do? In wartime Japan, a space where American behavior was vilified and Japanese behavior was championed, Nisei reordered their movements, mannerisms, and forms of expression as Japanese in order to survive during the years of total war.

The example of Nisei assimilation into mainstream Japanese culture takes even deeper roots in the broader process of citizen-making that had characterized Japan's empire-building since the dawn of its modern era in the late nineteenth century. Japan's answer to the process of making a citizen was two-fold:

denigrate the old identity (Ryūkyūan or Okinawan, for example) while valorizing the new identity (mainland Japanese). The government's efforts in *kōminka*
(making of imperial subjects) in the years of empire-building provide a vivid illustration of the power of institutions to shape individual attitudes and behaviors. Throughout the decades of Japan's territorial expansion around the turn of
the twentieth century, newly incorporated territories were utilized by the government as grounds for political experiments in *kōminka*, which included programs in language enforcement, control of the population by state-sponsored
communication methods and infrastructure planning, and ideological manipu-
lation to impose a Japanese national identity. Through these practices, the Japanese government attempted to integrate its diverse colonial citizenry as a unified
imperial populace. The focus of *kōminka* on shaping the population's attitudes by
targeting their customs illustrates that soft propaganda was assimilating the Japanese populace long before the start of World War II. Policies and messages designed to change individuals' behavior did so by encouraging people to recognize
the values and taboos reflected in their physical modes of self-representation
(such as the clothing they wore and the words they used).[37]

The education system was a pivotal access point through which government
officials in transwar Japan employed propaganda to shape public discourse. By
providing social cues for ideal roles and behaviors through *kōminka* education,
for example, the Japanese government endeavored to modify the actions and
emotions of the populace across the entire Japanese empire. In the Government-
General's curriculum in Korea, for example, students were instructed in Japanese etiquette, the Japanese calendar, the Japanese imperial legends, and tales of
ancient Japanese heroes. Moral education, employing State Shintō language, was
established as a primary avenue of cultural assimilation across the empire. The
explicit purpose of education was to cultivate loyal subjects. Across the Japanese
empire, school celebrations honored the Shintō deities, students memorized the
imperial *kami* pantheon, and pupils took ethics courses on the concept of loyalty
to the emperor and the Japanese state. In the Korean colony, the message of unification through Japanese supremacy was the Japanese state's "hard propaganda."
The everyday elements associated with that message—such as the classroom por-
trait of the emperor—were the elements of "soft propaganda" reinforcing state
propaganda subliminally in the physical environment.

With the onset of war against China in 1937, the Ministry of Education emphasized even more aggressively the importance of education to unify the spirit
of the Japanese imperial populace. National textbooks were revamped in 1937
to extract elements deemed Western in favor of glorification of the Japanese
national polity.[38] In April 1941, a new school year began with a major overhaul

of the education system: an edict from the Ministry of Education transformed the nation's *shōgakkō* (elementary schools) into *kokumin gakkō* (the people's schools) with increased emphasis on courses in Japanese history, ethics, national language, and geography. The Ministry described its renovation in patriotic language, extolling the new system as a means "to expand and maintain a foundational education for all of the nation's people," "to cultivate the roots of the national progress," "to renovate fundamentally the contents of education in accordance with the Imperial Way," and "to unify educational materials and unite the training of the Imperial Way."[39] Wielding this language, the wartime administration established a system of education geared entirely toward the cultivation of a national spirit, supported by unified minds, hearts, knowledge, and virtue.

In an effort to develop devotion to the national polity, the overarching emphasis of the *kokumin gakkō* education was to focus students' attentions on the figure of the benevolent emperor. Teachers trained students to value the sacrifice of individual desires, deeds, and personal emotions for the greater cause of supporting the emperor and his mission of leading Japan in a sacred war. Indeed, the national education system conditioned students to mediate their personal ambitions and desires through the nationwide goal of victory. The future, in effect, faded away as pupils across the empire prepared themselves to sacrifice their lives for the emperor. Sakuma Kunisaburō, a Japanese national who attended *kokumin gakkō* in Tokyo during the war, explained that Japanese boys were raised to believe that they could serve by dying for the emperor, and the girls could also contribute, for example, by going to a colony such as Manchukuo as the bride of a pioneer. "Of course," he said, "they didn't want to go, but everything was for Japan, for the emperor."[40] Hamazaki Shigenobu, who was also born and raised in Tokyo, described that the concept of sublime *gyokusai* (literally "shattering like a jewel") was venerated as a symbolic representation of the way that the imperial subjects could die honorably for their nation: "we were taught from elementary school on to die for the emperor."[41] Spokane-born Nisei Frank Hironobu Hirata (who moved to Japan as a nine-year-old in 1934) also remembered this philosophy of sacrifice: "*gyokusai* was openly taught in school . . . it means everybody vanishing all at once . . . scattered over . . . When Japan is attacked by the US, all one billion [subjects] will die together to defend the country."[42] By exalting the emperor and the national polity over the individual self, the education system in Japan also served to instill in the pupils a life of sacrifice by removing expectations of the distant future.

The Ministry of Education's efforts to reform the education system seeped readily into social discourse, and the values of self-sacrifice and emperor-centered word and deed reverberated far beyond the walls of the classroom. Weeks after the fall of Saipan, Japanese newspapers continued to trumpet the sacrifices of the heroic women who had died as *gyokusai* in dramatic headlines, such as the August 19, 1944, *Asahi Shinbun*'s claim that "Sublimely Women Too Commit Suicide on Rocks in Front of the Great Sun Flag" and, the following day, in the *Mainichi Shinbun:* that the women had "Changed into Their Best Apparel, Prayed to the Imperial Palace / Sublimely Commit Suicide in Front of the American Devils."[43] Across the home front, the discourse perpetuated by this sort of propaganda established for Japanese subjects a supreme goal: self-sacrifice was posited as the sublime achievement through which war-weary subjects could achieve ultimate greatness.

Whether or not the subjects believed that they should all indeed die gloriously for the emperor, this hard propaganda message seeped into material culture as soft propaganda and shaped behavior according to its ideals. As Hiromi Dollase explains in her analysis of the girl's magazine *Shōjo no tomo,* the concept of the "girl" transformed amid the wartime climate such that "*shōjo*" (girl) morphed into "*gunkoku shōjo*" (girls of the military nation). Whereas the *shōjo* had dazzled as a dreamy, imaginative paradigm of girlhood, the *gunkoku shōjo* was tasked with the responsibility to think of her lifestyle seriously—to live frugally with realistic goals, to work for the greater Pan-Asian goal, to encourage soldiers, and to live as a spiritual fighter on the home front.[44] Parents, neighbors, magazines, radio programs, and commercial institutions echoed this value system across the empire in every aspect of daily life, conditioning the nation's youth to peg positive value to self-sacrifice as a means to support Japan's efforts to exalt Asia and the Japanese race. In this way, Nisei youth—alongside their fully Japanese peers—were motivated by the ideals propagated in their everyday social environment to value the erasure of the individual as appropriate participation in the body of the Japanese nation.

Gendered Ideals of Japaneseness

In the space of a decade, the mood of everyday life in Japan had shifted—from an effervescent cadence wherein discourse, as historian Harry Harootunian describes, "continually pointed to the succession of events and looked to the future" to the absence of any future.[45] For children in Japan, the future had been displaced by soft propaganda peddling sacrifice in the here and now. Absent the promise of brighter days, the rhythms of everyday life became even more important. Women, who were tasked by the nation with ensuring the continuance of those rhythms, aspired to quell their own personal anxieties through those rhythms—by participating in the rituals of everyday life as volunteers, girls of the military nation, and pioneer brides. Through participation in these rituals on the home front, women were offered a means to shift individual intentionalities away from the uncertain future, and to mitigate discomfort in shared spaces and practices. In this way, the flavor of everyday life in Japan subliminally propelled women on the home front (young and old, Nisei and Japan-born, colonial subject and imperial citizen) to aspire to assimilate into the roles established by hard propaganda and reinforced through soft propaganda as ensuring the safety, security, and consistency of life in the empire.

Propaganda in media portrayals, shored up by government rhetoric and policies, posited the physical and behavioral attributes of ideal Japanese subjecthood for all members of the *ichioku* (the Japanese's empire's "one hundred million" moving as one). These ideals provided members of the populace who were marked as different—such as foreign-born Nisei and the non-racially Japanese residents in Japan's colonial empire—with paradigms to mimic so that they might hide or overcome their stigma. These wartime paradigms were the intensely gendered roles of the imperial soldier and the nurturing yet stalwart mother/sister/wife. These were ideals of self-sacrifice that would prove important models of assimilation for American Nisei endeavoring to mask their stigma of association with the enemy in order to survive and thrive in wartime Japan.

For a man in imperial Japan, *to thrive* meant to be brave, self-sacrificing, and patriotic. In the minds of the Japanese people, the figure of the soldier—he who had committed himself to die for the emperor—inspired ultimate respect. Despite the fact that the enemy targeted in the sights of their guns might be an old friend, neighbor, or even a relative, many American Nisei were influenced by this social tenor. Jimmie Matsuda, a Nisei from Hood River, Oregon, who became a suicide pilot (a member of the "*kamikaze*") in 1943, was one such Nisei. Jimmie described his decision to join the Japanese military in an interview with the researchers of Densho:

> After you graduate high school you have to volunteer in the military, they make you volunteer unless you're a handicap, so when I graduated, too, I had to volunteer and I figured that I won't pass, but when I took the test I passed the eleventh, yeah, I was the eleventh people that passed, took the test. But my uncle then, they were very proud because even though I was born in America I passed the test, and then after I passed the test, "Do you want to go to the navy or where?" I says air force, and then they told me air force is a tough place and I says, "I don't care. I'm gonna go to the air force." So I, that's when I went into the [air force] . . . To be, that time,

the, they were all good-looking people dressed up real nice, and if you walk in town, I mean, all the girls would come after you, to be honest with you.

In a society that glorified sacrifice of self for the nation, *kamikaze* pilots were treated, Jimmie said, like kings. "[W]e had, I mean, whatever we wanted. We had everything, from whisky, *sake,* tobacco, chocolate or anything, we had all those treatments and they were all free . . . Some elderly ladies would, out in the country, if we're walking, they, they'll bow to us and everything, saying, 'Thank you very much for fighting for the country.' "[46]

Hundreds of other Nisei men aspired to achieve respect and glory by serving the Japanese *minzoku* ("ethno-nation") as a soldier of the emperor. Edward Toru Horikiri, born in Los Angeles, had moved to Kagoshima with his family in 1931, and had been living in Japan since he was eighteen months old. He described his wish to become a soldier in these words:

> Right after I entered elementary school, war broke out between Japan and China, then, when I was in sixth grade, the attack on Pearl Harbor happened. Japan was swept up in a current of militarism; everyone was gung ho for nationalism. So, no doubt about it, I was to become a soldier. That is my wish, I said. I took the entrance exam for the military academy and was about to enter when the war ended.[47]

Minoru Teruya, who moved from Hawai'i to Okinawa at the age of ten in 1935, explained that as a boy in Hawai'i, observing the Japanese aircraft carriers that stopped at the port in Hawai'i before the war, "I often saw Japanese soldiers in navy uniforms around the downtown and Japanese navy officers visiting the Japanese embassy . . . I aspired to be like those naval men in their uniforms." When he moved to Okinawa, he explained, he truly "felt the *Yamato damashii* (Japanese spirit)," and although he failed his interview to be a navy captain (because of his American citizenship), "I wouldn't give up, and I took the Japanese Naval Academy entrance exam and passed it."[48]

Although service in the imperial Japanese military offered for Nisei a distinct opportunity to achieve irrefutable in-group membership in the *ichioku,* there were many Nisei men who did not volunteer to join the forces. Japan's policy of male conscription, however, left these Nisei men with little choice but to serve. Japan's draft system, which had been created in 1873, required three years of service from all Japanese male citizens when they reached the age of twenty. Dual citizens, such as Nisei who possessed both Japanese and American citizenship, were also required to serve these years of military duty. There were, however, exceptions to this rule, as demonstrated by the example of California-born George Tanbara, who shares his story in Kadota Ryūshō's *Sōkai ni kiyu*. George was living in Tokyo as a graduate of Waseda University when the war began. He was called in by the special police for an interview, at which he declared himself an American citizen and was released, never to be drafted despite his dual citizenship (perhaps because he declared himself unequivocally an American citizen instead of answering that he was a dual citizen). He spent the years of the war as an employee at an electrical equipment company. George's case, however, is extremely rare, considering that both of his parents were Japanese.[49]

There were exceptions to the dual citizenship conscription effort, but they are usually instances that implicate half-Japanese young men. James Harris, for example, who had taken his mother's Japanese citizenship as a young man in 1933 when his British father died, was working as a reporter for the *Japan Times* in Tokyo when war broke out. On the morning of December 8, 1941, he was arrested as an enemy alien and interned at the Yokohama yacht club despite his Japanese citizenship and was preparing to sail from Japan on one of the exchange ships for stranded civilian aliens during the war when he was abruptly released, conscripted by the Japanese army, and sent to the front as a Japanese solider.[50]

Japan's compulsory military service policy had compelled many Nisei males with dual citizenship in Japan to return to the United States before the declaration of war and had deterred numerous Nisei males from registering as Japanese citizens. After the attack on Pearl Harbor, however, Nisei males no longer had the option of sailing to the United States to avoid military service when they came of age. Furthermore, many Nisei possessing only American citizenship registered as Japanese citizens after the war began, either so that they might receive ration tickets or as a result of pressure from the special police. For many Nisei, the question of registration was beyond their control; they were registered by their relatives or by city officials, sometimes even without their knowledge. Henry Ueno, for example, was sixteen in 1941 when he received a letter from the district office in Katsuura, Wakayama, ordering him to report to the office for a physical required by a military training school. Born in Pendleton, Oregon, Henry had moved to Wakayama at age two upon the death of his father, but he had never registered for Japanese citizenship. Henry reported for the physical, but he remembered being uncertain about whether or not to tell the officials about his citizenship status:

> They asked me whether my mother, my parents were, approved of my joining the service. And I didn't really expected this because, young, but I start thinking, gee, what to answer this, you know. At that time, I knew

I was American citizen, but I just stop, think, and quiet for a while, then I thinking all the situations how my mother feels, all the relatives. My brothers, the Japanese army, and can I refuse? That's the biggest fear— can I refuse? If I refuse, tell them I can't serve, I'm American citizen, then how they feel, how they'll treat it? So I didn't answer that questions, and the city people said, "How come you don't answer all my questions?" Then I have to confide, you know. Finally, I'm American citizen, so that was it. They cannot draft me, draft American citizen. And then the day goes on. And about a few months later, my mother in hometown received from town hall that I was given Japanese citizenship. I wasn't asked for it, you know. So anyway, so they could technically draft me, I was dual citizenship, and they did.[51]

As a result of this unprompted registration, Henry was drafted into the army. Japan's surrender just before Henry's induction date in August of 1945, however, came just in time to save Henry from going to the battlefield.

Other conscripted Nisei were not so fortunate. Kei Tateishi, a Japanese-American journalist who was stranded in Japan during the war and was put to work as a translator for Domei (Japan's national news agency), estimated that thousands of Nisei were forced to serve in Japan's army and navy. Precise numbers are impossible, he explained, because the Japanese government did not record evidence of dual citizenship when it conscripted Nisei.[52] Using demographic calculations based on age and gender ratios of the Nisei population, historian Kadoike Hiroshi estimates that approximately three thousand Nisei served as soldiers in the Japanese military during World War II.[53] Especially as the conscription policies were altered as the war wore on (for example, by closing loopholes that previously permitted university students to postpone military service, and by lowering the draft age to nineteen in 1944), many Nisei who had been studying in universities were sent to the war offices of their ancestral hometowns to take the conscription exam and join a military unit.[54] Frank Fukuhara, who had moved from Hawai'i to Hiroshima in 1933, remembered that he tried to avoid the draft by applying to a technical college in Toyama:

To keep out of draft at that time, the only way to do for me was to either go to medical college or technical college. Then I can extend my draft. So I worked a little bit harder than I did because I found that out, so I took a test, about three schools that were public and technical, and I just passed one of 'em, so I went to that college, which was in Toyama, Japan.

And yet, even as a technical college student, Frank was drafted in early April 1945—to a suicide bomb squad. "If I had only American citizenship," Frank explained, "I would not be drafted, but it'd be hard to live in Japan because no more, they won't give you any rations to eat." As a member of the suicide bomb squad, Frank and his fellow soldiers "were to carry bombs and dive into American tanks if they come up. That was our mission at that time."[55] Thus, Frank, who had attempted to manipulate his career path so as to avoid fighting the country of his birth, found himself in a unit that would require him to commit suicide to kill American soldiers.

Many Nisei soldiers conscripted into the Japanese military put their English language skills to work, serving as communications monitors or as interrogators at POW camps. Morio Morishima, for example, of Fife, Washington, was drafted into the Japanese army and served throughout the war as a supervisor for a military academy and as an interpreter at the POW camp at Shimonoseki.[56] Warren Nobuaki Iwatake, born in Maui in 1923, had chosen to enter college specifically to avoid the draft, but when the draft stipulations were expanded in 1943, he was conscripted to serve as a communications monitor.[57] Other Nisei soldiers (like Frank Fukuhara) held jobs unrelated to their English language ability, and in many cases, they kept their American birth a secret. Sacramento-born Matsufuji Ōji had dreamed of being a diplomat so that he might facilitate peaceful conversation between his two countries, but at the age of twenty-one, he entered the Japanese navy *tokkō* (special forces). According to his friends, Ōji had never shared with anyone his concern for his family members in the United States after the attack on Pearl Harbor, and he did not mention to his military companions that he had been born and raised in the United States. On April 6, 1945, he became one of the nearly four thousand youths to die as a *kamikaze* pilot.[58]

Kay Nishimura was nine years old when he sailed with his family to Japan. Born in 1923 in Seattle, Kay was a dual citizen who had suffered the discrimination known well to Nisei. He was looked down upon as a "Jap" growing up in Palo Alto, California, in the 1920s, and was called *ketō* (a derogatory term used for foreigners) when his family moved to his father's hometown of Hiroshima in 1923. When Japan attacked Pearl Harbor, Kay's parents and three of his five siblings had already returned to the United States. Kay was living in Hiroshima with his grandfather, a strict, traditional man who would only let Kay go to sleep for the night after he had written one hundred *kanji*. Kay was drafted into military service in 1943 when Japanese policies shifted to accommodate students in the draft. He was in a *tokkō* unit, destined to become a suicide pilot, but was reassigned due to a hearing problem to serve instead as a trainer of suicide pilots in Pusan. "They were young kids—eighteen, nineteen years old. I trained them in how to go to *tokkōtai*. I would say, 'You are only gonna live maybe another fifty years, so why don't you do something for His Majesty the Emperor, and then you

昭和20年6月
朝鮮 釜山海軍航空隊
熊野克哉（現姓 西村）22歳
海軍少尉
甲板士官 勤務

Figure 3.1. Kei Nishimura in Korea at age 22 (June 1945).

Figure 3.2. Kei Nishimura at his home in Tokyo (June 2015).

will be [enshrined] at Yasukuni forever.'" No one in Kay's unit knew of his American citizenship until a telegram came from the Red Cross, informing him that his family was interned at a camp in Wyoming. Only then did Kay's commanding officer learn that Kay was American. "The officer said, 'You bastard, are you American-born?' And I said, 'I'm a dual citizen,' but he hit me for being insolent."[59]

Conscription policies rendered participation in the war against the Allies virtually inevitable for Nisei men. Women, however, were excluded from service in Japan's army. As a result, they were neither provided with this avenue to overcome their discrediting stigma, nor would they be able in the postwar to point to conscription laws as a way to absolve themselves of their contributions to the war effort. "Collaboration" on the part of Nisei women in Japan was not so overt as donning a Japanese military uniform and pointing a weapon at an Allied soldier. The ambiguity of collaboration represented in the actions of Nisei women in wartime Japan makes the history of these individuals an all the more compelling access point for a deeper examination of the very process of collaboration.

Making a Home on the Home Front

The contributions of Nisei women in World War II Japan were of a different nature than that of their Nisei brothers, but their actions were in effect compulsory as well: modes of assimilation into which Nisei women were guided by the realities of their environment. Like Nisei men making sense of their surroundings in the context of propaganda that idealized the imperial soldier, Nisei women made sense of their daily lives on the home front, struggling to survive by enacting ideals of a Japanese femininity that, in the years of total war, regendered women as soldiers defending the homeland.

World War II in Japan was a total war. Mass communication, psychological warfare, battle preparedness drills, and the atrocities of regular air raids rendered the home front a war zone. And yet, Japanese women had been tasked with upholding the myth of domestic security—of a wholesome, supportive, sacred sanctuary wherein returned soldiers could dissociate from the horrors of the battlefield. In the earlier days of Japan's participation in modern international warfare, state-supported women's associations established the Japanese woman's place in wartime as devoted nurturer. The nationwide Patriotic Women's Association was created in 1905 during the Russo-Japanese War as an organization through which 464,000 members comforted wounded warriors and supported the families of fallen soldiers.[60] By the late 1910s, women and their supporters in the Diet were lobbying for a woman's right to participate in politics, pointing to the contributions of women in the West who had supported their nations' cause during World War I through factory work, agricultural labor, and selling war bonds.[61] As Japanese women such as Hiratsuka Raichō and Ichikawa Fusae organized women's associations and spoke out publicly about the important functions of women in Japanese society against the backdrop of government programs such as the Seikatsu Kaizen Undō (Daily Life Improvement Campaign), modern womanhood emerged as two pristine ideals: effective motherhood and efficient household management. As Japan's soldiers went off to a new war in the 1930s, Japanese women were told that they could serve the nation as an updated version of a socially engaged "good wife, wise mother." Women were responsible for ensuring the nation's physical and mental vitality through good eating habits, safe and hygienic housing, and public displays of maternal support for soldiers by stitching belts, orchestrating care packages, sending off soldiers to the front, and grieving the fallen.

As the home front became a war zone, however, women in Japan faced the demand to serve as both supportive/distant mothers and prepared/engaged soldiers of the domestic war effort. While "good wife, wise mother" imagery of women as nurturers and providers persisted in magazines, on billboards, in films, and in newspapers, another paradigm of womanhood emerged: that of the de-gendered soldier in *monpe* (workpants), wielding a bamboo spear in preparation for defending Japan to the death in the final decisive battle against invading enemy troops. As Haruko Taya Cook described in her study of the propagandized *gyokusai* heroic death of women in imperial Japan, media portrayals heralding the heroism of women *gyokusai* during the fall of Saipan in 1944 mythologized a new extreme for the exemplar of womanhood—she who achieves the ultimate self-sacrifice: death.[62] The former domestic goddess paradigm of Japanese womanhood had expanded: as World War II wore on, the "home" became the "home front," and ideal womanhood was signified by the mother, herself a courageous defender of the home front who calmly faces death with honor, who takes pride in raising strong soldiers to die for the emperor.

Nisei women, though not conscripted as soldiers, were indeed drafted to work for the war effort. Labor enrollment in Japan officially began in November of 1941 with the Kokumin Tōroku Seido (Citizen Registration System), which required the registration of all unmarried women aged 16–25 and men aged 16–40.[63] Although women were required to register for possible service outside the home, the political discourse of the time emphasized that the wartime contributions women should make were those *inside* the home: rearing healthy children and running a thrifty household. As the Minister of Welfare Koizumi Chikahiko declared in February of 1942, "In order to secure its labor force, the enemy is drafting women, but in Japan, out of consideration for the family system, we will not draft them."[64] On this topic, Prime Minister Tōjō Hideki described that the "natural mission of the women in our empire" to serve as "that warm fountain-head which protects the household, assumes responsibility for rearing children, and causes women, children, brothers, and sisters to act as support for the front lines is based on the family system."[65] As a result of this rhetoric, the throngs of Japanese women supporting the war effort operated in a volunteer capacity as members of patriotic associations. As members of these *fujinkai* (women's associations), women raised war funds, visited shrines to honor war dead, found wives for wounded soldiers, led parades for soldiers, helped equip soldiers for the front with comfort kits or *senninbari* (thousand-stitch belts), and educated the populace in health, savings, and home economics. By October 1942, the Dai Nippon Fujinkai (an amalgamation of earlier women's volunteer groups) had 27 million members.[66] The group was under the control of the Diet, and although there was no law forcing women to join, it was considered one's patriotic duty to participate.

In addition to women's activities in volunteer patriotic associations, some women were effectively drafted by the government to fill labor gaps late in the war, despite the rhetoric of motherhood and the family nation. In early 1944, the government aggressively recruited women aged twelve to twenty-five, under the guise of urging women to become members of the *aikoku hōkokutai* (patriotic labor corps) and *joshi rōdō teishintai* (women's volunteer corps) to assist with war work in schools and in their neighborhoods, plus thirty days of factory work a year.[67] Women could be exempt from this, though, if they were married, or if they could prove themselves "pivotal to the family."[68] While the state was demonstrably reticent about forcibly putting women to work, social norms rendered volunteerism an absolute expectation of all Japanese women, including the Nisei on the home front.

Women in wartime Japan were cued to imagine themselves as assuring Japan's future (through bodily fertility, responsible mothering, thrifty home management, and compassionate nurse care), while simultaneously functioning in an environment that emphasized through ritual and rhetoric the total removal of any future—an environment that drilled women, men, and children alike in the script and choreography of self-sacrifice. Thus, in addition to the dissonance navigated by Nisei who found themselves engaged in a war against the country of their birth, the environment that shaped Nisei women on the home front was doubly cacophonous: the emergency conditions of total war Japan were out of tune with the myth of maternally nurtured national security. As the demands of their environment compelled Nisei women on the home front to function as Japanese citizens engaged in supporting the war effort, these Nisei women were simultaneously inspired by Japan's wartime policies to erase—or at least to hide—all aspects of America from their bodies in appearance, deportment, speech, thought, and activity. In this way, the everyday environment of the Japanese home front kindled in Nisei women the aspiration to purge their bodies of American—"enemy"—traits and to regulate their bodies in the image of Japanese femininity.

Mnemonic Sites as Ritual

The rhetoric of gendered ideals colored everyday life in families across the Japanese empire with the messages of Japan's holy war, and this discourse was further supported by government policies designed to inspire a spirit of self-sacrifice in the minds of the general populace. By creating opportunities for the populace to mediate individual thoughts and emotions on a popular, nationwide level, the administration endeavored to structure the lives of the people around the concept of a family state with the emperor as the benevolent head. This was accomplished through the development of what historian Takashi Fujitani calls "mnemonic sites"—material vehicles of meaning that either helped construct a memory of an emperor-centered national past or served as symbolic markers for commemorations of national accomplishments or potential.[69] Fujitani describes policies, objects, and celebrations designed to promote the idea of the "filiative bonds" between the people and the emperor, including markers in the physical landscape, imperial, and physical objects (from commemorative postcards to massive monuments and torii shine gates). Mnemonic sites pervaded the everyday environment of Nisei on the home front in wartime Japan, inspiring thoughts of the emperor, of union with the Japanese imperial citizenry, and of the nation's mission in war. As material and physical repositories of meaning, they serve as prime examples of soft propaganda in practice.

Mnemonic sites shaped the physical landscape of everyday life in wartime Japan, stimulating Nisei—as well as the Japanese citizenry—to consider themselves as fused to other members of the ichioku through the material environment. Collective experiences of cyclical celebrations and material objects served as rituals though which residents on the home front could focus their emotional energies and make sense of their grief, anxiety, ambivalence, and hope. Food, for example, served as one such physical mnemonic site. In support of the government's propaganda campaigns promoting frugality and home economy, organizations such as school groups and women's volunteer associations across Japan disseminated information on economical cooking and preserving practices, effectively rendering the kitchen a site at which individuals could contribute to the national war effort. In this way, the food one ate could serve as a manifestation of patriotism—especially, for example, when one packed a *hinomaru bentō* lunch (a red pickled plum resting in the center of a bed of rice, a design that replicated the Japanese flag), which students in Japan were encouraged to eat from 1939 onward, or ate *suiton* (a soup of flour dumplings and vegetable scraps consumed when resources were scarce near the end of the war).[70] Through mnemonic sites, the government's propaganda campaigns reverberated as soft propaganda, and Japan's imperial subjects literally swallowed the messages of self-sacrifice and patriotism.

Clothing also functioned as a material mnemonic site in wartime Japan by creating an environment in which the individual was encouraged to imagine herself as connected to her fellow Japanese citizens through similar dress. In April 1941, alongside the rebirth of *shōgakkō* (elementary school) as *kokumin gakkō* (the people's school), school uniforms were unified across the nation for both boys and girls. Instead of the previously popular Western-style "sailor" uniform, girls were required to wear a top with a standardized *hechima eri* (shawl-style collar) and a pleated skirt (which would be swapped for *monpe* pantaloons as the war intensified). The boys' uniforms were standardized as well, in a style reminiscent of soldiers' uniforms.

The government encouraged the adult population to wear standardized clothing as well. Looking to the example provided by the standardized dress of the Manshū Kyōkai (Manchu Association), which had been adopted in the puppet state of Manchukuo in 1937, Japanese ministers and bureaucrats started to explore the possibility of standardized dress for citizens on the Japanese islands. Inspired by both pragmatic economic concerns of limited resources, as well as a perception of the Manchu Association standard dress as a successful example of how patriotism, mental and physical preparedness, and *esprit de corps* could be achieved by a unification of the citizens' clothing, the Department of Health and Welfare organized a "Committee for the Consideration of Clothing" in 1938 to discuss possibilities of standardized *kokuminfuku* (citizen's clothing) for all Japanese male subjects not serving in the military. It took time, but their efforts, plus those of the War Ministry and the Ministry of Health and Welfare and designs solicited from the readership of the *Tokyo Daily News,* resulted in the official proclamation of *kokuminfuku* in the autumn of 1940 as Imperial Edict 725, one of more than twenty-seven thousand events marking the two thousandth anniversary of the Japanese imperial line. *Kokuminfuku,* which served as a uniform for the adult civilian male population, offered two options, both of which included a military-style jacket, cap, and pants, all in the khaki color of standard issue military uniforms. Although

the ordinance was not enforced through any means of punishment for viola-
tions, it was encouraged on a large scale, especially through print media, including a magazine called *Kokuminfuku,* a propaganda periodical composed
of photos, stories, and cultural "know-how" pieces released by the Kokuminfuku Cooperative.

In 1941, the Ministry of Health and Welfare held a similar contest to solicit
designs for *hyōjunfuku,* (standardized dress) for women. As with the men's *kokuminfuku,* a committee established two designs based on modified versions of the
entries. This time, the result was released not as an imperial edict but as an ap-
proved item of the vice cabinet (次官會議諒解事項). However, as Inoue Masahito points out in his study of the wartime standard dress movement, these
hyōjunfuku designs—unlike the men's *kokuminfuku* designs—were not widely
accepted. And yet, although *hyōjunfuku* achieved a much lower success rate, Japanese women in the total war climate *were* clad in a sort of standard dress: nearly
all women wore a *kimono* top with *monpe,* the trousers associated with farm
workers in the Japanese countryside.[71]

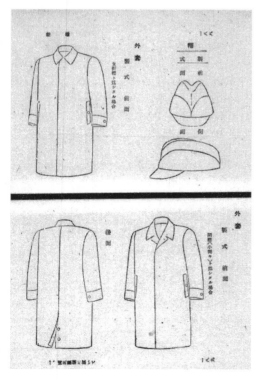

Figure 3.3. Samples of national dress
for men, from *Shōwa kokumin reihō:
Monbushō seitei* [Shōwa's National
Court of Justice Act established by the
Ministry of Education], 1941. Cour-
tesy National Diet Library, Japan.

As a result of the *kokuminfuku* efforts, as Minami Hiroshi describes in *Kindai shōmin seikatsushi*, from 1940 onward, Japan achieved a state of *"yunifōmu jidai"* ("era of the uniform").[72] According to data analyzed by Inoue Masahito, by 1944, virtually 100 percent of the Japanese non-military male population was wearing the *kokuminfuku* designs.[73] In this way, the mnemonic site of standardized dress subliminally prompted individuals in Japan to consider themselves as connected to their fellow Japanese citizens. Clad in dress that was coded by propaganda campaigns as economical, patriotic, practical in the climate of total war, and explicitly un-Western, members of the Japanese population were stimulated to consider themselves as participants in the category of "Japanese subject." Allured by the positive social codes accorded *monpe* and *kokuminfuku*—and compelled by the scarcity of alternative garments—subjects across the empire assimilated into a "uniform" populace.

To deviate from this idealized standard of dress—even in hairstyle—was to welcome distain. Japanese women who continued to perm their hair faced ridicule from neighbors and strangers alike, who accused them of vanity, individualism, and lack of patriotic spirit. As Takaaki Aikawa described in his wartime memoirs, young men with Western-style haircuts were reprimanded by soldiers, who would demand, "Why do you want to look like an American? It's antiwar feeling and you are a defeatist." The order for even civilian men to shave their heads in the style of Buddhist monks, Aikawa continued, "came to us from some unknown source. It was not a formal order from the government, but it had such a strong and uncanny power that it caused one school after another to yield to this magical voice."[74] The government's widespread *kōminka* policies had evidently succeeded in convincing Japanese society of the imagined connection between outward appearance and individual conviction. As a result, the normalizing gaze of society itself further bolstered administrative policies encouraging unified Japanese hairstyles, clothing, food, and decorative objects.

The minds of the population were united, additionally, through mnemonic sites of celebrations and commemorative days developed to stir feelings of patriotism in the populace. In 1942, for example, the eighth day of every month was established as *taishō hōtaibi* (Imperial Rescript Proclamation Day), when all of the nation's newspapers would carry the imperial proclamation of war on their front pages. Japanese citizen Utsunomiya Fumiko remembered of her girlhood that Imperial Rescript Proclamation Day was celebrated at her school on the eighth of every month with great fanfare, including performances by the school's drum and fife band and the flag corps show. During these celebrations, Fumiko wrote, students would sing and pray for success of army and navy, ever mindful of their duty to think of "nothing but the victory" and "self-sacrifice."[75]

Through mnemonic sites of material culture—such as food, dress, images of the emperor, and shrine altars installed in every home—as well as through mnemonic sites of celebrations in which voices sang and bodies moved in unison, members of the imperial Japanese populace could imagine themselves united in time, movement, appearance, and expression. Honor and patriotism required foregoing individual concerns to champion national goals. Through these rituals of material culture, members of the Japanese populace were given outlets to mediate their individual emotions of grief and fear by participating in collective mnemonic sites. This social atmosphere inspired members of the population to direct their individual energies ever toward the collective whole, and private life was virtually absorbed into public life. The demand for individual sacrifice spread throughout the entire population, including to the Nisei who were living in wartime Japan. As their environment was purged of Western ideas, words, and physical items, their minds were re-focused on Japanese clothing, Japanese language, Japanese food, and celebrations of Japanese history and government actions. In this way, the physical environment guided the assimilation of Nisei in Japan by providing avenues for participation in the category of the Japanese ethno-nation.

Material objects in the physical environment of everyday Japan were imbued with patriotic, victory-oriented, emperor-focused meaning. In schools, teachers drilled Nisei children in the attributes of nationalistic education designed to shape pupils who believed in Japan's mission to lead Asia—pupils who saw the influence of the West as antithetical to Japanese autonomy. Outside of school as well, in the magazines they read, the conversations they heard, and in the physical environment surrounding them, Nisei confronted calls to economize and to sacrifice their individual desires for the imperial cause. They held, ate, and wore material objects charged with positive meanings—elements of culture coded as expressive of patriotism and national pride. They observed and participated in ceremonies celebrating the glory of Japan and the emperor. Nisei in wartime Japan directed their behavior and appearance toward the mission of the Japanese ethno-nation, and they were thereby absorbed into the imperial populace in action, appearance, and expression.

The channels of the physical environment and material culture that fused foreign-born Nisei into the imperial populace were the same channels that severed Nisei from their American past. The speech, thought, physical appearance, and bodily movements of Nisei in Japan were not only directed away from the concept of America, but were redirected toward the Japanese imperial cause. Nisei youth faced the image of ideal patriotism within the reformulated imperial education system; Nisei men became soldiers who would die for the emperor in battles waged against their former friends and neighbors; and Nisei women adopted the mannerisms associated with Japanese patriotic womanhood—in the home as well as in fields, in factories, and in military support offices.

Making assumptions about perceived shortcomings (stigmas) being detected by their audience, Nisei in wartime Japan edited their mannerisms to minimize the threat posed by detection. Before the declaration of war, Nisei had existed in a gray area, recognized as neither fully Japanese nor fully American. But the start of World War II marked a striking shift in social differentiation. Nisei were at least provisionally included in the Japanese populace—the *ichioku*—a single family with a single soul.[76] Their survival rested on their ability to perform the ideals of Japaneseness that permeated their everyday environment.

CHAPTER FOUR

Visible and Invisible Discipline

The aspiration of Nisei in wartime Japan to perform as Japanese was shaped not only by subliminal messages of soft propaganda (the carrots, so to speak), but also by the disciplinary methods of the Japanese wartime state (the sticks). The Japanese administration's methods of discipline appear in its policies of race-based segregation, hypersurveillance, and daily life regimentation. This chapter takes a closer look at these methods of discipline in the everyday environment of wartime Japan to underscore that Nisei collaboration, assimilation, and obedience in wartime Japan were not so simple as *deciding* to be disloyal to the United States, but were rather the product of psychological forces that compelled Nisei to regulate their behavior in "Japanese" ways.[1]

As Mary Kimoto's memoirs relate, she and her fellow Nisei passengers disembarked the *Tatsuta Maru* at Yokohama port, underwent some questioning by police, and were released to face the years of war among the fully Japanese citizenry. Uncertain of where to go and what to do, Mary took a train from Yokohama to Tokyo, to the residence of her previous host family, but they were unable to take her back into their home. With little recourse, she found a position as a housekeeper for a female doctor who ran a small clinic. "I sold everything I could," she wrote, "—the kimonos, dried mushrooms, and tea that I had bought for presents to take home. So I am not absolutely penniless yet. But now there won't be any money coming from home as before."[2] With no hope of passenger ship traffic to ferry her home across the Pacific and no more financial support arriving from her parents in California, Mary was left to fend for herself in a country that was unfamiliar to her in many ways.

When Japan entered full-scale war against the Allied powers after the attack on Pearl Harbor, Allied nationals living on the main islands of Japan as well in Japan's territories and colonies became "enemy aliens." However, whereas white citizens of Allied nations disembarking the *Tatsuta Maru* were taken directly to a newly established Kanagawa prefectural enemy internment facility (or, in the case of diplomats, to their respective embassies), passengers like Mary Kimoto who were of Japanese descent were released after questioning, regardless of the details of their citizenship.[3] At the time, Mary possessed only American citizenship; she was, therefore, an "enemy alien" who was nevertheless permitted (and expected) to meld into the Japanese citizenry on account of her Japanese heritage.

In wartime Japan, white and other non-Asian enemy aliens faced entirely different circumstances from those experienced by Mary and her fellow Nisei. Even before the official declaration of war between Japan and the Allied powers, many of Japan's white residents found themselves relieved of their positions as teachers and managers. In a letter to Miye dated September 23, 1941, Mary Kimoto wrote that her former classmate Fritz Langer "was rather disappointed because he was dismissed from his job of teaching at the government Naval College. Now he doesn't know what to do. They fired all foreigners from the military schools."[4] Fritz, the son of an artist killed in World War I, had been living in Japan for several years, but as nationalism rose to a fever pitch in Japan in late 1941, not even the fact that Fritz was German (and therefore an Axis ally) could save him from the fate endured by many white teachers in Japanese schools.

Across Japan, white teachers, school administrators, and businesspeople found themselves replaced by Japanese nationals, regardless of their ancestral country's political alignment. Yayoi Cooke, a Nisei from California who had moved with her family to Japan in 1938, had been attending a mission school called Tōyō Eiwa, where the presence of English-speaking, foreign teachers had eased her transition into Japanese society, but in 1941, "I think three of the white teachers had to be taken away, and we had a Japanese vice principal . . . a Japanese man. He became the principal. He took over and of course everything had to change."[5] Such anti-white sentiment on the part of government agencies, businesses, and educational institutions demonstrated to Nisei the fundamental importance of Japaneseness to career and social advancement. As schools and businesses shifted their leadership to fully Japanese, Nisei—many of whom were in Japan to gain better employment—plainly saw that Japanese citizens were eligible for positions of power and respect, whereas "Western" attitudes, expressions, and appearance constituted grounds for dismissal.

While Nisei like Mary Kimoto and Iva Toguri continued their daily activities as members of the Japanese populace, non-Japanese heritage foreigners—missionaries, merchants, teachers, clergy, diplomats, and journalists—were segregated, marked as different from the rest of the population. According to the records of Japan's Interior Ministry, as of December 8, 1941, there were 2,138 enemy nationals living in Japan, including Americans, British, Canadians, Dutch, Australians, Belgians, Norwegians, and Greeks.[6] This population count does not include Nisei, who numbered in the tens of thousands at that time. In addition to the numbers of enemy nationals recorded by the Interior Ministry were 1,150 "neutral nationals" (French, Soviets, White Russians, and stateless individuals such as displaced Jews), as well as 2,482 Germans and 246 Italians.[7] The enemy aliens, marked as racially different from the Japanese citizenry and politically different from members of Axis-affiliated nations, were extracted from the Japanese populace by a variety of methods of wartime segregation.

Segregation: Distancing Nisei from America

Imprisonment was the most severe method by which enemy aliens were removed from the homes and jobs they had known in Japan. Immediately following the attack on Pearl Harbor, police rounded up more than one hundred Allied nationals—now enemy aliens—and imprisoned them in jails such as Tokyo's Sugamo Prison. Those targeted by such raids were primarily white male journalists as well as those who had demonstrated leftist leanings. British lecturer John Morris, who was still living in Tokyo at the time of the raids, relays in his memoir the conditions of such imprisonment, as described to him by his friend Frank Hawley, the director of the British Library of Information and Culture:

> The cell was six feet by nine and had a small cupboard, flush toilet, and a wash basin fitted with a cold water tap. There was no furniture, the only alternative to squatting on the floor being to sit on the lavatory seat. There was in addition a twig brush for cleaning the cell, a paper dustpan and a wooden waste-paper basket into which the dust from the floor was emptied; it was removed once every week. There was one barred window two feet by four; it was of opaque glass covered with wire netting, hinged at the top and so arranged that it could not be opened for more than six inches. There was no heating of any kind in the winter and the cell was stifling in summer. One 30-watt bulb hung from the center of the ceiling; this was kept burning throughout the night, and since all prisoners are required to sleep in such a way that their faces can be seen by the duty warder on his rounds, it is impossible to avoid the glare of the unshaded lamp. The door of the cell was of steel, with an observation hole three inches in diameter. This hole was closed during the day but kept open throughout the night.

Prisoners were to be examined within two months, but officials often ignored this policy, and the suspected spies and subversive detainees could be held interminably at the will of the special police. In this manner, the journalists and ideologues who had once struggled to represent the realities of Japanese politics and affairs to the world were removed from the realm of human activity, silenced in their thirty-six square-foot cells. Morris adds that the police also imprisoned scores of Japanese citizens in such raids—and that these prisoners received even worse treatment in jail than did white prisoners.[8]

While foreign members of the media faced imprisonment, other enemy aliens in Japan in the wake of the Pearl Harbor attacks were placed in one of thirty-four internment camps across mainland Japan. More than half of these facilities— repurposed churches, monasteries, activity centers, and schools—were somehow related to Christian organizations.[9] In her comprehensive study of World War II enemy alien treatment, Komiya Mayumi identifies four phases of the history of alien internment. In Phase One (December 8, 1941, through August 1942), the residents of Japan's internment camps were primarily adult men who received relatively fair treatment. During this phase, the Home Ministry specifically listed as its internment targets: soldiers, those with flight crew qualifications, eighteen- to forty-five-year-old male enemy nationals, individuals with special technical abilities (such as radio operators or munitions engineers), and those suspected of involvement as foreign intelligence operatives.[10] Although the enemy aliens interned during this phase were predominantly male, in Tohoku, Okayama, Hiroshima, and Nagasaki, several nuns were also interned.[11] Phase Two of internment (September 1942 through September 1943) represents a shift sparked by Japan's defeat at Midway. This phase saw stricter treatment at the facilities, as well as an expansion nationwide to include female missionaries and nuns among the number of interned. Komiya's third phase (October 1943 through early 1945) marks the inclusion of Italian citizens in internment facilities after Italy withdrew from the Axis powers. Finally, Phase Four (early 1945 through August 1945) marks the preparation for the final decisive battle on the homeland, during which residents at the camps (like all Japanese citizens by that time) were in constant danger of firebombing and starvation. During this phase, the Allied victory in Europe resulted in the addition of Germans and French to the internment camp population.[12]

Many of the remaining enemy aliens who were neither imprisoned nor interned faced a third form of segregation from the Japanese populace: house arrest. This method of segregation was primarily intended for diplomatic officials and their families, who were ordered to remain in their embassy buildings or their diplomatic residences until repatriation could be realized. In addition to the house arrest imposed on diplomat families, some Japanese districts with few white foreigners—such as Shimane prefecture and Kumamoto prefecture—required those foreigners to remain in their own homes in a state of house arrest in lieu of placing them in internment camps. Other methods for managing enemy aliens in these regions included imprisonment or transfer to an internment facility in a different prefecture, as in the case of Robert Harrison Crowder, a teacher from Illinois. Crowder was incarcerated in a Kumamoto prison for three months and then placed in "a defunct leprosarium" until being transported to an internment camp in Nagasaki.[13]

A fourth means by which white Allied nationals were erased from the landscape in wartime Japan was through evacuation. Several hundreds of enemy alien residents—many of whom had previously been imprisoned or interned—sailed from ports in Japanese territories on official exchange ships coordinated by the governments of Allied nations with Japan through the mediation of neutral nations. The first exchange ship *Asama Maru* departed Yokohama on June 17, 1942, repatriating to America some 1,500 American men, women, and children.[14] These passengers arrived in New York harbor more than two months later, after an exchange at the port of Lourenço Marques (present-day Maputo in Mozambique). Two additional exchange ships would follow: the *Tatsuta Maru* on July 30, 1942, and the *Teia Maru* on September 14, 1943.

Not all enemy aliens eligible for repatriation on the exchange ships were able to make the journey. Iva Toguri and her Nisei friend Chieko Ito, for example, had both applied at the Swiss consulate for passage on the exchange ship, but without official US passports, they were unable to establish their citizenship through correspondence with the State Department in time to join the voyage.[15] And despite what other scholars have recorded, Nisei with American citizenship were indeed eligible to apply to sail home on the evacuation ships, and immigration records reflect that a handful of Nisei were able to make the voyage. According to Max Hill of the Associated Press, who was one of the passengers aboard the first exchange ship, the few Nisei on board spent the journey apart from the other American passengers. Upon their arrival to New York, these Nisei were detained for special questioning to clarify the particulars of their citizenship.[16]

Others chose to remain in Japan to stay with their spouses and children, or because they knew no other home. Robert Harrison Crowder, who was living in west-central Kyushu at the time of the attack on Pearl Harbor, was transferred to the Bund Hotel in Yokohama after several months of incarceration to await repatriation on the *Asama Maru* in June of 1942. In Crowder's words: "My name was on the list. But at the last moment we were asked if we wished to go or to stay in Japan. Like many others who had so bonded with the country and its people that it was difficult to imagine leaving, I decided to stay."[17] Crowder and the other enemy aliens who had elected to remain in Japan were transferred to an internment camp in a vacated Catholic school building near Mount Fuji. Fourteen months in the internment facility evidently wore down Crowder's resolve; he elected to leave Japan at his next opportunity, the September 1943 exchange ship.

As the war wore on, evacuation policies for foreign residents in wartime Japan extended beyond enemy aliens to include large numbers of white foreigners categorized as stateless or neutral, as well as those hailing from countries aligned with the Axis powers. Many of these foreigners were also extracted from Japanese cities—not aboard the exchange ships but instead via quasi-compulsory evacuation to specially-designated foreign districts. In some cases, Japanese officials compelled foreign residents to move to these foreigner districts, but other stateless, neutral, and Axis-affiliated civilians moved there by choice to avoid suspicion or to seek a region remote from the threat of air raids. George Sidline, who was born in Japan to stateless parents (refugees from the Russian Revolution), explains in his memoir, "The government issued travel permits on a case-by-case basis, but for foreigners headed to Karuizawa, it was readily given."[18] Other foreign families chose alternative rural locations where they hoped to escape the threat of air raids, as did Heinz Altschul (a half-Jewish German rendered stateless when the German consulate confiscated his passport in the early years of the war) and his German wife and son, who moved to the more remote Ashiyagawa after seeing a plane from the Doolittle raid soar over Kobe in 1942.[19]

Lucille Apcar, born in Yokohama in 1926 to an American-born mother and a Japan-born (white) father of Armenian descent, was among the stateless residents evacuated to the resort town of Karuizawa in the mountains of Nagano. When Lucille's father was released after fourteen months of imprisonment (for suspected spy activities of the Masonic Order of which he was a senior officer), Lucille explained, "We were given three choices of location by the Japanese authorities, one of these Karuizawa, our home for the next two years."[20] Karuizawa had boasted a thriving international community before the war and had been popular as a summer resort, but the conditions were evidently harrowing for foreigners who weathered the war in this town nestled in the mountains of Nagano prefecture. In her memoir *Shibaraku: Memories of Japan,* Lucille recalls living in a small home in the Mikasa area of Karuizawa "with insulation nonexistent, with doors and windows ill-fitting and leaking cold air," where "keeping warm during the bitter winters became almost impossible."[21] Lucille and her family had to store food underground lest it freeze inside the walls of their home.

The parents of Austrian-born Beate Sirota Gordon (who was raised in Japan but was attending college in America at the time of Pearl Harbor) were another such family sequestered in Karuizawa. As Beate's memoir *The Only Woman in the Room* relates, Karuizawa's bitterly cold, snowy winters left Beate's mother— who was also Lucille Apcar's piano teacher—extremely ill.[22] George Sidline remained with his family in Kobe for the early years of the war, but as bombing intensified, the Sidlines, too, moved to Karuizawa. George remembered that wartime Karuizawa "had its contingent of Hitler *Jugend*, the Hitler Youth, who frequently marched down the main street in their brown shirts, Sam Brown belts and swastika arm bands, holding high the Nazi flag," a practice which quickly ceased after Germany surrendered.[23]

In addition to Karuizawa, the towns of Hakone (Kanagawa prefecture) and Yamanakako (Yamanashi prefecture) also served as special locales wherein foreigners were isolated from the rest of the Japanese population. These areas were primarily intended for residents of Axis nations or neutral nations (by 1943, there were two hundred German families living in Karuizawa),[24] but in practice, the districts' membership was more nebulously based on race, gender, and pre-war association with foreign contacts (through business or leisure) than on enemy-versus-ally nationality. The population in evacuation districts such as Karuizawa and Hakone also included "mixed-blood" residents who were deemed unlikely to be spies, such as Pia and Jaye Kurusu, the half-white/half-Japanese daughters of Japanese special envoy Kurusu Saburō and his American-born wife Alice, as well as two of American entrepreneur Thomas Laffin's half-Japanese daughters (Mary and Mildred). While Mary and Mildred Laffin lived with their mother in the family's Hakone vacation home, their sister Eleanor who had remained in their Yokohama home was interned when rules were tightened in 1943. Their brothers Thomas Junior and William sailed home on the first exchange ship after arrest (Thomas Junior) and internment (William).[25]

The complexities introduced by the experiences of biracial ("Eurasian") children and by Nisei possessing Allied citizenship during World War II provide a window through which to consider the wartime Japanese government's calculation of the security threat posed by enemy aliens and their offspring. During the war, the Japanese government lacked the resources necessary to intern all Allied nationals living on Japanese soil. Authorities endeavored, therefore, to find expedient methods for assessing the potential threat to national security posed by this heterogeneous enemy alien population. An ambiguous formula emerges: one in which factors of race, gender, and "suspicious" activity were considered more important than official nationality. Ostensibly, when Japan officially entered a state of war against the United States and Britain on December 8, 1941, any citizen of America or the British Empire living on Japanese soil became an "enemy alien" who should be the target of the government's anti-spy procedures of extraction from the populace through the methods discussed above. In practice, however, even Nisei who did not possess Japanese citizenship were spared this designation, demonstrating that the nationality represented on one's passport carried less weight than blood-based membership in the Japanese ethno-nation.

The rationale for this differentiated treatment of non-Japanese enemy nationals and racially Japanese Nisei is supported by the assumptions that underlay the *kōminka* efforts discussed in Chapter Three. Amid these efforts, ideologues in Japan touted the "mixed" ethnic origins of the Japanese people and other Asian populations as a testament to the assimilative prowess of the Japanese people— and as justification for Japan's territorial expansion throughout Asia.[26] As a result of this discourse, the concept of "Japanese subject" expanded alongside Japan's quest to build the Greater East Asia Co-Prosperity Sphere. The concept of the "Japanese subject" could transcend national boundaries to apply to members of conquered nations—Asian peoples whose ancestry was represented as intertwined racially with Japanese ancestry.[27] The 17,277 Chinese residents in Japan as of June 1942, for example, weathered the years of war under police surveillance but were not subject to other methods of extraction.[28] The argument supporting mixed racial heritage of the Japanese, while paving the way for incorporation of other Asian peoples, precluded the inclusion of ethnically non-Asian peoples. Race—kinship in blood—could transcend the intricacies of citizenship in the case of racially Asian individuals, but this kinship did not extend to white foreigners.

Nisei—even those without Japanese citizenship—were not interned or forcibly evacuated to foreigner districts. Indeed, when "Tokyo Rose" Iva Toguri, who possessed only American citizenship, requested to be interned alongside the other American citizens, the special policeman assigned to Iva reasoned, "Well . . . since you are of Japanese extraction and a woman, I do not think you will be very dangerous. So we will not intern you. For the moment we will just see how things go."[29] Evidently, this treatment also extended to Nisei men. When Paul Rusch, an American professor at Rikkyō University, returned on an exchange ship in 1942, he reported that many Nisei "have been placed in internment camps under conditions similar to those of enemy nationals. The government will not allow the Nisei to leave Japan."[30] And yet, in her extensive study of the wartime internment rosters, Komiya Mayumi found no record of Nisei detained in internment camps.[31] The "interned" Nisei to whom Rusch refers were likely interned Eurasians.

In practice, the segregation of enemy aliens from Japan's cities and towns has less to do with birthplace, professions of neutrality or loyalty, or passport designation. Even white "foreigners" who had been born and raised in Japan were forced into internment facilities. Rather, the segregation practices were driven by suspicion of spy activities, and based on the records of those imprisoned, interned, placed under house arrest, and evacuated, Japanese authorities determined potential for treason or loyalty primarily according to race and gender.

White enemy foreigners were suspected as potential spies, and white men in particular were seen as dangerous to Japan's war effort, regardless of where they were born or which nation they considered "home." In these ways, the Japanese government's wartime practices of race-based definition and segregation of "enemy aliens" purged Japan's neighborhoods, marketplaces, and schools of non-Asian enemy foreigners.

In the lives of Nisei in wartime Japan, segregation—the establishment of a physical enclosure, a vivid partitioning of Nisei Americans from white Americans—functioned as segregation from *without*. The enemy aliens incarcerated in prisons and interned in monasteries and schools were disciplined through enclosure and partitioning, to be sure. But the Nisei excluded from incarceration or house arrest on account of their Japanese racial membership were nevertheless disciplined by the same segregating partitions. American Nisei were placed outside the "enclosure" of Americanness by the segregation policies enacted by the Japanese government, leaving them physically cleaved from Americans. In this sense, barriers of enclosure discipline not only those within the enclosure but also those who must consider why they are kept *outside* the enclosure. The government's policies of segregation and enclosure made manifest in the physical environment that Nisei were granted reprieve from the fate of internment or compulsory evacuation on account of their membership in the Japanese race, but that they must train their bodies in accordance with the other Japanese bodies "on the outside."

Surveillance in Wartime Japan

Although Nisei were permitted to continue their daily lives among the fully Japanese citizenry, they were expected to substantiate the trust granted them by assimilating into the Japanese populace in action, expression, and emotion. Their prison, therefore, was of a different sort: the prison of hypersurveillance, both by official policies and representatives of the Japanese law, and by members of society who protected and enacted these policies. The Japanese government's propaganda efforts reverberated throughout the populace. Just as the environment of hypersurveillance encouraged average citizens to be ever on the lookout for spy activity, so were these average citizens on the lookout for any behavior or expression that might be deemed "pro-West." This message was also resoundingly reinforced in the education system, where Nisei were particularly susceptible targets.

The primary force of hypersurveillance in wartime Japan was the Kempeitai (literally "corps of law soldiers"), a military police division of the Imperial

Japanese Army established in 1881. Originally, the main purpose of the Kempeitai was to track down individuals who did not report for duty upon conscription into the Japanese army, but after Japan's annexation of Korea in 1910, the powers of the Kempeitai expanded to include maintenance of public order within Japan (under the auspices of the Home Ministry) and in Korea (under the War Ministry), with a primary aim of silencing voices opposed to the Japanese government.[32] By the start of the Shōwa era in 1926, the Kempeitai had offices in fifteen cities across Japan, plus several international branches, including posts in territories that were not under Japanese rule.[33] After the Manchurian Incident in 1931, the Kempeitai rapidly ramped up their activities of policing the general population, earning notoriety across the Japanese empire for their brutal interrogation tactics. The severely intimidating reputation of the Kempeitai was entrenched well before Japan's declaration of war on the Allied powers, and their notoriety expanded as the environment of militarism escalated in Japan. The *Japan Times* reported that between 1933 and 1936, 59,013 people had been arrested by the Kempeitai and the Tokkō (the Tokubetsu Kōtō Keisatsu, formed in 1901 as a civilian counterpart to the Kempeitai) for harboring "dangerous thoughts."[34] Under particular scrutiny during the war years were those who had strong ties to the West, including Nisei.

With the start of World War II, the powers of the Kempeitai extended beyond intelligence and espionage to include the operation of prisoner of war camps, civilian internment camps, and the comfort woman system, as well as commando-style combat and the coordination of propaganda campaigns and warfare experiments. The increasingly menacing reputation and scope of the Kempeitai cowed the Japanese population to fall in line with government policies.[35] Kempeitai officers hailed from top military academies, and they had higher educational and physical standards than ordinary soldiers. The unit was ostensibly a volunteer corps, but in reality, members were selected based on military examination scores and the soldier's ability to demonstrate a warrior spirit above all else.[36] As Private 8th Division Australian IF Roy H. Whitecross (POW 1942–1945) remembered:

> The Kempeitai were without doubt the elite of the Japanese military forces. In Japan, any member of the Kempeitai was saluted by army personnel with meticulous correctness. When a member of the Kempeitai was within sight of civilians, no matter how far away, the civilians went down on their knees and then bowed their faces only an inch or two from the ground. And they stayed in that position until the Kempeitai was completely out of sight.[37]

Adding further to the daunting estimation of the Kempeitai was the free hand with which they reigned as the thought police of the Japanese population. They required no warrant to arrest anyone suspected of spying, or of leftist or anti-government activities. Once arrested, suspects were subject to violent interrogation tactics designed to purge them of their unpalatable ideologies. Prisoners were forced, for example, to write their thoughts and political opinions until they had produced the sort of material the Kempeitai demanded.[38]

The Kempeitai shadow particularly haunted the lives of Nisei, and of Japanese citizens who were associated with "the West" through foreign work or study experiences, or through religion. Mary Kimoto, for example, was a member of the Holiness Church, an evangelical congregation thriving among Japanese immigrants in her home community of Ceres, California. A Japanese minister of the Holiness Church, Reverend Kaoru Itō, had shown Mary particular kindness as she adjusted to life as a Nisei in Japan. Mary was horrified and saddened to learn that Reverend Itō had been jailed "as were all ministers, mostly of the Holiness Church, who refused to renounce their faith" and that the Kempeitai had grilled him and his wife for countless hours about whether or not they believed that "the emperor is God."[39]

Under this sort of constant surveillance—and the threat of brutality should they fall suspect to some crime against the government—Nisei in Japan were careful not to behave in ways that would cast suspicion on themselves or their relatives. Frank Hironobu Hirata, a Nisei from Spokane who moved with his family to Japan as a boy, remembered his constant fear of the Kempeitai, whose wrath would surely be felt by those who dared to "talk openly." "There was two dangerous things," he explained. "One is to speak bad about the imperial family, next is about the warfare, how it's going on, the truth."[40] Bill Hashizume, a Nisei raised in Mission, Canada, who moved to Wakayama to live with relatives in 1938, shared:

When I went to Japan, I heard that the emperor was revered as a living god. And a living god, my goodness. He's no different from an ordinary person. And, but my relatives, you know, they warned me. Says, "Don't ever say that, because the special police or the military police are going to come and pick you up." And not only that, it's not myself, it's the full family . . . will be in trouble. They wouldn't be able to get good jobs, they wouldn't be able to do business. So, "keep it under your hat," which I did. I didn't want anything to happen to my sisters or my mother, any of my brothers. So I kept it all on my thing, but you know, all this, to me, from a person that went to thing and had, grew up in Mission, in Canada, that seemed to be a lot of hogwash, but I just kept that to myself.[41]

Any leeway granted Nisei for their "Western" or "American" brashness and inde-
pendence before Pearl Harbor melted away with the declaration of war against
the Allies. Nisei in Japan quickly learned to keep mum about their personal
opinions, especially on matters relating to the emperor and the war. Before the
war, Nisei bodies had been on display to their communities as "zoo people" and
"mannequins," but in the climate of wartime Japan, being watched was equivalent to being in danger of Kempeitai wrath. This environment of hypersurveillance stimulated Nisei to amplify their Japanese features and stifle their
American ones.

Across wartime Japan, acknowledgement of constant surveillance was a fact
of life. Propaganda campaigns emphasized to all members of the populace that it
was a citizen's duty to police his neighbors, and all Japanese citizens were on alert
for any behavior that smacked of "pro-West" attitudes. Nisei—at least those who
were known to be Nisei by their neighbors and colleagues—and Japanese citizens who had affiliations with Western organizations or English language ability
were natural targets for suspicion and even harassment. For example, as Jimmie
Matsuda of Hood River, Oregon, recounted of a run-in with an agent of the Kempeitai (which he calls the "Japanese FBI"):

> [T]hey thought we were spies. So even during the daytime or nighttime,
> they would come in the house without even knocking. They'll just open
> the door and say, "How are you guys doing?" and things like that, too.
> When we were having dinner they'll do that. And one day, I didn't go to
> school, but the FBI says, "Hey, Matsuda-san," he said, "How was school
> today?" I said, "Oh, it was very good." He says, "Nope, you didn't go to
> school. You played hooky, 'cause you were at the coast swimming with
> the other friends." They caught me right there . . . they were watching us
> all the time . . .[42]

California-born Rose Ito Tsunekawa, too, remembered that the constant surveillance from the Kempeitai effectively severed her ties to America. The special police
took particular interest in her family, which had settled in Tsushima just one week
before the attack on Pearl Harbor. She recalled, "Japanese police were almost every
day checking up on my parents, the radio that we had, make sure we weren't listening to shortwave . . . they were all very authoritative, very . . . no-nonsense."[43] Jack
Dairiki of Sacramento, who also moved to Japan in 1941, faced a similar reception:
"We were, [of] course, well-known as we were foreigners, of course anybody who
comes from a foreign country were known as the *gaijin* or the foreigner, and we
were under suspicion of the police department at all time . . . all the radios were
confiscated, any other thing they could, thought was suspicious were taken away

from us."[44] As these Nisei individuals' experiences illustrate, Nisei in wartime Japan were suspended in a liminal position of being "foreign" but not so "foreign" as to warrant internment, provided that they were careful not to raise any flags for the Kempeitai that might lead to suspicion of spy activity.

The fearsome authority of the Kempeitai had been enabled by the addition, in 1941, of laws that essentially gave the special police a free hand to arrest whomever they pleased. The National Defense Security Law of March 6, 1941, penalized residents for revealing information that might aid Japan's enemies. The revamped Peace Preservation Law of May 1941 abolished the appeals court for thought crimes, gave the Ministry of Justice the right to appoint defense attorneys for those on trial for thought crimes, and declared religious organizations as under the auspices of Kempeitai oversight. And shortly after the attack on Pearl Harbor, the Press, Publication, Assembly and Association Special Control Law of December 19, 1941, banned all unauthorized publications, assemblies, and organizations. Newspaper censorship laws, too, grew increasingly stringent. In January 1941, the Newspaper and Publication Control Ordinance granted the government the power to punish any newspapers seen as failing to follow a set of severe guidelines.

The Kempeitai served as a visible reminder, a marker in the everyday environment of the requirement of all residents to behave according to the government's stipulations. Indeed, the Kempeitai were ubiquitous, especially in Tokyo. The Kempeitai wore special white armbands inked with the characters "Soldier of the Law." "Everyone pretty much knew who they were," explained Abe Teruo, a Japanese boy who lived in Tokyo during the years of war. "They weren't the regular police or the special police. They were the people who came around if you said anything against the emperor or Japan or the war."[45] In addition to the visible presence they maintained in the streets and neighborhoods across Japan, Kempeitai also made their threats of violence visible. Kempeitai in mainland China, for example, displayed in public the severed heads of dissidents.[46]

The policing forces were not always visible, though, and their power was also stifling in its invisibility. Sometimes, officers dressed in plainclothes, blending in with the rest of the population to eavesdrop on conversations or spy on gatherings of friends and neighbors. Furthermore, one never knew when the special police might come calling. Michiko Usui Kornhauser, a Japanese girl living in Okayama during the war, remembered that people would be sitting around at home, and then someone would whisper, "'The Kempeitai is coming! Kempeitai may listen to you or come get you,' that was enough to keep us all quiet."[47] Acquiescence to surveillance as a fundamental duty of the citizenry—and, indeed, as a part of patriotic duty—permeated the everyday atmosphere of wartime Japan with a flavor of suspicion not only from government agencies, but also from the general populace. By July of 1941, the state had introduced the first of what would become annual antispy weeks, during which Japanese subjects were encouraged through films, banners, posters, handouts, and even matchboxes to be on the lookout for spy activity.[48] As John Morris wrote of the increasingly paranoid atmosphere surrounding him in 1941 Tokyo, "Anti-spy posters appeared on every hoarding, and the people were warned against the activities of the ubiquitous fifth column. This campaign was directed, of course, primarily against the British and Americans."[49] In this climate of surveillance, Nisei on the home front knew that their stigma of Americanness could be detected at any moment. This ever-present threat sustained in Nisei an affective intensity that shaped the way they presented themselves in public.

Amid this atmosphere of suspicion and conformity, average Japanese citizens were cued to consider their personal contributions to surveillance a part of their patriotic duty. The wartime format of district organization, the *tonarigumi* (neighborhood group), bound together individual family units, making each family responsible for the actions of the others. By extension, families were responsible for policing the actions of the others within their *tonarigumi*. In his autobiography *Unwilling Patriot*, Aikawa Takaaki wrote, "We were threatened with severe punishment if we failed to report to the town office any anti-war sentiment or comment in the neighborhood." Even on a streetcar full of complete strangers, when the car passed the Imperial Palace, "the conductor would tell the passengers that they were near the palace. Then all the passengers rose and made the special profound bow. It was rumored that someone was always watching and that those who would not make the bow were taken away to the special police office when they left the car." When families were ordered to have small Shintō shrines in their homes in the second year of the war, the heads of most *tonarigumi* inspected residents' homes to be certain that the shrine was present.[50]

Nisei therefore had to be wary of their actions, appearance, and expressions as observed not only by the special police, but also of the members of their *tonarigumi*. This resulted in an increased pressure for many Nisei, who were flagged as ultra-suspicious due to their foreign ways. Should they engage in activities detrimental to the war cause, the members of their neighborhood association would ostensibly also be punished for failing to police properly. Understandably, this caused tension among Nisei and their Japanese neighbors, contributing to the cold environment that pressured Nisei to assimilate—by conforming to Japanese standards and by participating in the war effort.

Under this surveillance, Nisei regulated their bodies as Japanese in action, speech, and appearance. At the same time, they stifled their American mannerisms and ways of thought in public, and they bit their tongues about their opinions on the war between their two nations. California-born Yayoi Cooke, for example, recalled that at her school in Yamanashi, a fellow Nisei pupil organized a speech contest, only to be brought to tears upon hearing the comments of the judges—that her speech was "too Americanized." "It seemed that the teachers had eyes on us," she mused, "[so] that we wouldn't do anything that's too, I think they called it 'liberal' because that was a Western idea which was not allowed in Japan."[51] Years after the war, many Nisei shared that because they were familiar with America's advanced industry and military might, they knew that Japan had little hope of winning the war. Hawaiian Nisei Paul Yempuku, for example, who spent the war as a student in Hiroshima and later Tokyo, remembered that his whole family knew "how big America is, and we shouldn't fight against America."[52] But, as his mother added, although they all knew that America would win the war, "we couldn't talk about this with others because we feared possible police action."[53]

Nisei faced pressure from their neighbors and from the special police not only to conform to Japanese ways in word and deed, but also to make their affiliation with Japan official by entering their names in the family register, or by renouncing their American citizenship. As Masayo Duus explains in her biography of Iva Toguri, this pressure was "part of the effort by the Japanese government to conscript Japanese Americans into the army and make them pledge their loyalty to Japan."[54] Iva refused to register for Japanese citizenship and maintained only her American citizenship throughout the war, but the majority of other Nisei in Japan who had not yet been registered for Japanese citizenship (such as Mary Kimoto) did eventually sign their names to the registers—for reasons such as school enrollment, Kempeitai pressure, and to receive rations.

Body Regulation on the Home Front

Life in wartime Japan was characterized by regimentation: organized time schedules, requirements for efficiency in gesture, empire-wide coordination of rituals, and mobilization of the citizenry in factories and fields on behalf of the war effort. A consideration of the Nisei body in motion in World War II Japan reflects the power of such regimentation to discipline the behavior of Nisei and Japanese subjects alike. While mnemonic sites of material culture and public celebrations propelled Nisei bodies to mimic other members of the imperial Japanese populace, Nisei bodies were also put to work—for the emperor, for the war cause, and for the Japanese nation. Thus, while propaganda directed Nisei thoughts and emotions toward Japaneseness, the realities of daily life such as curricular requirements, conscription policies, social pressure, and financial obligations directed Nisei bodies toward the concept of the Japanese nation and race as well. Through physical education and military-style drilling at school, and also through war mobilization, including service for the Japanese war machine, Nisei hands were repurposed to do the work of the Japanese nation.

British professor John Morris, who was living in Tokyo as an instructor at Keio University when Japan attacked Pearl Harbor, described the military-style training implemented at Japanese schools (including at Japanese universities) in the late 1930s:

> Every educational institution in the country has a number of army officers attached to it . . . The amount of time devoted to military instruction is supposed to be about five or six hours a week, but "special" periods of instruction are now often added, usually in the hours allotted to one or other of the foreign teachers, or at some time when the students would otherwise be studying what in the senior officer's opinion is some unnecessary subject, literature or philosophy, for instance. The military instruction includes lectures on discipline and the merit in dying for one's country. There is also a certain amount of field work, which includes route marches of anything up to twenty-five miles.[55]

Nisei students attending Japanese schools endured this type of military training alongside their Japanese classmates. Jack Dairiki, who was on a visit to Hiroshima from Sacramento when the war started in 1941, recalled of his training at school in Japan: "[T]hey wanted to train children to become strong to become a future soldier of the emperor . . . So we gathered for school, marched to school about two or three miles, depending on where you lived, in rows of two. We had a leader—the eldest of the group became the leader—and we marched to school every morning."[56] Henry Ueno, who moved from Oregon to Wakayama at age two, started basic military-style training such as marching and handling rifles in the fourth grade of elementary school. When he reached the seventh grade, though, the training progressed to "fencing, the bayonet trainings, and the sports like baseball and small wrestling, . . . how to shoot the gun, how to throw the hand grenade, and that type of thing."[57] This type of military training was not limited to boys' schools. Young women, too, engaged in physical preparation for battle. Marion Tsutakawa Kanemoto, who was born in Seattle in 1928 and moved to Okayama on an exchange ship during the war, describes that she and her classmates would strip down to a white top with *monpe* in the mornings to practice *naginata* drills, learning swordsmanship with sticks or bamboo spears.[58] Boys and girls in schools across Japan underwent such physical training, often practicing fencing techniques on straw dummies identified as Franklin Roosevelt, Winston Churchill, or Dwight Eisenhower.

In addition to military-style physical training of the body, pupils across Japan were put to work for the Japanese war effort in myriad capacities, ranging from childcare to agricultural labor to line work in armament factories. As Japan braced for total war, the very flavor of education changed, and all energy and coursework shifted focus to the question of how students might devote their energies to benefit the nation. The pupils at Japan Women's University, for example, saw their entire curriculum restructured according to the contributions women could make to the war. Their school's Department of Home Economics expanded to include Divisions of Child Care, Hygiene, Administration, and Domestic Science, and the students in these divisions dedicated their attention to practical application of the skills they learned. For example, they opened a day care center for children in the busy farming season in Suge Village. They also developed an exhibition on thrifty skills for home economics that, through the support of the Ministry of Education, Ministry of Finance, Ministry of Health and Welfare, and the Ministry of Commerce, toured the nation from 1938 to 1939, opening in department stores in Sendai, Osaka, Kobe, Kyoto, Nagoya, Fukuoka, Kumamoto, Okayama, Shizuoka, Hamamatsu, Niigata, Hiroshima, and Sapporo.[59]

Across Japan, the school year for high school and college students was shortened by three months in 1941, and again by six months in 1942 to allow for students to dedicate themselves to labor outside of the classroom. As schools reorganized their schedules according to the increased demand for student labor, they also responded by reformatting the classes themselves to accommodate student mobilization. Rikkyō University, for example, required its students to participate in *tanren* (drill) daily, often in place of elective courses such as English and Philosophy. For *tanren,* students were divided into groups and engaged in agricultural labor and special labor tasks, "national defense exercise" such as forced marches, swimming and strength tests, and "national defense competitions" of softball, tennis, volleyball, and canoeing.[60]

By the end of 1944 students across Japan were forfeiting essentially all classroom learning so that they and their teachers could work in Japan's factories and fields. Nisei pupils were expected to participate alongside their Japanese classmates, regardless of any ambivalence they might have felt about the war itself. As a student at Tsuda College, for example, Yayoi Cooke and her classmates spent only half of their time at study. With the other half of their time, they worked in the school gymnasium, which had been converted into a factory for airplane parts. Every night, American bombers would swoop down so close to the factory that the girls could see the faces of the pilots.[61] Mary Kimoto, who was also a college student during the war, explained that, "As the war went on, we were unable to do much studying. We had to work in the fields to supplement our diet. It was probably around the spring of 1944 that we went to munitions factories in Tokyo to work. I helped to make small batteries."[62] Seattle-born Marion Tsutakawa Kanemoto sewed buttons on army uniforms in Okayama.[63] Hiroko Nakashima, who moved from Spokane to Yamaguchi in 1939, was mobilized to work in a factory in the nearby town of Hikari. "I don't know what kind of parts we were making," she reflected, "but it must have been for the submarines or boats or something. So . . . during the junior and senior year we didn't learn too much in school because we were working all the time."[64]

Japan's total war mood, which demanded seriousness and war readiness from all members of the population at all times, pervaded the students' work as well, effectively rendering the students as soldiers and the factories as war fronts. The martial conditions in which mobilized students worked were extremely austere. In Aichi prefecture, Rose Ito Tsunekawa of Salinas, California, was mobilized first to help local farmers and then at a textile factory, weaving blankets from synthetic material alongside her high school classmates. "We hardly did any studying," Rose explained. "We had to work in the fields, because all of the men were at war or were working for the war . . . [At the textile factory] we each had a machine, and we were only able to talk to the supervising employees." Rose and her classmates—all in their early teens—worked ten-hour days under strict conditions with only one day of rest each month. "When the war escalated," Rose remembered, "we were really happy that the B-29s would come, and the sirens would blast out every day"—because it meant that they could have a break from their furious sewing.[65] Peggy Furukawa of San Jose worked at the Mitsubishi airplane factory, manufacturing airplane wings. Wherever she and her classmates went in the factory, they had to run. "[W]e cannot walk. They let you run to the work, run to the bathroom, and you cannot talk to guys. It was strict like army . . . And we worked sometimes all night, sometimes to midnight, all like that. And then I wasn't absent at all. And they, yeah, they treat you like you're army."[66]

Hawai'i-born Atami Ueno remembered similarly strict conditions. Atami was studying English in Nagasaki at a school called Kasui Women's College, and when all of the students (except the medical students) were mobilized, she was sent to a Mitsubishi factory to make torpedoes. It was dangerous work, done entirely by hand by students who typically had no experience in such machinery. She described that she and her fellow students wanted to talk to one another to pass the time, but "I guess a means of punishment, they separated you, . . . they separated you in morning shift and the night shift or whatever so that you can't work together. And I guess that was fortunate for me because they put me to a night shift, and I worked until about midnight, then I kind of slept there."[67] Atami's daily life—and the lives of Japanese students mobilized for the war effort as

Atami was—focused entirely on her work at the factory. There, she moved like a soldier, dedicating herself solely to the precision of her work.

Nisei boys who were too young to be soldiers were also mobilized alongside their fellow classmates. Izumi Hirano, for example, who moved from Hilo, Hawai'i, to Hiroshima at the age of four in 1933, was put to work in the nearby fields during his middle school years. Once he entered the ninth grade, his courses completely stopped, and he went with all of the students in his class to work at a factory, making rifles and airplanes.[68] Fellow Nisei Jack Dairiki worked at a factory in the city of Mukainada, operating the machinery that carves steel bars. "I worked from eight o'clock in the morning to five in the afternoon. We had a lunch break at noon, and I took a seven-thirty train to get to Mukainada station and then walk a, maybe about a, maybe a mile or so to get to my particular station," remembered Jack.[69] Paul Yempuku was mobilized to work at a submarine factory in Kure, which was far from his home in Hiroshima. "We didn't have no class or anything," he explained, "and [we] worked the whole day, seven days a week at the Kure Navy Base." When he graduated from high school, Paul was admitted to Waseda University, a top school in Tokyo, but in lieu of coursework, he and his Waseda classmates were sent to Nagoya to work in a factory for the military.[70] Mobilized for the war effort, boys and girls in Japan had no time for leisure activities, and hardly any time for study. Their daily lives revolved entirely around their work. They were not to let their minds wander from the task they were performing. They were required to direct all energy, all thoughts, and all focus toward the war effort.

Everyday Realities and "Collaboration"

Nisei living in total war Japan were inspired to assimilate into the category of the Japanese ethno-nation by multiple forces: by the sway of the soft propaganda-infused public discourse and physical environment, by ritual and mnemonic sites in their everyday surroundings, and by disciplinary methods enacted by the various wartime policies of the Japanese administration. But perhaps the most immediate layer of coercion impacting their everyday lives was the situational force of economic and familial realities that induced Nisei to align themselves with Japanese ideals and to participate in the war effort.

As noted in Chapter Two, Nisei living on Japanese soil during the years of war were a heterogeneous group in terms of domestic and economic situations. Nisei children of *dekasegi* families were more likely to find themselves in rural areas, in large, multi-generation households in a parent's hometown. Other Nisei had sailed to their ancestral homeland alone to seek employment or education and were more likely to be living in dormitories, in rented apartments, or in host families in Japan's cities. Many such young adult Nisei had been relying on stipends mailed from America by their parents—financial support that abruptly ended when passenger and mail traffic halted in the wake of Pearl Harbor. In short, of the thousands of Nisei in Japan, each had her own individual economic factors, familial considerations, and personal anxieties that would influence her actions in wartime.

Mary Kimoto, for example, gained employment as part of Japan's military effort due to economic necessity. She signed the family register (which equated to registering for Japanese citizenship) so that she might receive a rice ration. Near the end of the war, Mary was recruited by the navy along with several other Nisei and began work at a listening post in early 1945. "At the listening post," she explained, "the navy provided a house for Nisei in which a dozen of us lived together. At night we listened to short-wave radio messages of American airplanes which by that time were coming closer to the Japanese mainland. I was never able to make much sense out of those messages, but we were told to write down whatever we heard."[71]

Economic reasons also compelled Honolulu-born Muriel Chiyo Tanaka to seek employment with the war effort. Muriel was one of the three Nisei women (and six or seven Nisei men) who were, in her words, "so-called conscripted" by the army to work at a secret outpost, monitoring English-language broadcasts. "I was the highest paid employee with English monitoring, for eighty-one *yen* a month," Muriel remembered. As a special employee of the military machine, Muriel had access to food and resources that were beyond the reach of average citizens struggling to survive hardship and starvation.[72] Nisei melded into the Japanese imperial populace as a means to cope with their anxiety during the war, as well as out of a desire to survive in the increasingly dire war conditions.

Especially in Japan's large cities, food became extremely scarce during the war. Mary Kimoto captured the hardship she faced in 1943: "Our rations are becoming pitifully meager and I am always hungry. All we think and dream about is food. Once in a while, a restaurant will be open, but only for *zosui,* a soup supposedly made of a rice base with everything from weeds to fish bones thrown in."[73] Frank Fukuhara, whose family members were back in Hawai'i when he was first mobilized as a student and then drafted into the Japanese army, explained that he had little energy to devote to thinking about his family members back in America: "We were so scarce on everything it was hard to get anything. That's all we worried about, trying to get enough to eat and things like that. We couldn't pay much attention towards our family in the States all the time."[74] As the war intensified, Nisei in Japan were suffering alongside the rest of the Japanese population from hunger, from grief over lost loved ones, and from the constant fear of air raids. In such dire circumstances, they had little incentive to ponder questions of the meaning of loyalty behind their actions. Rather, they could find solace by knowing that that they shared their suffering with their friends and neighbors.

In Yamasaki Toyoko's novel *Two Homelands,* the Amo family of Los Angeles is one of the many Nikkei families divided across the Pacific Ocean by World War II.[75] The protagonist Kenji, the eldest son of the family and a Nisei journalist at a prominent Los Angeles Japanese-language magazine, is interned in the Manzanar camp with his Issei parents and his two younger siblings. Tadashi, the second son in the family, was living with a relative in the family's ancestral hometown of Kajiki, Kagoshima, at the time of the attack on Pearl Harbor. His family in Manzanar assumes (correctly) that because of his age, he has been drafted into the Japanese army. Kenji, a "Kibei"[76] who spent several years earning his education in Japan, wrestles with his own divided loyalty to both Japan and the United States. Eventually, he is compelled to serve in the United States army as an interpreter in the Pacific, where by a twist of fate, he meets and shoots (though not fatally) his brother Tadashi on the battlefield.

Although the story is fiction, it underscores that the decisions Nisei made during the war—both in America and in Japan—were not their decisions alone to make. Kenji is the epitome of a self-sufficient Nisei; he is among the oldest of his generation, established in a successful career and esteemed by his fellow Nikkei in America as a man who stays true to his convictions, even when those convictions land him in an FBI camp. And yet even independent Kenji cannot clearly define his loyalties and live exclusively according to those convictions throughout the war between his two nations. Instead, he must struggle (along with his siblings) to cope with the pressures placed upon him by his parents, who are in turn responding to the social pressures of their fellow Nikkei. Kenji is also bound by his duty to protect his wife and children, and out of fear for their safety, he goes against the wishes of his parents and accepts a position as an interpreter for the US military.

While Kenji struggles to rationalize his own behavior as something that will help the war end more quickly and, thereby, save more Japanese and American lives, his former work colleague Nagiko is also torn between her two nations. Disgusted with her Nisei husband for his efforts to ingratiate himself with white US Army higher-ups, Nagiko sails with her mother and father on a mid-war exchange ship to Japan, where the special police pester her to work for the English-language propaganda outfit. When Nagiko repeatedly refuses the Japanese detective's recruitment, the detective is irate: "You got your nerve! I'm not going to take any smart talk from you. You got a sister and an ex-husband in America. If I want to, I can put you on a blacklist of Nisei to be watched. You won't even be able to eat." Out of fear for her family and for her own safety, Nagiko relents and accepts the position making propaganda broadcasts. "It was her miserable lot as a Nisei woman," writes Yamasaki, "to have to endure the insults and abuse of the special police. In the end, there was no way around it."[77]

As represented in the characters of Kenji and Nagiko, the demands of survival in everyday life guide people to take certain jobs, and to commit to certain causes. Only in the aftermath of the conflict—when a victor is determined, when a right "us" and a wrong "them" is demarcated—do such actions appear to be clear-cut "collaboration." The stories of Kenji mobilized for the US war effort and of his friend and lover Nagiko mobilized for the Japanese war effort illustrate that even Nisei who were older members of their generation, even those living in homes of their own, were bound by family connections and concerns. They could not act solely based upon their individual convictions and loyalties.

The historical experiences of Nisei like Mary Kimoto and Muriel Tanaka bring to life the fictitious Kenji and Nagiko. Their examples serve as reminders that in addition to soft propaganda, disciplinary methods, and the power of ritual to guide human behavior, Nisei collaboration during World War II was also deeply entangled with individual demands: one's family relationships, the fear for one's own safety, and the everyday necessities of survival. These forces, too, prompted Nisei to assimilate—to stifle their Americanism and participate in a performance of Japaneseness.

As related by Mary Kimoto at the beginning of Chapter Three, Nisei passengers on the *Tatsuta Maru* were segregated from non-Japanese enemy aliens and, regardless of citizenship details, were released to face the years of war as members of the imperial Japanese populace. With no hope of passenger ship traffic to ferry them home across the Pacific and no more financial support arriving from family in the United States, Nisei like Mary were left to fend for themselves in a country that was hostile to the nation of their birth. After the attack on Pearl Harbor, as Part Two has described, Nisei were no longer free to don their American costumes. The Japanese administration enacted policies designed to unite the spirit of its disparate subjects, connecting them through shared material culture such as clothing and food, as well as through shared activity. As a result, material objects coded as "Japanese" carried positive connotations of patriotism, loyalty, and cultural pride, whereas material objects coded as "Western" were negatively charged. At the same time, students underwent a curriculum that praised the sacrifice of individual concerns and desires, emphasizing one's actions in the present as contributions to a collective future rather than an individual one. Forces in the everyday environment generated in Nisei the aspiration to regulate their actions and expressions according to Japanese ideals. This is precisely the process of cultural assimilation: the integration of a minority culture (the individual) into a dominant culture (the whole). The power of soft propaganda in wartime Japan functioned to assimilate not only Nisei but the entire Japanese population through the sway of paradigms for ideal imperial subjects—the volunteer mother, the self-sacrificing soldier, the dedicated student-worker.

By uniting the populace in shared mnemonic sites of material culture and group activities, by valorizing the sacrifice of self, and by requiring the hands of the entire population to do work for the shared cause of Japan's victory, the power of the Japanese administration was acting not monolithically but rather rhizomically, like a root system spreading on a horizontal plane under the ground, growing from several points rather than a single root. The hegemony of ideal Japanese culture pulsed dynamically throughout the everyday environment of imperial Japan, through a broad network of subconscious internalizations and associations.[78] Furthermore, through policies of physical segregation, hyper surveillance, anti-English language movements, and anti-Western propaganda, the concept of the "American" was equated with the image of the self-indulgent, excessively independent, brutal, and perhaps most importantly, *white* American.

Thus, the everyday physical environment and social discourse that surrounded Nisei in wartime Japan reiterated in all aspects of daily life that because of their Japanese blood, Nisei were categorically different from the countrymen of their birth nation. They were not the enemy; they were unlikely to be spies; rather, they were the North American pioneers of the ever-expanding Japanese empire, whose loyalty could be cultivated and whose bodies could be put to work for the imperial cause. Whether or not they consciously recognized it, Nisei were guided by the forces of cultural hegemony to regulate their own behavior according to restrictions established for them by government policies, the opportunities available to them in their social environment, and the ideals posited for them by soft propaganda.

Soft propaganda, modes of bodily discipline, and economic and familial demands were the everyday elements that encouraged Nisei in wartime Japan to perform Japaneseness and stifle Americanness in order to survive and to thrive. Even Nisei who had never registered for Japanese citizenship were entrusted with jobs that required their loyalty and contribution to the Japanese cause against the Allied enemy, working in factories that built weapons and airplanes, cracking codes, disseminating propaganda, and even fighting in the Japanese army. Although they did face stringent hypersurveillance by official police and by their own neighbors, this oppressive hypersurveillance was endured by all Japanese residents throughout the war.

American Nisei in Japan—although not thoroughly trusted—were considered less threatening than other foreigners because of their membership in the Japanese race. These Nisei weathered the years of war in a climate so hostile to the paradigm of the power-hungry white conqueror that their own speech, mannerisms, and dress were re-ordered in the very image of Japaneseness. At the same time, their "Japanized" bodies were put to work for the imperial cause. Nisei in Japan were thereby inspired subliminally by their environment to perform Japaneseness and eschew Americanness in thought, word, and deed. As this environment extracted white, English-speaking America from the lives of Nisei, it thereby encouraged the compliance of Nisei in Japan to perform racial Japaneseness, including loyalty to—or at least not treachery of—the Empire of Japan.

The process of assimilation delineated here is discernable not only in the lives of Nisei struggling to survive in total war Japan. The power of soft propaganda to shape behavior is also commutable to many historical and contemporary examples in which members of minorities edit their behavior and appearance in order to achieve goals. As the next chapter of this book will discuss, the power of the physical and discursive environment to inspire collaboration is visible, too, in the experiences of Nisei in occupied Japan. Indeed, mimicry in occupied Japan parallels mimicry in wartime Japan; when Nisei emerge from the battlefields and factories of war and enter the offices of the Allied occupation, they collaborate by assimilating to new preferences promulgated by soft propaganda in the everyday environment. In postwar Japan, it is the hegemon—not some conscious and all-directing force of loyalty—that has changed.

PART III

Postwar

CHAPTER FIVE

Where Loyalties Lie

Hong Kong, September 1945: Donald Yempuku descends the staircase in the lobby of the grand Peninsula Hotel alongside the other representatives of defeated Japan. Donald, who was born and raised in Hawaiʻi but served the Japanese military as an interpreter during the war, has come to Hong Kong to continue his interpreting duties on behalf of Japan at the surrender ceremony. Through the crowd, he spies a soldier in an American uniform. Although the man's back is turned, Donald recognizes the figure as his brother Ralph, the only member of Donald's immediate family still in America when World War II began. "For a brief second," Donald recalled, "I felt the urge to call out. But I couldn't let myself do it. In my mind the war was still going on and we were still enemies. It was the most trying moment of my life as I marched past Ralph and past the crowd."

The Yempuku siblings are just one example of the countless Nikkei families who weathered World War II as houses divided, fighting on opposite sides of the same conflict. Their parents had spent twenty-five years in Hawaiʻi but had returned to Japan and were living in Atatashima in Japan's Inland Sea when war broke out. All of the Yempuku boys had been born in Hawaiʻi as American citizens. Four Yempuku brothers spent the war years in Japan: Donald served as a translator for Japan's military press bureau and for the Domei news agency; Toru and Goro were conscripted into service for the Japanese army; and their youngest brother Paul was put to work in a war plant near their family's hometown Hiroshima. But one Yempuku brother had remained stateside: Ralph, the oldest, was living in Hawaiʻi when the war began. He volunteered to serve for the United States, first in the Varsity Victory Volunteers and then (when Nisei were permitted to enlist) as a captain in the Office of Strategic Services. When Donald heard the news in December 1941 that Japan and the United States had declared war, he explains, "I felt bad that it was the United States, because a part of me was American. It was a real tragedy. The two countries that were part of me. I knew I had to choose. I did a lot of soul-searching . . . I made my choice when the war came." He filed for Japanese citizenship, renounced his US citizenship, and "threw my support behind Japan. I told myself, 'I'm Japanese now. I can't be loyal to two countries.' But I still didn't want to fight America."[1]

Donald, sharing this story with reporter Tomi Knaefler of the *Honolulu Star-Bulletin* more than twenty years after the end of World War II, styled his decision to renounce US citizenship and serve the Japanese war effort as a conscious choice to become Japanese. How might the outcome of the war, the passage of decades, and the listening audience (a Japanese-American woman composing a commemorative article for a major American newspaper) have influenced the way Donald framed his experience? How might the narrative frame differ for a Nisei woman, who supported the war as a civilian on the Japanese home front rather than among soldiers in the Pacific? The postwar self-representation of Nisei is directly related to their wartime experiences, and the way Nisei in transwar Japan frame their stories must be excavated in the context of postwar anxieties, preferences, and memory.

In the wake of the Allied victory in August 1945, American GIs and journalists flooded into Japan, and the American and Japanese public watched with interest as war criminals and public enemies were rounded up in the early weeks of the occupation. Iva Toguri—who had adamantly refused to renounce her American citizenship during the war—was arrested and imprisoned as part of a sensational media hunt for the radio propagandist Tokyo Rose. Amid this spectacle, the American-born Nisei who had cooperated with the Japanese during the war were left to question whether their actions, too, might be designated as grounds for punishment—or at least as a barrier to returning to America or reinstating lost American citizenship.

But the struggles faced by Nisei in wartime Japan were far more complex than a conscious decision to "become Japanese." And their "collaboration" in Japan during the war was the result of countless moments of conscious and subconscious self-regulation, of behavior that manifested fear, anxiety, and aspiration to thrive. Rather than dismiss the actions of Nisei in wartime Japan as the behavior of brainwashed collaborators, it is more fruitful to examine those myriad moments, to walk alongside Nisei navigating the everyday wartime and postwar environment. This chapter hunts for specific evidence of the power of the physical and discursive environment to shape Nisei behavior and attitudes in the postwar era. In considering Nisei stories, it also tempers the narratives with the knowledge that historical outcomes, the passage of time, and shifting hegemonies color memories and shape self-representation.

As Nisei rationalized their wartime behavior in occupied Japan, they coded their self-narratives with the starkly shifted preferences and expectations crafted for them in the postwar era. The pages that follow take a transwar focus on the experiences of Nisei in occupied Japan, considering how Nisei in Japan made sense of their wartime collaboration, and examining Nisei collaboration with the postwar hegemon: the Allied occupiers. In Nisei postwar collaboration, too, a process of assimilation is at work: conscious and subconscious self-representation shaped by discourse, the physical environment, and economic realities. As the narratives shared in this chapter demonstrate, collaboration and making sense of collaboration are processes of self-regulation that are far too complex to be understood as directly reflective of loyalty or treason. Nisei collaboration—with Japan during the war and with the Supreme Commander for the Allied Powers during the occupation—must instead be considered in the context of changing anxieties and hegemonies, and with an understanding of how the human brain shapes behavior.

Making Sense of Collaboration

When war broke out between the US and Japan in 1941, American Nisei in Japan—many of whom identified with both Japanese and American culture—faced the fact that their birth nation was now their enemy nation. Throughout the war, Nisei men living in Japan fought as soldiers in a war against the country of their birth, and Nisei women and children supported the Japanese war effort in factories, communications outposts, and in the fields. While their non-Japanese American countrymen were extracted from the streets of Japan through internment, imprisonment, house arrest, and evacuation, American Nisei were put to work for the sake of the Japanese imperial cause. As they toiled alongside their Japanese classmates and neighbors, these American Nisei were severed physically and emotionally from the culture of their birth country. Somehow, each Nisei found ways to rationalize her actions in support of a war effort targeting the United States, where many Nisei still had friends and family.

What were these Nisei thinking? How do they describe their wartime actions, and how do they explain the flexibility with which so many of them transitioned from roles in support of the Japanese war effort into roles supporting the Allied occupation? The answers to these questions must be tempered with several key important findings about how the human brain navigates the environment, and how we humans (mis-)remember the past and (mis-)judge the reasons behind our actions. Although many human beings think of themselves as sitting in the driver's seat of their lives, ever in control of their own decisions and behavior, neuroscience has shown this to be far from the truth. Instead, explains behavioral economist Dan Ariely, human behavior is shaped by the shortcuts our brain takes to help us process the world, such as categorization, reproducing social norms, and understanding things only in relativity.[2] So much of human behavior is charted subconsciously that we can seldom accurately predict how we will act, much less describe the reasons behind our actions to someone else. This is especially true of an individual in a heightened ("hot") state, such as hunger or fear—both of which were the norm for much of the populace in Japan during the years of war. In such an agitated or passionate state, the reptilian brain takes over, and humans behave in ways they could never have expected to behave, and have trouble rectifying upon reflection.[3]

In evaluating the oral histories provided by Nisei throughout this book, one must also consider the fragility of memory, and the weakness of the human brain to remember details from the past with accuracy. Humans remember moments from the past as through a hazy, distorting lens, remembering not true details but rather the feeling of what it was like to experience that moment. Explains theoretical physicist Leonard Mlodinow, "Our unconscious takes the incomplete data provided by our senses, fills in what's missing, and passes the perception to our conscious minds . . . Our brains use the same trick in memory."[4] As a result, human recollections of the past do well to capture the visceral affect of a moment but fail miserably as a source of accurate detail.

Yet another element of psychology to consider when evaluating Nisei self-representation is that of hindsight bias, which psychologist Daniel Kahneman describes as the human brain's "imperfect ability to reconstruct past states of knowledge, or beliefs that have changed."[5] An individual's view of the past is inevitably colored by her new perception of reality. After Japan's defeat, many Nisei insisted that they knew Japan had little hope of winning in a war against America. Familiar with America's advanced industry and military might, many said they were certain all along that Japan would lose in a war against the United States. But, they explain, they dared not share that opinion publicly during the years of conflict. Peggy Furukawa of San Jose, for example, who moved to Okayama at age eleven in 1939 for schooling, insisted that she knew Japan would lose the war. "I can't understand why these Japanese people want to fight . . . Oh, I know America going to win. I know that, well, Japan didn't have the paper and pencil [for students at] school, and America had everything. And then Japan is this small and America is this big. How could Japan win?" And yet, she continued, "I didn't want to say nothing . . ."[6] Despite such postwar reflections of confidence that America would eventually defeat Japan, the principle of hindsight bias suggests that these Nisei indeed may not have realized that they were supporting a losing cause in the moment.

Human beings do not remember accurately. We do not understand the real reasons that inspired our actions. Our knowledge of a historical outcome taints our perception of our past selves, and our audience and circumstances color our self-representation in the moment of retelling. So why conduct interviews about historical events at all? When layered with archival data, retellings of past events can confirm details about a moment in time. But more importantly, oral histories are fruitful for what they tell us about the *feeling* of a moment—constriction, pain, comfort, pleasure, anxiety: the affect of experience. Moreover, the frames subjects use in telling their stories reflect the norms of their moment of action and of their moment of delivery. There is, therefore, a great deal to learn about ideals and taboos from the retellings themselves, whether or not the facts shared are perfect in their historical accuracy. In the words of Leonard Mlodinow, "When asked to explain why we feel a certain way, most of us, after giving it some thought, have no trouble supplying reasons. Where do we find those reasons, for feelings that may not even be what we think they are? We make them up." Just as humans replace gaps in their memory with a falsification believed to be true, we also fill in gaps about our feelings with similar falsifications. How does the brain come up with these "confabulations"? Mlodinow explains: "It searches your mental database of cultural norms and picks something plausible . . . When asked how we felt, or will feel, we tend to reply with descriptions or predictions that conform to a set of standard reasons, expectations, and cultural and societal explanations for a given feeling."[7] In other words, self-narrative provides direct access to the social norms and discourse of a historical moment.

The Nuances of "Brainwashing"

The public propaganda of democratization, de-feudalization, and de-militarization promulgated by the occupying Allied forces in postwar Japan provided Nisei— and indeed all Japanese subjects—with one frame in particular through which to make sense of their wartime actions: they had been brainwashed. Occupation policies were designed to undo the work of a militaristic Japanese administration that had succeeded in brainwashing the populace. As these policies were developed and enacted, the rhetoric of brainwashing emerged as a rationale through which Nisei could make sense of their cooperation with the war effort. Frank Hironobu Hirata, for example, described that he was brainwashed during the war to believe that Japan could never lose the war: "we were completely brainwashed . . . Whatever is taught, just swallow the whole thing as a truth, fact. Like the *kamikaze* and so forth, . . . Japan was never defeated or the foreigner stamped their foot on the Japanese soil and so forth. And I was a strong believer in that kind of a teaching."[8] Hawai'i-born Albert Hajime Miyasato, too, framed his collaboration at the Heishikan during the war as the result of brainwashing, saying:

> I was a traitor. I was willing to die for Japan. I was willing to die for the emperor. I gloried in what the military leadership called "the cause of the Greater East Asia Co-Prosperity Sphere." . . . After a few months [in Japan], I was thoroughly brainwashed. Although I wistfully thought of my parents and younger brothers and sisters in Hawai'i, I found myself willing to die for the emperor at any time.[9]

In the postwar, removed from the atmosphere of total war, Nisei were questioning their wartime actions in the context of the occupation's efforts to undo ultra-nationalist propaganda. Iwao Peter Sano, who moved from California to Japan in 1939, depicted his wartime outlook as completely colored by pro-war propaganda. He remembered, for example, that one day during the war a teacher at his school received a draft notice from the Japanese army. He overheard one of the teacher's coworkers saying, "I don't know . . . if I should congratulate you or tell you, 'Gee, too bad you got this notice.' . . . I thought to myself, 'Wow, what does he mean? It's nothing but good opportunity to serve your country. Why can't he see that there's no two ways about it?"[10] Peter was, like the Yempuku family introduced above, just one of thousands of Nisei whose families were divided by the Pacific Ocean during World War II. Despite the fact that Peter's parents and three younger siblings were still living in the US throughout the war, Peter dedicated himself to his duties as a soldier in the Japanese army. "I was going to be Japanese," he explained, "I really felt that this was my duty. I tried really hard to be Japanese . . . in some ways I was more Japanese than the Japanese."[11] He mulls over the contradictory emotions he experienced about being a Nisei in the Japanese army in his memoir:

> I had passed the physical with excellent marks, and I knew that I was healthy and strong, fit to be a model soldier on any battlefield. World War II was in its fourth year, and the press and radio continued to headline the victories of the Japanese military in the South Pacific. I eagerly waited for the day I would be drafted to serve my country. Eagerly? Perhaps. Was my feeling one of true patriotism or a sense of duty, knowing that I had no other choice in the matter? Memories of my days in California swept through my mind. What are my old friends at school and church doing now? I would be fighting against them this time. My parents must be worried and agonizing about my being here, knowing that I am of

draftable age. I felt pain and wished that things were different. I also knew, however, that I had become a true Japanese in a very short time. I felt a strong sense of loyalty to Japan, or perhaps I simply acquiesced to the situation in which I found myself. After all, all Japanese were being called to make concerted efforts and even sacrifice their lives to ensure Japan's victory. We took seriously the government propaganda slogan, "We shall not ask for anything until victory is ours!"[12]

In his memoir, published fifty years after his enlistment as an imperial soldier, Peter struggles to make sense of the passion he felt to support a war against the nation of his birth and his family. Peter remembers being unafraid about his assignment to be a "human bomb" who would commit suicide to destroy an enemy tank. Of the so-called *kamikaze* way, Peter writes: "I, too, swallowed the whole notion without question."[13] Framing his narrative of collaboration this way, Peter leans on his reader's sympathetic understanding of the power of propaganda in wartime Japan to mold citizens into soldiers.

Many American Nisei living in wartime Japan describe that they, too, absorbed the propaganda and even began to fear Americans. Fumiye Miho who moved to Japan after graduating from the University of Hawai'i in 1939 and spent the war in Japan working for the Japanese cabinet's information office, explained that by July of 1945, "it was clear that the end was near for Japan, but the news on the radio and in the newspapers kept saying that Japan was winning— and I believed them." And to those who whispered that Japan was losing, Fumiye—who had spent her entire girlhood in the US and still had three brothers living there—would admonish them: "I would say, 'You're only drinking in American propaganda.'" Steeped in Japanese messages about fearsome and inhumane American soldiers, Fumiye recalled that when she first saw an American GI after the war:

> I was covered with goose bumps and I trembled with fear . . . Imagine! . . . Me! Born and raised in Hawai'i! Afraid at the sight of Americans! . . . I had actually come to believe all the Japanese propaganda without realizing it . . . The propagandists had pounded over and over again that if American troops got into Japan, the GIs would rape all the women . . . Women were advised to look as dirty as possible.[14]

Decades after Japan's surrender, Fumiye highlighted the irony of her situation, emphasizing the authority with which propaganda controlled her fears. An American raised among Americans, she began to fear Americans. Propaganda, she explained, was directing the change.

Mary Kimoto, who weathered the years of war in Tokyo and, in the very end, in Wakayama, wrote of wartime propaganda that painted Americans as completely apathetic about indiscriminately killing Japanese women and children. After watching American planes soar over Tokyo in an air raid, Mary described, "The papers said the 'cowardly enemy' had picked out schools and hospitals for bombing, even machine-gunning schoolchildren at play." In a later entry, she asked her friend Kay, "Did you read in the paper of how American soldiers ran tanks over wounded Japanese soldiers in the Philippines? And that one GI had made a souvenir out of a Japanese soldier's bones and given it to Roosevelt?" In the immediate aftermath of the war, before any encounter with American troops, Mary heard from a rather staunchly nationalist Japanese acquaintance that "the Americans will sterilize all the Japanese men, just as they did the Nisei men in the relocation camps. We are warned to keep out of sight or we will be raped." Mary, piecing together letters and memories to compose her memoirs as a term paper at Boston University in 1947, highlighted the intensity of wartime propaganda as a way to make sense of her attitude in Japan during the war—and to communicate that attitude to her American audience.[15]

These postwar Nisei portrayals of wartime brainwashing—of being completely blind to fact by the force of Japanese propaganda—are congruent with the way the Japanese populace was depicted by General Douglas MacArthur, the five-star American general in charge of orchestrating the Allied occupation of Japan. MacArthur spoke broadly of the Japanese citizenry as child-like victims who suffered in ignorance at the hand of an ultra-militarist government. As he declared to the Senate in 1951:

> The German people were a mature race. If the Anglo-Saxon was say 45 years of age in his development, in the sciences, the arts, divinity, culture, the Germans were quite as mature. The Japanese, however, in spite of their antiquity measured by time, were in a very tuitionary condition. Measured by the standard of modern civilization, they would be like a boy of twelve as compared with our development of forty-five years. Like any tuitionary period, they were susceptible to following new models, new ideas. You can implant basic concepts there. They were still close enough to origin to be elastic and acceptable to new concepts.[16]

To MacArthur, Japanese women were doubly duped: victims not only of the authoritarian administration but also of the feudalistic societal structure that had subjugated women for centuries. A deeper dimension of women's portrayal in occupied Japan, explains women's studies scholar Mire Koikari, was the perception that Japanese men had unambiguously challenged the United States as soldiers during the war, but "Japanese women had been at home, manipulated by the state ideology of 'nationalistic mothers' and forced into war efforts—and were thus not directly accountable for the war."[17] MacArthur's depiction of Japanese subjects (and especially Japanese women) as brainwashed victims set the tone for the occupation's approach to the Japanese people in its policies and in its own propaganda. Nisei questioning the motivation for their actions in support of the war were provided with the rhetorical frame of brainwashing to help them rationalize their own stories.

In trying to understand and explain their participation on the Japanese side of World War II decades after the war had ended, many Nisei—and fully Japanese citizens as well—portray themselves as brainwashed by Japanese propaganda. And yet, to invoke "brainwashing" yields a problem similar to that posed by the term "collaboration." Nisei who reflect on their cooperation with the Japanese war effort during World War II as "brainwashing" are looking backwards, cognitively considering actions through the lens of postwar discourse on propaganda in wartime Japan. Someone who is "brainwashed" does not rationalize her actions as the result of "brainwashing" in the moment. Only from an alternate position—an outsider or even a self altered by changes over time—can a person apply the label of "brainwashed." The trope of "brainwashing" as an explanation for Nisei collaboration is useful not as a rationale for their actions, but rather for what it reveals about the discourse of the postwar era—and how Nisei found themselves and understood their actions in the context of that discourse.

Constriction as Affect

Brainwashing offers Nisei a backward-glancing explanation in the postwar, but how did American Nisei understand their performance of Japaneseness *during* the historical moment of total war? These Nisei, mobilized by the Japanese government to build weapons, submarines and airplanes, to crack codes and translate broadcasts, surely must have paused to consider that they could have been cracking the code that might kill their own brother fighting for Uncle Sam, or polishing the wing of the plane that would crash into an old friend's battleship? Again, research on the human brain suggests that to ask subjects to explain the reasons behind their behavior is futile; not only do we misremember, but due to the supreme power of our subconscious mental pathways, we also are rarely fully consciously aware of the true reasons why we act in certain ways. And yet, though we may not be able to describe the reasons for our actions, we can recall the visceral feelings we experienced in a given moment. The words subjects select to convey that affect can paint a picture of their frame of mind in a historical moment.

When questioned about what they were feeling as Americans in Japan during the war, many Nisei describe feeling trapped or ensnared, code-switching into the phrases "*shō ga nai*" (also *shiyō ga nai*, "nothing can be done") or "*shikata ga nai*" ("it can't be helped.") Both phrases imply a sense of inevitability—a lack of options. For example, when asked how she and her Nisei co-workers felt about their intelligence work for the Japanese military, Muriel Tanaka explained, "[We said,] '*Shō ga nai, ne?* You can't help it."[18] A student at Waseda Kokusai Gakuin employs similar language as he reflects on his liminal position as an American Nisei in a composition written in 1942:

> Although I hold the rights of American citizenship and all of my family members live in America, I somehow came to feel glad on that the day of Japan's declaration of war against England and America. Of course I am worried about my parents and siblings, but this is an individual matter, and the Greater East Asian War is the war that will liberate all the *minzoku* of Asian peoples from oppression, and if for this my parents must die in as sacrifices, I can just think *shikata ga nai*.[19]

The personal reflections of Jack Ishio, who grew up in Tacoma, Washington, and served as an anti-aircraft gunner for the Japanese army, echo this sentiment. Jack, a dual citizen who moved to Japan with his family in 1938, recalled shooting down four American dive bombers in a battle near the end of the war. Jack explained that as he fought alongside his Japanese comrades, he was living in the present rather than the past, saying, "I had no resistance whatsoever to being drafted. In a war what can you do? You can't be thinking two things at once."[20] Repeatedly in individual accounts of Nisei who weathered the war in Japan, co-operation with the Japanese war effort is represented as simply accepting one's fate, and of either ignoring or not permitting themselves to dwell on questions of loyalty, treason, and identity. As many Nisei have done when giving personal accounts of life during World War II, Jack spoke of "*enryo*-ing," meaning "holding back" or "being reserved." Even in English interviews, this term frequently appears in Japanese as a code-switch. Constriction: this is the affect of Nisei collaborating in wartime Japan.

In *Nihon gunheishi ni natta Amerikajin tachi* (*Americans Who Became Japanese Soldiers*), historian Kadoike Hiroshi shares interviews of several American-born Nisei who fought in the Japanese military during World War II. As Kadoike summarizes, a common theme in his conversations with these Nisei is this same phrase, "*shikata ga nai*," to communicate: "I had no choice" or "it can't be helped." This expression, Kadoike maintains, represents a manner of resigning oneself that is familiar in Japanese culture. Kadoike cites Japanologist Donald

Keene, who once asserted that this *"shikata ga nai"* spirit demonstrates that the Japanese are quick to resign themselves, that they are reluctant to put up resistance against the flow of history.[21] In the quest to re-imagine collaboration, though, it is more fruitful to examine *"shikata ga nai"* not as uniquely Japanese but as a non-culturally specific feeling of being bound to act in a proscribed way—again, the affect of constriction, of what it feels like to be psychologically disciplined and charted upon a path proscribed by the exigencies of one's physical and discursive environment.

To understand the *shikata ga nai* feeling that characterized the lives of Nisei in transwar Japan is to consider the circumstances, values, and opportunities of these Nisei during the war itself. In so doing, it becomes clear that although Nisei like Donald Yempuku, Peter Sano, and Jack Ishio described themselves as deciding to become Japanese, there were other extenuating circumstances, such as family considerations, economic situations, and the regulatory power soft propaganda in the physical and discursive environment inspiring Nisei to perform Japaneseness and distance themselves from America during the years of total war. Consider, for example, the constant anxiety plaguing Nisei on the home front, who suffered not only the malnourishment, horrific air raids, and bereavement known by all Japanese subjects during the war, but also the added anxiety of affiliation with the enemy due to their American roots—and of dread as they speculated about the fate of Stateside friends and relatives.

To alleviate some of this anxiety, and to earn money and achieve a greater sense of security, some Nisei sought positions serving the war effort. One such Nisei is Masao Ekimoto, who had renounced his Japanese citizenship in 1940 before moving from America to Japan. As Masao described to historian Michael Jin, he felt anxiety about living as an American citizen in Japan during the war, and so in December 1942 he applied to the Heishikan, a government-sponsored training program that had been established in 1939 to prime Nisei for careers in the media and in international relations. The Heishikan pupils were assigned duties during the war such as monitoring English-language short wave radio broadcasts in the "Radio Room" of the Foreign Ministry's Broadcasting Section and translating and summarizing these reports for the Foreign Ministry. At the Heishikan, Masao immediately began working in the Radio Room, relieved that he could be safe as a student at a government-run institution. Nori Hideo of Wapato, Washington, also joined the Heishikan and worked as a monitor for the Radio Room. When he visited a friend in Fukuoka during one summer break, he "was stunned to find that almost all of the men from the village had been conscripted into the military. His enrollment at Heishikan and service to the Foreign Ministry thus had allowed him to avoid the possibility of being drafted and taking arms against his country [of] birth."[22] Albert Hajime Miyasato, who was sent by his family from Hawai'i to Fukuoka to train as a Buddhist priest, recalled that he watched many of his classmates leave to join the Kamikaze Youth Corps, saying, "I would have gone with them, but I wasn't a Japanese citizen." Instead, Albert enrolled at the Heishikan, where he recalls passing the years of war with about thirty other Nisei. The Foreign Office, he explains, provided them with free room and board plus fifty *yen* of spending money for books and entertainment.[23]

According to research by historian Paul Spickard, of the American Nisei living in Japan in 1942, an estimated 15,950 (45 percent of the total 35,420 American Nisei estimated to be in Japan at that time) were under the age of twenty.[24] Living mostly with their immediate family members or with relatives in their ancestral hometowns, these Nisei in many ways lacked the autonomy to act according to personal convictions during the war. Paul Yempuku, for example, remembered talking to his parents about the war, and about fighting for Japan. His parents, to whom he was looking for guidance, "just told us . . . to do whatever you're doing for the country."[25] Jimmie Matsuda, too, was influenced by his parents to commit himself to sacrificing his life for the imperial cause. As he left on a train for his army service, Jimmie remembered:

[M]y mother, she come running to me and as the train is moving she said, "Jimmie, Jimmie, Jimmie," and she says, "I don't want you to come back alive." She says, "If you're gonna go," says, "you got to fight for Japan, so I want your ashes to be at the Yasukuni Jinja. And you speak English, but," says, "no, never be a POW either, and if you get hurt or something . . . you got to suicide, take suicide." That was the last word I heard from my mother . . . saying, "So never give up on anything. Be sure that when you do your duties, do what you're supposed to do. I don't want you to come back." Boy, that was really a shock to me, though. But during the war, I guess, any country, the parents would say something like that.[26]

In addition to the demands of family relationships, many Nisei regulated their actions in wartime Japan to avoid certain punishment for straying from the tight path established for them by their superiors. Toru Yempuku, one of the Yempuku brothers conscripted into the army, explained, "You couldn't say no when they called you. You either got in [to the army] or got shot or ended up in prison. There was no choice."[27] Frank Fukuhara said that he did not think too much about fighting against the country of his birth until he was assigned to the suicide bomb unit, but that "I didn't know what to do, but I just had to obey orders. If I don't they're gonna shoot me anyway."[28] Shigeo Yamada, who served as an officer in the Japanese Imperial Navy after his family moved from Idaho to

Japan mused, "It was a dilemma in my mind, but what else could you do? There was nothing I could do other than object to the conscription and be thrown into jail."[29]

Despite emotional connections to American culture and to American people, Nisei in Japan were living in a war zone, and the planes dropping the bombs that burned their schools and houses were American planes. Nisei in that environment could easily develop animosity toward the American enemy. For many American Nisei, such feelings of animosity compounded with existing anxieties over associations with the enemy and uncertainty about friends and family in the US, instilling in Nisei a sense of powerlessness and resignation. Jack Dairiki's reflections, for example, depict just this sort of heartache. Jack, who sailed from Sacramento to Japan in August 1941 for a short visit with a sick grandfather, was only ten years old when the start of the war severed him from his mother and siblings back in California. When asked how he felt about his position during the war, he explained, "Well, I was just caught in the situation, as age, age ten you couldn't do much. Just horrible feeling that, not being able to see my mother and siblings again, that was sort of a sad feeling, and what's gonna happen to me now? So you couldn't do much anyway, whatever my thought was."[30]

Mary Kimoto's depiction of her own wartime mood echoes Jack's despondency. In her 1947 memoirs, she attempts to recapture her state of mind in the last months of the war, when she was under constant bombing: "I feel now that I don't care whether I live or die. At times I think death would be a welcome rest. It is only if we live that we must continue to struggle in this insane world."[31] As Mary's entry relates, there was little time in total war Japan for brooding over questions of loyalty or for resisting the work assigned to her. She merely yearned for a swift end to the fighting. Years later, Mary reflected, "My life was so miserable, lonely, and hopeless that I felt it didn't matter whether I lived or died. The war seemed to go on forever, and I had nothing to look forward to."[32]

The phrases "*shō ga nai*" and "*shikata ga nai*" convey precisely the sense of entrapment Nisei in wartime Japan faced as a result of these multiple factors shaping their behavior, inspiring them to assimilate by performing as Japanese subjects. They were hemmed in by their family's expectations, by their struggle to survive food shortages and air raids, by the forces of hyper-surveillance, and by the threat of violence due to their association with "the enemy." Nisei self-regulation as Japanese in wartime Japan was the culmination of multiple input factors, including familial and economic responsibilities, the disciplinary policies of the government, and the influence of soft propaganda that inspired mimicry of Japanese ideals. The physical and discursive environment shaped Nisei self-regulation by establishing and reinforcing Nisei goals and social preferences. The actions of Nisei during the war, therefore, are not direct representations of their convictions of loyalty. They are much more complex than that. The expression *shō ga nai* conveys precisely this notion of the overwhelming force of the kaleidoscopic demands placed on an individual—demands that propel an individual into actions that may not be directly reflective of emotions and convictions.

The remembrances of Marion Tsutakawa Kanemoto illustrate precisely this disconnect between cognitive elaborations and behavior. A "Kibei" from Seattle who had sailed with her family as repatriates to Japan on an exchange ship in 1943, Marion recalled that her Japanese principal tried to convince the students that the brown eyes of Japanese soldiers permitted more accurate sight than the blue eyes of "golden-hair Americans." Listening to the principal, Marion said, "I thought, 'How stupid.' And I couldn't even tell any of my friends this. So it's a very private thought that I thought. 'How sad. Does he expect people to believe that?' I mean, I certainly didn't believe it." When she trained alongside her classmates with bamboo spears, she said, "I kept thinking, 'How foolish.' Because, you know, the American soldiers have guns and here we have a bamboo stick. But then, you just, you're, it's a mass thing. So, just like a puppet you just follow. I mean, I couldn't cause any wave and I couldn't cause any disgrace to my parents so I continued to do the thing."[33] Marion was ensnared by familial obligations and societal expectations that gave her little option for resistance, despite what she claims are her personal convictions about the conflict. Marion's attitude toward the war, shared decades after Japan's defeat and therefore colored by memory and war legacy, illustrates the struggle of Nisei identity—of self-representation and self-understanding—both in the moment of action (when confronting ambiguous emotions, anxieties, and demands) and in the moment of retelling (when confronting a different set of ambiguous emotions, anxieties, and demands). There is no clear-cut, direct correlation between conviction and action. Rather, self-representation continues to oscillate, buffeted by the undulations of preferences in the physical and discursive environment.

A sense of entrapment, of being unable to act according to cognitively elaborated feelings, further complicates the struggle to understand Nisei emotion and action in transwar Japan. Many Nisei expressed that because they believed that their actions were not entirely in their own control, they tried to block out all emotion. They spoke of trying not to let their minds wander to questions of loyalty—or to friends and family back in the United States. For example, when interviewing Nisei *kamikaze* pilot Jimmie Matsuda (born in Oregon in 1927), Steve Fugita asked, "When you were training for this, did, did you ever think about, well, maybe these Americans might be some kids from your school on that, might be on the destroyer or the battleship or the carrier?" Jimmie replied: "I never did think about that."[34] Toru Yempuku, one of the younger brothers of the Yempuku family, was in high school when his family moved to Japan and was in college in Osaka when the war started. When asked about his feelings during the war, he described himself as "not pro-American or pro-Japan. I just went with the tide. I didn't let myself think about much."[35]

The memorable narrative of Frank Fukuhara offers a similar example. Frank moved from Hawai'i to Hiroshima in 1933 with his family, but his sister Mary and brother Harry had moved back to the United States in the late 1930s. Frank, who was mobilized as a freight train laborer alongside his classmates, was drafted into a suicide bomb squad for the imperial army in 1945. When asked how he felt about a war against America, Frank described food rationing, clothing rationing, and the requirement of constant work, implying that in a war zone, there is little time for personal feelings. "I didn't think about Harry or Mary much," he explained. "I was just worried about my mother staying home all alone all the time. But when I was assigned to this suicide unit, that was, I thought that, well, I'm not gonna live long anyway, so I'll just go along with it and I might be lucky and live through it, but I just didn't have any hope, no fight."[36]

Through years of bi-cultural performance, many Nisei in transwar Japan had been conditioned to consider their actions as performative and, therefore, as detached from their true emotions and opinions. Attempting to recover the "true" emotional state of Nisei during the years of war is futile, because their emotions were only one factor charting the course for their behavior. Emotion itself cannot serve as a direct indicator or predictor of behavior. Rather, emotions are the stories told about affective experiences and behavior. Emotions are cognitive appraisals—the meaning ascribed subsequently to a situation or reaction.[37]

The role of emotion adds an additional layer of complexity to reconciling Nisei emotions and behavior in transwar Japan. Cognition and emotion, argues cognitive appraisal theorist Richard Lazarus, can be dissociated, and "the way one interprets one's plight at any given moment is crucial to the emotional response."[38] In the personal narratives provided by Nisei, the representation of emotion is influenced not only by appraisals of one's plight in the historical moment of action itself, but also by appraisals of one's plight in the moment of retelling. The "feeling rules" at play in these depictions of past action and emotion span not just cultures—but decades, too.[39] Therefore, the emotions (cognitive appraisals) shared by Nisei in contemporary oral histories are necessarily different from the appraisals made by those Nisei during the years of war. And because of this, to recapture fully the emotional state of Nisei collaborators in transwar Japan is impossible. Instead, it is more valuable to look to self-narratives of

collaboration for what they tell about the preferences and taboos of a given historical moment: to unravel collaboration by looking to soft propaganda in the
everyday environment that shaped behavior both during the war and during the
postwar.

By assessing Nisei behavior as embedded in the physical environment, it becomes clear that Nisei actions both during and after the war were shaped by multiple situational and environmental factors—and not just by a sense of loyalty.
Examining self-regulation as shaped by the environment is a more precise means
of unpacking collaboration than asking Nisei to rationalize their behavior and
loyalties in personal narratives (which are shaped by collective war memory,
hindsight bias, and the inability of humans accurately to identify, much less recall, the reasons behind their actions). The self-narratives of Nisei, especially
those shared many years after the war, are valuable for the norms and narrative
tropes that they reflect. The brainwashing of Nisei collaborators is not interesting
as a reason for their actions, but rather as a pervasive postwar frame that Nisei
employed to rationalize and explain past behavior. And from the *shikata ga nai*
mentality of ensnarement, the takeaway is not that Nisei truly had no other avenue or option for action, but rather that the *feeling* of being constricted captures
the visceral experience of life as a Nisei in Japan during the war—and that this
constriction must have been all the more jarring in light of the oscillation and
cultural flexibility that characterized Nisei life in the years before the war.

To recapture the historical moment of Nisei in Japan during the war years,
Part Two discussed Nisei wartime performance as consciously and subconsciously shaped by the preferences of the propaganda-infused physical and discursive environment. A parallel process was at work in Nisei performance in
occupied Japan. The same forces that shaped Nisei behavior in wartime Japan—
surveillance, propaganda-coded discourse and material culture, familial obligations, and economic realities—shaped Nisei behavior in occupied Japan.
Although the names and uniforms of those in power had changed, the power of
hegemonic preferences to shape behavior was the same. During the war, the various government ministries of imperial Japan coordinated surveillance policies,
propaganda campaigns, censorship strategies, consumer culture, and economic
affairs. In the era of occupation, these same forces of regulation were coordinated at the hand of the Supreme Commander for the Allied Powers (SCAP).
Discourse and physical and economic realities in occupied Japan inspired Nisei
collaboration with a new hegemon: their former enemy, the Allies.

CHAPTER SIX

The Passage Home

On August 15, 1945, the hegemony wielded by the Japanese war machine abruptly flatlined. At noon that day, Emperor Hirohito delivered a radio address across the Empire to announce the unconditional surrender of Japan to the Allies. For the millions of Japanese subjects, and especially for the tens of thousands of Nisei living in imperial Japan, life was immediately different. California-born Yayoi Cooke recalled that even though she had prayed for a Japanese victory throughout the war, she was relieved to hear the emperor's announcement—even as all of the girls around her burst into tears. She looked out the window and saw that some girls were already walking around in skirts, which had been verboten for years.[1]

The skirts Yayoi noticed outside the window were harbingers of a new era of Western hegemony on Japanese soil. In a few weeks' time, Allied units would descend upon Japan, permeating not only Japan's urban centers but also the hamlets of her interior, driving new preferences for behavior, fashion, movement, and expression in an effort to overhaul Japan into a democratic nation. Just as the everyday physical environment and social discourse had inspired American Nisei to manifest Japaneseness during the years of total war, so did the shift toward American hegemony influence Nisei to manifest "American" behavior through soft propaganda in the era of Allied occupation.

Throughout the war, Nisei in Japan had been suspected of clandestine pro-American activity by the special police and by watchful neighbors, and many Nisei had endeavored to downplay or hide their American past—and even to overcompensate for it by participating on behalf of Japan during the war. After the announcement of defeat, however, these Nisei no longer had to "act Japanese." Instead, Nisei in occupied Japan would face a new challenge: how to hide, explain, or obfuscate their cooperation with the Japanese war effort in the presence of the Allied conquerors. Positioning themselves in the context of this demand, Nisei sought ways to highlight their cultural dualism, and in so doing, they relied on the resurrection of *kakehashi* rhetoric of Nisei as bridges between American and Japanese cultures.

In 1941, just before the dawn of war in the United States, Louis Adamic published a manifesto calling for a new era of world peace wrought by the contributions of American-born children of immigrants. Adamic's *Two-Way Passage* describes a vision for second-generation Americans to close the circuit of their parents' "passage here" by making a "passage back." Just as their parents escaped the old world to a land of freedom and opportunity, so might the second generation return provisionally to their parents' homeland as advisors capable of orchestrating an American democratic revolution. Adamic, a naturalized American citizen who had immigrated from the Austro-Hungarian Empire in 1913, called upon second-generation Americans to serve as cultural interpreters who might explain, extol, and facilitate American-style democracy in their ancestral homelands. Written in a moment of heightened anxiety as America yet clung to the hope of isolationism, *Two-Way Passage* targets a style of peace for the future that is mindful of multiculturalism as an asset to American ingenuity, rather than a hindrance to its unification. The United States, "a nation made up of all the peoples of all the world," Adamic insists, is "the only conceivable intercessor in this situation."[2] Bureaucracies such as the League of Nations, he argues, fail to achieve international understanding thorough their style of authoritative imposition. The offspring of immigrants, however, might succeed in imposing democracy from *within,* inspiring an obliging audience to embrace democracy and diplomacy through the natural understanding of their ancestral culture.

Five years (and a world war) after the release of Adamic's book, Frederick A. Orehek, a former Marine correspondent in Japan, notes in the opinion paper *Trends and Tides* (published by Adamic himself) that the second-generation Japanese Americans working for the occupation in postwar Japan exemplify the "two-way passage" idea advanced in Adamic's pre-Pearl Harbor book. Just as Adamic had advocated, these American-born children of immigrants were making use of their cultural finesse to facilitate understanding between the Japanese and their American conquerors, and to advance the occupation's aims of democratization and equality. "Alert to the Japanese moral traditions and customs," writes Orehek, the Nisei "commanded the mutual respect of both the Americans and the Japanese. He realized that he was there to do a serious job and that the natives watched his every move," thus making him "the perfect bridge between the Orient and the Occident."[3] Although Orehek's vision of Adamic's "paradigm fulfilled" refers to male Nisei GIs he observed in occupation roles, his analysis sheds light on the public perception of all Nisei who served as intermediaries between the Allied victors and the defeated Japanese in the postwar period.

Two years before Orehek's article, when war was still raging in April of 1944, American journalist Carey McWilliams had predicted that the Nisei stuck in

Japan throughout the war would be instrumental to the success of an Allied occupation when the fighting ended. As McWilliams summarized in the *Far Eastern Survey*:

> Unquestionably Nisei are fighting on both sides in the Southwest Pacific
> today. It is quite likely that many Nisei who were trapped in Japan on
> December 7, 1941, are either in concentration camps or under close sur-
> veillance. The fact that they have not found it possible to adjust them-
> selves to life in Japan, and that many of them are now under suspicion
> there, does not necessarily mean that they are ardently pro-America or
> pro-Ally. However, instead of remaining a maladjusted apathetic minor-
> ity group, they might be encouraged to fulfill a valuable function in the
> difficult postwar period, through their knowledge of Japan and of the
> United States.[4]

McWilliams's forecast, Adamic's appeal, and Orehek's assessment of the importance of Nisei as cultural intermediaries in postwar Japan highlight the resur-
gence of an ideal popularized in both America and Japan in the 1920s and 1930s
that second generation Japanese Americans might serve as cultural "bridges"
(*kakehashi*) or "wedges" (*kusabi*) between their two cultures. This ideal—and the
social discourse surrounding it—shaped the actions and expressions of American Nisei both in the US and in Japan. The postwar resurrection of the pre-war
kakehashi/cultural bridge paradigm placed social pressure on Nisei to navigate
nimbly the languages and cultures of both Japan and America.

This ideal performance of dual cultural dexterity, however, marks a dramatic
shift from the demands for assimilation placed upon Nisei during the years of
the war itself. As discussed in Part Two of this study, throughout the years of
war, the tens of thousands of Nisei living in Japan were conditioned by stimuli in
their everyday environment to manifest Japaneseness and purge themselves of
Americanness in their physical appearance, expressions, and behavior. In order
to thrive—and indeed to survive—American Nisei who weathered the years of
World War II in Japan were required to hone their prowess at cultural performance. As they endeavored (consciously as well as subconsciously) to highlight
or stifle "American" or "Japanese" elements of their appearance or behavior according to the moment's preferences for an ideal Nisei societal role, American
Nisei in Japan developed a cultural flexibility that severed self-understanding
from behavior and expression.

Two weeks after the emperor's announcement of surrender in August 1945,
General Douglas MacArthur, the Supreme Commander appointed to oversee the
Allied occupation of Japan, landed at Atsugi Air Base just outside of Tokyo. His

arrival was followed by a cascade of military transports bringing thousands of troops to take over military bases in the Tokyo area and beyond—and to carry out the occupation's missions of disarming and demobilizing the Imperial Army and Navy and their factories, arresting suspected war criminals, disbanding the special police, purging ultranationalist leaders, and completely overhauling the political, economic, and educational systems of the defeated Japanese empire. The social expectations, privileges, and discrimination challenges facing Nisei in Japan during the Allied occupation shaped the ways in which Nisei regulated their behavior, as well as the ways they considered and represented their wartime actions. The pressures of idealized cultural duality informed Nisei interaction with the Japanese populace and with GIs, and assumptions about Nisei multiculturalism shaped these individuals' racial, gender, and ethnic self-representations throughout the 1940s.

The Supreme Commander for the Allied Powers, responsible for administering the occupation's goals, sorely needed employees who would be able to facilitate interaction among the Allied personnel, the Japanese administrative officials assisting in the transition, and the Japanese populace at large. Nisei living in Japan, many of whom had some language ability in both English and Japanese in addition to knowledge of American and Japanese culture, were instrumental in filling this demand. In all, more than 5,000 Nisei worked in occupied Japan as both military personnel and civilians.[5] Their number includes Nisei who had served in the American army during the war, as well as Nisei who came to Japan seeking job opportunities in the immediate postwar years. Their number also includes American-born Nisei who had, either by choice or by unforeseen consequence, weathered the years of war in Japan. These were the same Nisei who had been mobilized against the country of their birth as translators, broadcasters, code-crackers, soldiers, and factory workers for imperial Japan. These Nisei served critical roles in occupied Japan, utilizing their bilingual skills and cultural fluency in the postwar as interpreters, translators, censors, and monitors for SCAP, as well as in the private sector.

During the war, hypersurveillance, segregation of non-Japanese foreigners, anti-English and anti-Western propaganda, and physical mobilization had prompted American Nisei to stifle their American ways and fuse with the Japanese imperial populace. In the postwar period, however, they were called upon—just as they were in the years before the war—to serve an important mission as cultural ambassadors between their ancestral nation and their birth nation. Whereas during the war Nisei in Japan aspired to stifle their Americanness, in the postwar, their connection to America was a positive attribute—and indeed, was a key to survival in a war-torn, impoverished, famished country. Positive social coding sparked in many American Nisei the aspiration to "re-assimilate" by performing American traits with Japanese bodies.

Social discourse establishing "the Nisei" as a cultural ambassador inspired Nisei in postwar Japan to seek ways to serve the occupation's mission in line with the *kakehashi* paradigm. Through years of changing demands placed on Nisei to be "American" and/or "Japanese," many American Nisei had developed a cultural flexibility enabling them to regulate their behavior and appearance according to ideals posited in their physical and social environment. In postwar Japan, Nisei endeavored to survive and thrive by enacting the paradigm of the dual-heritage cultural ambassador. Functioning in a social environment that valued cultural flexibility as an asset, Nisei could make sense of their wartime and postwar actions in the terms established by this ideal.

In the immediate aftermath of Japan's surrender, bilingual Japanese-English speakers in Japan were in high demand for a variety of jobs. Even Nisei with limited Japanese ability or limited English ability found employment in a variety of positions available in the occupation, ranging from translators of intricate documents to janitors and drivers.[6] California-born Nisei Rose Ito Tsunekawa, who worked for the occupation in Nagoya, insisted that, "as long as you could pronounce 'one, two, three,' you were able to get a job [with the occupation], and it paid pretty well."[7] Mary Kimoto, who had lived in Japan throughout the war, wrote in a letter in 1946: "Right now I am working as a typist at the Signal Office at the I Corps, Osaka. You know that I can't type, and I flunked the typing test that they gave me at the Military Government Labor Board, but it just goes to show how hard up they are for typists."[8] Former occupation employee Beate Gordon, recalling one group of girls from Hawai'i roller-skating in their negligees through the streets of Tokyo, reflected that "some of the caliber of the secretaries and so on who had been brought in was a little bit doubtful because apparently people were recruiting all over the place, just on the basis if they knew a little bit of Japanese."[9]

Many of the Nisei who came to Japan in the postwar to serve in occupation roles were members of the American army's Allied Translation and Interpretation Service (ATIS), an intelligence outfit tasked with code-breaking, map reading, radio interception, POW interrogation, and Japanese language propaganda during the war. They were graduates of the Military Intelligence Service Language School (MISLS), which had been developed specifically to train soldiers in these tasks. After Japan's surrender, many of these MISLS graduates applied their skills as linguists in various duties for the occupation. In addition to these military personnel, there were thousands of Nisei employed as civilians in the occupation apparatus, primarily in communications roles. The Central Liaison Office (affiliated with the Japanese Ministry of Foreign Affairs), which was established to coordinate between the Japanese government and the occupation, posted employment advertisements almost daily in the *Nippon Times* for the first few years of the immediate postwar.[10] Nisei were also recruited in America, but the majority of the Nisei civilian employees of SCAP—especially in the critical first years of the occupation—were recruits from the population who had weathered the war on Japanese soil.

Nisei employees—both military and civil—were particularly fundamental to the operation of the G-2 Intelligence arm of General Headquarters (GHQ), including the army-run Civil Censorship Detachment (CCD), which was responsible for seeking intelligence through media and correspondence censorship, as well as spying on Japanese citizens to root out dissent and potential instigators, and for assessing efficacy of occupation policies. According to Masaomi Mita, who worked for the CCD, "[The CCD] was a fancy name for reading other's people's mail without them knowing about it."[11] Employees at the Press, Pictorial and Broadcast Division of CCD monitored media of all forms, from telegrams to films to sewing patterns, scanning all material for "questionable items" which, if found, would be passed along to American superiors.[12] Employees were trained to flag correspondence and publications that mentioned taboo topics of censorship, misconduct of Allied personnel, atomic bombs, food shortages, black markets, Japanese Americans, war criminals, reparations, mixed-blood children, and fraternization. Employees also kept statistics about public opinion on topics discussed in correspondence, such as food problems, public health, occupation personnel, and education.[13] G-2's more broadly known Civil Information and Education section (CI&E), too, relied on Nisei employees to assist with GHQ domestic propaganda policies designed to rid militarism and promote democracy in media contents.[14] They scoured media to assess public opinion on fundamental areas of reform, such as education, religion, the arts, and information. These employees were also responsible for submitting recommendations to the Supreme Commander regarding the purging of personnel in Japan's education system, and for "reorienting and rehabilitating" Japanese thought patterns and customs.[15]

There were many Japan-born Japanese citizens who had studied enough English to be helpful to the occupation (indeed, Japanese civilians accounted for more than 40 percent of all GHQ personnel), but Nisei were critical not only because of their language skills, but also because of their familiarity with American culture.[16] Nisei could function in Japanese society as both Japanese and American, helping to align the Japanese population with SCAP ideals of democracy and social reform. Nisei played a critical role as buffers, diffusing tension between the

Japanese citizens and the Allied victors in the tumultuous postwar period. By interacting directly with Japanese citizens with a helpful, approachable manner, they could work to undo the propagandized idea of the brutal *oni*—the American "devil" imagery that had been promulgated throughout the war. The shock of bad news seemed somehow softer when delivered to the Japanese public by Japanese Americans who could present themselves as sharing marginally in the pain of defeat. Harry Fukuhara, for example, was a graduate of MISLS who was tasked with explaining to Japanese POWs the series of events leading to Japan's surrender, including the news of the devastation wrought by atomic bombs on Nagasaki and Hiroshima—where he, too, had several family members.[17]

SCAP benefitted not only from the linguistic abilities of its Nisei interpreters, clerks, and translators, but also from the ability of Nisei to serve as intermediaries engaging members of a population who were receptive to Nisei as marginal kinsmen. In communities across Japan, Nisei—even those who were not SCAP employees—facilitated interaction between the Japanese and Allied personnel in tense moments that might otherwise have boiled over into violence. For example, Jimmie Matsuda of Hood River, Oregon, who had served as a soldier for a *kamikaze* unit of the Imperial Japanese army during the war, shared that in the immediate postwar, the local Japanese city hall officials came calling at his family's home, bearing expensive fish as gifts, entreating the family to come to city hall and the police station to serve as interpreters once the American marines arrived. Jimmie, his brother, and their three sisters reported a few days later to introduce the Japanese city police to the officials of the 24th Infantry Division, and to assist the marines in their weapons inspections of local homes and schools.[18] Across Japan, Nisei like Jimmie and his siblings who were not directly employed by SCAP assisted the occupation in its tasks and in the promotion of its goals, and many such Nisei were looked to for guidance by the Japanese population in this era of sweeping change. In this sense, American Nisei in postwar Japan emerged as those who might galvanize the Japanese populace *from within* as it transitioned from traditional Japanese ways of life toward SCAP's vision for a postwar Japan.

In addition to buffering interaction between conquered Japanese and Allied victors, Nisei also were instrumental to facilitating communication due to their understanding not only of the literal meanings of English words but also of cultural context. Rose Ito Tsunekawa was only fifteen years old when an army jeep pulled up to her all-girl school in the countryside outside of Nagoya. The American forces had caught wind of a Nisei teenager who worked on Sundays in a little café in Nagoya, and they had come to collect her to assist them in translating for a court martial of an American soldier accused of raping a Japanese girl.

The Japanese national they had hired to interpret at the trial was a professor of English who "was trying to sound intelligent, but those Yankees couldn't understand his British English," and so Rose stepped in to assist in interpreting. One day at the trial, a witness used the word "*ketatamashii*," and the Japanese professor serving as interpreter was absolutely flummoxed as he tried to come up with an obscure, impressive equivalent. The judge turned to Rose and asked what the word meant, and everyone chuckled when she candidly answered, "Well, that's just a big word for 'noisy.'"[19] As Rose's anecdote demonstrates, communication between Japanese and Americans in the strained period of the immediate postwar required more than linguistic capacity. Nisei could help mend the fractured relationship between their two countries through cultural understanding and—though in many instances tentative—trust.

Nisei functioned as mediators, diffusing tension and facilitating communication in postwar Japan. They also served as living testimonies, demonstrating to the Japanese people that Japanese, too, were capable of understanding democracy and of finding success in a democratic society. As Yujin Yaguchi discusses in his study of Japanese portrayals of Hawaiians in the 1940s and 1950s, Nikkei living in Hawai'i had been depicted in the prewar period as marginalized pioneers of the Japanese imperial expansion struggling to eke out a living in American society, but in the postwar, the Nikkei emerged as proof that Japanese could "do" democracy. To demonstrate this shift, Yaguchi analyzes a small photograph book published in 1956 entitled *Nikkei Amerikajin—Hawai no* (Japanese Americans of Hawai'i) to argue that portrayals of American Nikkei in postwar Japan emphasized the "successful acculturation" of Japanese in Hawai'i to American society.[20] Such representations of Nikkei success in American society provided a Japanese audience with positive imagery: even Japanese could adapt to the "Western" ideology and culture that had been so vilified during the years of militarization and war. In this way, Nisei served as models of cultural assimilation, demonstrating that membership in the Japanese race did not preclude acculturation to Western values and ways of life.

A Rose by Any Other Name

Social discourse informed Nisei that their contributions as cultural ambassadors—through language interpretation, interpersonal interaction, and by serving as positive role models—would ensure both the healing of their ancestral nation and the establishment of a positive relationship between two former enemies. Rhetoric extolling Nisei as cultural ambassadors stimulated Nisei in Japan to find ways to serve as intermediaries so that they might fulfill the two-way passage paradigm. For example, Mary Kimoto, who first found employment as a clerk at the American Red Cross canteen in Osaka and later as a secretary with I Corps in Kyoto, wrote in her postwar letters that she was disappointed with herself for not devoting more energy to worthy projects that would build a brighter future for Japan and its war victims. Eager to contribute, Mary began developing side projects in addition to her daily work at the I Corps office, penning a Japanese-English slang dictionary with her fellow Nisei friend Kay, and later helping to establish a public library that might provide the Japanese public with American reading material. After successfully assisting in the establishment of the CIE-Kreuger Library for the Japanese public in Kyoto in 1946, Mary framed her contribution in language emphasizing cultural understanding, writing to the *Nippon Times* that:

> [T]hrough renewing contact with the world by means of modern literature, people will gain knowledge and truth, thereby laying the foundation for rebuilding a new and peaceful Japan. All thoughtful Americans, and especially those who are members of the occupation, realize that the Japanese themselves must be the ones to reconstruct their war-torn country.[21]

The rejuvenated rhetoric of the Nisei cultural bridge provided a paradigm that encouraged Nisei to understand their dual ethnicity as advantageous in postwar Japan, rather than contentious (as it had been during the war).

Eager to recast themselves as willing assistants in a new era of Japan-America relations, many Nisei sought opportunities to fulfill this ideal, with or without official affiliation with the SCAP apparatus. Jack Dairiki, for example, born in Sacramento to Japanese immigrants in 1930, was a fourteen-year-old boy living in Hiroshima when the atomic bomb fell on his city. In the aftermath of the surrender, he was so eager to help the occupation forces stationed near his home that he would often go out to the camp as a volunteer interpreter: "I didn't get paid. I'd just, just go there and help out because I could translate and it was very helpful for them when they were making the rounds, doing search, research, security type thing."[22] During the years of war, Jack had reverently bowed every morning in the direction of the imperial palace alongside his fellow Japanese schoolmates. As the war wore on, classes were cancelled, and in lieu of schoolwork, Jack labored from eight o'clock in the morning until five o'clock in the evening operating a lathe at a factory in Mukainada. And yet, as soon as the war ended, he was volunteering to assist the American conquerors against whom he had been mobilized.

The enthusiasm of Nisei such as Jack and Mary to participate in the occupation suggests not only their aspirations to fulfill the ideal of the cultural ambassador, but also a subconscious drive to atone for their wartime contributions to the Japanese war effort. When the fighting ended, many Nisei who had served Japan as soldiers, and in factories, offices, and in the fields realized that their wartime actions might be perceived as willful collaboration with Japan against America. On the day of the imperial surrender broadcast on August 15, 1945, for example, Mary Kimoto and her fellow monitors "were warned by the officer in charge not to say anything about our work at the listening post because, if we did, we would never be allowed to return to the United States."[23] Even decades after the war, Nisei continued to employ the *kakehashi* trope of cultural ambassadorship as they narrate their wartime collaboration. In a letter to his fellow Heishikan alumni penned in 2006, Norio Hide of Wapato, Washington, coded his own wartime experience as a Heishikan student during World War II as an example of living the *kakehashi* ideal: his work there had strengthened his "international understanding" between his two nations and had been fundamental to the forty-seven-year career he built in service to the US Department of Defense in the years after the war.[24]

Throughout the early postwar period in particular, Nisei who had lived in Japan during the war faced the challenge of distancing themselves from two Nisei famously tried and convicted as traitors: Iva Toguri and Tomoya Kawakita. The arrests and trials of these two California-born Nisei captured public attention through the years of 1945–1952, and this notoriety compelled Nisei in occupied Japan to distance themselves from the popular images of "Nisei as traitor" represented by these two antiheroes. For example, two of Iva's Nisei colleagues at Radio Tokyo, Kenichi Oki and George Mitsushio, both of whom had become Japanese citizens but had never formally renounced their American citizenship, were compelled to sign pre-composed depositions incriminating her. "'We were told,' one of them admitted decades later, 'that if we didn't cooperate, Uncle Sam might arrange a trial for us, too. All of us could see how easy it was for a mammoth country like the United States to crucify a Japanese American—all we had to do was look at Iva.'"[25] By seeking ways to contribute to the healing of Japanese-American relations in the postwar, Nisei could demonstrate that their wartime actions had been the result of force and circumstance rather than a reflection of true loyalty.

Within the Nisei community in postwar Japan, however, tension was brewing regarding the wartime actions of Nisei who had been in Japan throughout the years of war. Many Nisei veterans who had joined the American army during the war envisioned their own service for the US as a means to advance the social standing and rights of Japanese Americans at home, and to prove that Japanese American loyalty to the United States was just as strong as that of white

Americans. The historical reality that Japanese Americans living in Japan during the war had "traitorously" supported the Japanese war effort seemed to challenge this understanding, and to undo the contributions of Nisei veterans to the American victory.

Many Nisei veterans who arrived in Japan in the postwar were surprised to see that these same Nisei who had supported the Japanese war effort were enjoying special privileges (such as preferential employment and special rations), despite their wartime behavior. A back-and-forth in the "Comment & Query" column of *Pacific Stars and Stripes,* the free newspaper distributed by the US armed forces in postwar Japan, demonstrates this tension. On October 13, 1946, "A Nisei Veteran" laments:

> When I think of the many Niseis who gave their lives to serve their country and of the many thousands who served their country in uniform, I cannot help but compare these men with Niseis who chose to stay Japanese, and who are the sudden recipients of so many privileges . . . How many, I wonder, had the chance to leave Japan, but refused? Many of them played meekly along with the Japanese authorities and contributed to the Japanese war effort.[26]

A few days later in the same column, "Another Nisei Veteran" seconds this opinion on so-called pseudo-Niseis,—these "quick change artists, who, like the floating leaves, ride with the tide of victory" and are now "clamoring for reinstatement [of citizenship] on grounds of their birthrights, a birthright they failed miserably to fight for."[27] There was clearly a schism in the postwar Japan Nisei community. Nisei who arrived to work for the occupation after the fighting ended deemed the actions of "pseudo-Niseis" living in Japan during the war as shameful collaboration, and saw their eagerness to find SCAP employment in the postwar as opportunism and turn-coating. Many Nisei who had been in Japan during the war, however, hoped to demonstrate through postwar cultural ambassadorship that they, too, had America's best interest at heart—and that their contribution to the Allied occupation was proof of their support of America's mission.

Mary Kimoto read the gripes of the Nisei vets in *Stars and Stripes* with disgust. On October 18, she wrote indignantly to her friend Kay (who was then living in Tokyo):

> It made me so sad that they should be so narrow-minded. And that they should censure us Nisei who remained in Japan from before the war. Yes,

I see their point. They fought for America, and now, when they get discharged, they cannot get WD [War Department] civilian positions because some Nisei who have been in Japan and not even fought for America has beaten them to it. But they made such broad accusations. And should our Nisei problems be brought up to the light of the army newspaper, which has circulation in all the Pacific area? Why should we be fighting among ourselves? We have our hands full in fighting the prejudice against us from the outside. We ought to stick together, at least. These veterans are wonderful, I know, and I do want to give all due honor to them. But they fail to understand the circumstances we [faced] in Japan. Besides, [one] said that many who had contributed towards the war effort in Japan were now enjoying all of the privileges of American citizenship. Doesn't he know that if there is any doubt at all that any of us helped the Japanese during the war, we would not be reinstated?[28]

Mary's response letter to *Stars and Stripes,* printed in the "Comment & Query" column on October 25, accuses these Nisei veterans of making ill-informed overgeneralizations, spiritedly recounting the realities faced by Nisei in wartime Japan:

I believe that the Niseis definitely have NOT amalgamated themselves with the Japanese. Any Japanese will tell you that he can distinguish a Nisei from his countrymen. During the war, we were looked upon with suspicion and contempt because of our American ways. The police and kempeitai were on our tracks, and Nisei girls were slapped by ultra-nationalistic Japanese men because they read English books or spoke English. And have we ever really been congenial with the Japanese? No. Sad years of experience in trying to understand and to harmonize with them have only emphasized the fact that we are basically different.

Not only Niseis, but many servicemen have realized what home meant only when they first left it. To the Nisei veteran's question of whether we reinstated Americans can appreciate the meaning of American citizenship, I can answer a definite yes. Having witnessed the disastrous effects of militarism and a life inhibited by old customs, we realize the privileges and responsibilities of being Americans.[29]

In Mary's understanding, assimilation—for the sake of personal safety, quelled anxieties, and eschewing violent penalties—was not tantamount to treason. Although in hindsight the behavior of Nisei living in wartime Japan may look like voluntary collaboration, there were many other factors that encouraged Nisei to blend into the Japanese population in order to survive. Their cooperation with the Japanese during the war must therefore be understood in the context of the disciplinary forces, familial obligations, and the soft propaganda-infused environment that also shaped their wartime behavior. Furthermore, although the *kakehashi* paradigm offered a means for Nisei to redeem themselves by supporting the Allied mission in occupied Japan, it also demonstrates the duality of immigrant groups, whose subject positions are constricted according to the ways those in charge *expect* them to act. In interpreting their self-representations, it is important to look not only to the philosophical rhetoric of their contributions, but also to the everyday realities of their situation. Just as the physical and discursive environment during the war compelled Nisei to regulate their bodies as Japanese, so did soft propaganda in the postwar compel them to seek ways to align with the occupation.

In addition to the more abstract benefits of social advancement and self-esteem sought by Nisei who functioned as cultural intermediaries in the postwar, there were more tangible, practical factors that motivated Nisei to align themselves with the occupation and its missions. The first such incentive was financial: in war-torn Japan, SCAP salary was significantly higher than the pay offered by most Japanese employers. For example, the interpreters at the Tokyo Tribunal received 1,800 *yen* per month (around 120 dollars) plus a per diem of one hundred *yen* (around seven dollars) at a time when the Japanese government had established 500 *yen* a month as the standard cost of living in Tokyo.[30] Censors at CCD made twice the monthly salary of the average Japanese worker at the time, and employees who reported more effective information to CCD officials received higher salaries.[31] For the first few months of the occupation in Okinawa, employees were paid in much-needed food, clothes, and tobacco (until the wage system began in 1946).[32] Whether distributed as wages or as material items, occupation pay was extremely attractive, especially considering that there were few other jobs available in postwar Japan, where families were homeless and destitute, and entire cities had been destroyed.

English ability and understanding of Western culture—two features of Nisei life which had been cause for suspicion and discrimination during the war—now served as lifelines for Nisei who could ensure their family's survival by seeking employment with the occupation. Yoneko Dozono, for example, a Nisei from Portland who had married a prominent Japanese educator and had spent the years of the war in Okayama, was left with little choice but to seek work when her husband was one of the first to be purged by the Allied authorities. "I had to become the breadwinner of the family," she recalled. "And because of my background [as a Nisei], I was asked to work for the military government."[33]

All SCAP employees enjoyed significant pay and benefits compared to what they might have earned from other employers, but the degrees of pay and benefits differed according to the employee's nationality status. Japanese citizens hired by the occupation were "Japanese nationals," paid in *yen* and excluded from many of the special access privileges granted to Allied nationals and foreign nationals. Allied nationals received their salary in US dollars, and they were also able to use the commissary, to shop at the Post Exchange (PX), and to use the Army Post Office (APO) for mail. Nisei who had lived in Japan during the war were—as Mary Kimoto puts it—"lumped" together as "foreign nationals."[34] With this designation, they too received special privileges, though not as extensive as the privileges enjoyed by Allied nationals (civilian and military).

Mary Kimoto's letters from occupied Japan demonstrate that foreign nationals working for SCAP enjoyed a variety of benefits. At a time when Japanese subjects faced famine, inadequate shelter, and limited and overcrowded public transportation options, Mary could receive free medical care at the dispensary. She had permission to ride American Red Cross vehicles. She received a uniform of gray wool and slacks. She could get free donuts anytime at the I Corps Canteen, and she had an option of free housing (with meals) provided by the Army. Her supervisor also granted her permission to stay in their (heated) office as long as she wanted, even after hours, so that she might keep warm in the biting Kyoto winter. She also enjoyed leisure benefits, such as use of the CI&E reading room, and access to theatre and cinema shows.

Even with the special privileges that distinguished Nisei from other Japanese citizens, Mary was often frustrated that she was not considered equal to other Americans working for the occupation. "We foreign nationals," she wrote, "are at the mercy of anyone who happens to have the power over us. We work for the army but we have to abide by Japanese regulations . . . Kicked around by the Americans on one hand, and bled by the Japs on the other." Foreign nationals like Mary were banned from using the Army Post Office mail system (which was the only system available until September of 1946). Although they were generally paid better salaries than Japanese nationals, they could have received significantly higher pay in civil service jobs open only to American citizens. Mary's dormitory for foreign nationals in Osaka did provide three meals a day, but Mary lamented that the dormitory was unheated, that it was just one room shared by twenty Nisei girls, and that the meals were all composed of canned goods.[35] Even so, access to these benefits was critical to the survival of Nisei and their Japanese relatives and friends. Atami Ueno, who was born in Hawai'i in 1927 but was attending school in Japan throughout the war, found employment as a foreign national at CCD. Each morning at the hotel breakfast, she and her Nisei friend Jill "would order hard boiled eggs because we could take it home, see, to our families, and so we would order seconds of the hard-boiled eggs."[36]

Although many Nisei employees like Mary and Atami were categorized as foreign nationals, scores of other Nisei employees were designated instead as Japanese nationals, because their contributions to the Japanese government (such as military service or voting in elections) had resulted in automatic loss of their American citizenship. Despite their comparatively diminished access to special privileges, though, these Nisei still had the ability to gain access to much-needed food and other benefits, simply via their connection to the occupation. Even Nisei who were not employed by SCAP earned tangible benefits simply by developing connections with SCAP personnel. Hawai'i-born Frank Fukuhara, for example, who had been drafted into the Japanese army during the war, was traveling with his brother Harry (an American soldier who had lately arrived in Japan on an occupation mission) when they stopped by the American 41st Division camp near Kure to visit for a few days. At the camp, Frank was told by the commanding officer that "I can live on base, I can go to any mess hall . . . I can eat any[thing], so I was really hungry, so I ate about five meals, sometimes six meals a day I'd eat."[37] Oregon-born Jimmie Matsuda, a former soldier for a Japanese *kamikaze* unit, assisted at a postwar military camp, where the quartermaster—who knew that Jimmie was from America—let him take whatever he wanted, enabling Jimmie to feed his family with the steak and bacon he received from the mess hall.[38] The food, clothing, and other supplies squirreled away by those who interacted with American GIs (either socially or on the job) also helped foster positive opinions on the part of the Japanese public of their American occupiers—and of Nisei.

American Hegemony in the Physical Environment

The privileges accessible to Nisei "foreign nationals" and "Japanese nationals" who either worked for or associated with SCAP employees and GIs, however, paled in comparison to the privileges enjoyed by the arriving conquerors themselves. American military personnel in Japan lived a "soft life" of cheap food, free rent, lavish entertainment, access to golf and sailing clubs, and gas for a mere fifteen cents a gallon at army filling stations.[39] This stark contrast resulted on one hand in significant animosity from many Japanese citizens who had the extravagance of the victors rubbed in their faces. According to Nisei Yayoi Cooke, the Americans blatantly flaunted their superior lifestyle:

[They] associated among themselves, they stayed among themselves, they lived their own way with material abundance which the Japanese didn't have at all. And that also made the Japanese very hostile to the Americans. They had cars, they had clothing, they had food. They had a comfortable way of living. They took over a lot of the good buildings, where the Japanese didn't have any buildings.[40]

On the other hand, the aura of luxury that surrounded GIs and other American personnel of SCAP reinforced to Nisei that the more American a person is, the more tangible benefits he is able to receive. Nisei who befriended or ingratiated themselves to SCAP higher-ups could see rewards in the form of better food and special privileges (such as transportation and leisure activities). Thus, just as soft propaganda in the wartime environment had emphasized the performance of Japaneseness (in appearance, mannerisms, and expression) as the means to advancement and security, so in the postwar did Nisei see that the performance of Americanness would provide access to better opportunities and benefits. The hegemony associated with American behavior, appearance, and expression in postwar Japan inspired Nisei to gravitate toward American behavior, appearance, and expression in order to thrive. Explained Mary Kimoto, "Our lives were completely reversed, for in the Japanese eyes we were no longer the hated enemy. Rather we were identified with the conquerors who had plenty of food, cigarettes, and other scarce things."[41]

Changes in the physical environment also subconsciously inspired Nisei to perform as American in postwar Japan. Just as Nisei in wartime Japan had seen America purged from their surroundings, now in the postwar, they could see and feel America everywhere. Immediately upon its establishment in Japan, SCAP commandeered all major buildings that were still standing in Tokyo and Yokohama for billets, officers' clubs, entertainment facilities, PX and administrative offices. SCAP hoisted the Stars and Stripes and forbade the display of the Rising Sun in Japan's streets. Within weeks, nearly all of Japan's major cities were teeming with GIs—and with the sounds of the English language, with American music, and with jeeps. As a result of a directive by MacArthur himself, public notices throughout Japan appeared in Roman letters as well as Japanese, and in Yokohama and Tokyo, street signs were either in English and Japanese or just English.[42] The everyday physical environment of Japan, once so hostile to even tinges of "the West," was now in many ways approximating an American setting. In an environment infused with a shock of Americana, American Nisei could again feel at ease to behave, dress, and speak as Americans.

Under the pressure of wartime hypersurveillance, most Nisei had been careful to toe the line and obey the rules, but amid postwar refrains of "democracy" and "freedom," Nisei began to push boundaries, buck authority, and test the limits of SCAP's red tape. The opportunity to "act American" again offered Nisei an outlet for the stress they had endured during the war when trying to blend into the Japanese populace. Once targets of criticism due to their affiliation with the American enemy, Nisei like Mary Kimoto could now seek retribution by aligning themselves with the American conqueror. A letter dated May 4, 1946, captures this newfound freedom:

> Yesterday, I had an interesting time because I went with the chaplains to a Buddhist temple [in Kyoto] to witness some kind of dedication ceremony. It was a lot of fun, especially because I did not have to bow and act like a Jap, as I've had to for years. Now I could stick up my nose at them— but I didn't, I only acted natural. And they had to excuse me for being that way, since I had on my uniform complete with cap, and had four American officers with me.

Mary, who describes herself as a "skinny, nervous . . . worry-wart," who meekly did whatever she was told during the war, resumed her former brassy, strong-willed attitude in the postwar. Mary's postwar letters reflect that she and her friends would often test the limits of their benefits as American-born SCAP employees by bending the rules—and asking questions later. For example, of the ice-cream bar on the third floor of her GHQ office building—stocked with ice cream, pie, coffee, and donuts technically off-limits to foreign nationals—Mary, undeterred, wrote that "We intend to go until we get kicked out."[43] In a similar manner, she rode in GI cars until getting kicked off. She also took advantage of opportunities to express her opinion publicly (as in the *Stars and Stripes* column mentioned above).

As an employee of I Corps in July of 1946, Mary petitioned the supervising Postal Officer in a formal letter to request that foreign nationals be granted access to the Army Post Office. Her letter appeals to the rhetoric of brotherhood and togetherness:

> To us, who have never even met our loved ones for six or seven years . . . And also, is not correspondence a means toward the making of 'one world'? We who have suffered here the war years know and understand the Japanese people. With this experience added to our background of American upbringing and schooling, surely we can contribute towards mutual understanding, and thus, the shortening of the occupation and the prevention of future wars.[44]

Stimulated by the social discourse positing Nisei as promoters of American values in the postwar, as well as the physical environment's demonstrations of American behavior and expressions as valuable, Nisei like Mary both consciously and subconsciously regulated their behavior according to these ideals.

It is important to mention here as counterpoint, though, a different group of Nisei in postwar Japan: the approximately eighteen hundred "renunciants"—internees who had been stripped of their US citizenship and shipped to Japan along with about eight thousand persons of Japanese descent (a group which included Issei as well as American citizens who had not renounced their American citizenship but accompanied parents who had renounced).[45] Unlike Mary Kimoto and other Nisei who had suffered alongside the Japanese populace during the war, these Nisei faced a different sort of undoing of their wartime experiences. Keige Kaku was one such Nisei. Born in 1915 near Fresno, California, Keige had

Figure 6.1. This photo, taken by Nisei US army photographer Ted Akimoto during the occupation, depicts three styles worn by Japanese women as they transitioned from wartime to postwar: the workpants *monpe* (at right), Western-style clothing, and traditional kimono for festival days. Courtesy of the Theodore Akimoto Family Collection, Densho Digital Repository.

joined the US army in 1941, but after the Pearl Harbor attack, his Commanding Officer forced him out of service and sent him home to California. He was interned during the war in Arizona and later at Tule Lake, having refused to answer Question 27 on the infamous "Loyalty Questionnaire," which asked internees if they would be willing to serve in the United States military. Keige, indignant that the army that had rejected him would later ask for his support, was stripped of his American citizenship. He and his family were among the 4,406 internees "repatriated" from Tule Lake to Japan. As Keige's son related in an interview with *Nikkei West,* the family "wanted no one to know we were once American." Although Keige was qualified to send his children to the American Army School, he sent them instead to neighborhood Japanese schools, and the family never spoke English, until they returned to the United States in 1956, having regained their US citizenship through litigation.[46]

The reflections of George Masayuki Kikuta, a Sansei (third generation Japanese American) whose family was repatriated as renunciants from the internment camp at Manzanar to Fukushima in the immediate postwar, shed light on why Keige and other "repatriated" families may have been so hesitant to "act American." As George describes of his childhood in postwar Japan, "I was treated like a foreigner, immigrant . . . they called me an American spy and tried to segregate me and my brothers because we were from the United States." Nisei repatriates and their families, many of whom were shocked to see the devastation in war-torn Japan when they reached Japanese shores, faced a different sort of future: the need to assimilate with the Japanese populace that they (or their parents) had "chosen." As complicated as it may have been for such families, their connection to America and their ability to navigate American culture and an English-speaking environment could still be used to their advantage. After about six months in Japan, Keige Kaku and his brother were hired by the Army Corps of Engineers to work for the occupation. And as George Masayuki Kikuta continues:

> But we, we used to get the American foods and chocolates, gum, and that type was shipped from U.S. And my relatives, I think, tried to help us. We distributed that among our neighbors, and that really made us look really good. [Laughs] . . . I think after the initial sort of teasing or discriminatory comments, we were treated rather in a positive way, more elite type of, coming from U.S.[47]

Access to such employment, food and privileges was a matter of life and death to some Nisei and their families in war-torn Japan. Keige may have endeavored to hide his American background from his Japanese neighbors, but the Army

Corps of Engineers undoubtedly relied on him and his language ability in an environment starved for people who could navigate both American culture and Japanese culture.

The *kakehashi* paradigm's emphasis on Nisei as cultural intermediaries also functioned to mitigate feelings of shame in a tenuous postwar atmosphere in which fraternization and cooperation with the former enemy were reviled by many Japanese nationals. Whereas Japanese citizens who sought employment with SCAP were viewed by friends and neighbors as serving the enemy, Nisei employees could rationalize their employment as simply taking advantage of the knowledge of American language and culture that was their birthright. Their Japanese-born coworkers considered their own work for SCAP as dishonorable. Indeed, post-postwar inquiry into the lives of Japanese nationals who worked in the Civil Censorship Detachment reveals that it was considered a badge of shame to work for "the enemy," and many of the Japanese civilians employed by the CCD did not even talk about their experiences with their own family. As Kawada Takashi, a Japanese national who worked for the postal censorship division, expressed, "Of course, cooperating with the American army is [seen as] despicable. It's embarrassing." Kōno Shigeko, another Japanese employee of CCD, remembered feeling cut deeply by the reactions of her countrymen when she told people where she was working: "[They said,] 'Wow, it's just appalling what you're doing there.'" The *kakehashi* paradigm—which rather encouraged Nisei to find ways to contribute to SCAP's mission—offered a way for Nisei to differentiate themselves from Japanese, and to sidestep feelings of disgrace which many of their Japanese friends and neighbors associated with SCAP employment.[48]

The flexibility of interaction offered by the *kakehashi* paradigm also influenced the freedom of Nisei women in their social interactions with GIs. Japanese nationals—women in particular—who sought access to privileges through friendships or romantic interludes with American personnel were accused of "fraternization," which was discouraged by Japanese and American officials alike. Newspapers, too, disparaged personal contact between Japanese and occupation personnel, cautioning readers to behave with decorum. Signs that warned against "fraternization with the indigenous personnel" greeted occupation workers in the streets, and women were cautioned against wearing too much make-up and responding to soldiers' greetings.[49] MacArthur, however, refused to issue a non-fraternization order like the one issued in Germany, instead encouraging his staff to associate with whomever they pleased. Even so, as Takaaki Aikawa described, in many cases the benefits of interacting with a GI outweighed the social shame heaped upon Japanese women who associated with them:

Once a street girl got an American soldier, she ceased to be a Japanese, it seemed. She could go shopping with her mother to the PX, which was off-limits to other Japanese; she could walk through the special passage in the station for the occupation army—where no other Japanese was permitted to step . . . Looking coldly at the mass of her own people, the street girls passed by like queens with their hand in the arms of American soldiers.[50]

The situation was different, though, for American Nisei, who had more flexibility associating with the American occupiers. Because of their own American background, these Nisei for the most part did not encounter the same intensity of social shame as that heaped upon the so-called pan pan girls, the non-English-speaking Japanese women who offered their attentions to GIs in exchange for tangible benefits such as *pan* (bread). Many Nisei felt comfortable palling around with American GIs, whom Seattle-born Marion Tsutakawa Kanemoto remembered as "very accepting. That's the neat part of Americans, they're so open. You know, much more than the Japanese . . . I actually befriended [GIs] very readily."[51] Additionally, Nisei women who were able to speak English were better equipped to protect themselves from the advances of soldiers. Mary Kimoto heard that most of the officers kept private homes with "temporary wives"—"girls from good Jap families," and that the officers "want women who can't speak English, for then they can keep their tracks covered more."[52] Mary Kimoto wrote to her friend Kay of numerous evenings spent in the company of soldiers named Pat and Paul, two young "wolves" living in the basement of her building. She assured Kay not to worry, though—"They don't do any wolving on me."[53] The freedom of the democratizing social environment, in addition to the leeway provided by social rhetoric that championed Nisei who assumed roles supporting the occupation, both enabled and encouraged Nisei like Mary to seek advancement and opportunity by engaging with American personnel, and re-assimilating by "acting American."

Imaginary Bridges and Cultural Flexibility

The presence of the two-way passage paradigm in social discourse granted Nisei in postwar Japan license to code-switch between Japaneseness and Americanness. The demand that Nisei serve as cultural bridges made this oscillation possible. In return for their cooperation with the conqueror and promotion of SCAP goals, Nisei who had lived in Japan during the war received tangible benefits critical to their survival, as well as less tangible benefits, such as an outlet for the accumulated stress of war experiences and a means to cope with shame. And yet, although they were discussed as essential "bridges" between two cultures pitted as opposites, in practice Nisei were underutilized by SCAP. In a 1961 interview conducted by Beate Gordon, Burton Crane (a veteran from the Office of Strategic Services who returned to Japan in 1945 as an economic correspondent for the *New York Times*) described the prejudice in SCAP—perpetuated by MacArthur's leadership style—against anyone who had extensive familiarity with Japanese history, language, or culture. "[MacArthur] tried to have no BIJ's anywhere around him—that is, Born in Japan people. There were some Nisei, yes, but they knew nothing about Japan; not if they spoke good enough English."[54] In the re-membrances of occupation employees recorded in Beate Gordon's oral history project, SCAP emerges as a closed-door, "Old Boys' Club" in which women, per-sons of color, and Japanese partners were permitted limited say in the design of SCAP policies and the implementation of SCAP goals.

Nevertheless, the *kakehashi* ideal of Nisei in prewar and postwar Japan pro-vided Nisei with a forum to exercise both Japaneseness and Americanness. Soft propaganda positing Nisei as cultural intermediaries encouraged Nisei to con-sider their wartime participation and their postwar mobilization as simply ebbing toward opposite sides of their cultural dualism. The two-way passage ideal represents the social expectations of Nisei in postwar Japan and illuminates the opportunities available to Nisei as they adjusted to life under the occupation. By placing value on the role of Nisei as intermediary, the paradigm gave Nisei in Japan freedom to associate with Americans, providing them with an avenue to demonstrate their support of America in the postwar regardless of what conclu-sions might be drawn of their wartime actions in Japan. As *kakehashi,* Nisei acted as buffers who could diffuse tension, deliver bad news, censor difficult doc-uments, and facilitate communication not only on a literal level but on a social level as well. The paradigm served Nisei, too, by providing them with a means to cope with issues such as shame regarding mobilization during the war and fraternization after the war. Thus, the discursive concept of the *kakehashi* influ-enced expectations of Nisei in postwar Japan and, accordingly, shaped Nisei self-representation by establishing the ideal for Nisei behavior.

The *kakehashi* paradigm emphasizes the understanding of Nisei identity as dual—as two cultures functioning in opposite realms within the body of the Nisei. This reinforces the image of bicultural individuals not as hybrids, but as possessing dual characters. Nisei were stimulated to consider themselves as possessing a Japanese sensibility and an American sensibility, between which they were able to shift according to their own goals and the preferences of their audience. Unlike the *shikata ga nai* constriction that characterized their wartime experiences, Nisei in the postwar years were again expected to oscillate between the two sides of their cultural identity. Seattle-born Marion Tsutakawa Kanemoto, introduced earlier in this analysis as a Nisei driving bamboo spears into straw Americans in wartime Japan "like a puppet" animated by Japanese militarism, conveyed such malleability when narrating her postwar support of the occupation. After Japan's surrender, when the American soldiers of the occupation arrived in a jeep at her school, Marion's principal sent a messenger to "get Tsutakawa . . . And I happily went down to the office and reported to the principal and, well, the GI would start talking, well, that was no problem, greet a friend. So this was role acting . . . I had to be careful not to be too happy, and, but then we chit-chatted." Both during the war and during the occupation, Marion described, "I just played my game. I mean, and knowingly, and it was a survival kind of thing . . . I just had to kinda, oscillate."[55]

While Nisei themselves oscillated between Japanese and American performances, public discourse manipulated them as alternately Japanese and American, as seen in the example of Hanama Tasaki, a Hawai'i-born novelist who fought in the Japanese army during the war. After traveling to Japan to enlist in the Imperial Army in 1936, Tasaki served in the army's campaigns in China, worked as a reporter, and later served combat tours in the South Pacific during World War II. After Japan's surrender, he worked odd jobs while penning his English-language novel *Long the Imperial Way*, which gained readership first among occupation personnel in Japan in 1949, and later among a broader international audience. As Edward Tang points out in his research on the novelist, "Tasaki and the promotional material about *Long the Imperial Way* selectively masked and acknowledged aspects of his life story, especially regarding his ethnicity and US citizenship."[56] This selective characterization—whether intentional or not—highlights key tensions in the narrative of Japanese American identity overall in the postwar era, and especially of Hawaiian Nisei. A novel in which a soldier questions the morality of militarism and expansionism requires delicate public relations when released amid a backdrop of Japan's occupation by the victorious Allies—all the more so if that novel's author is Hawai'i-born, raising yet another specter of America's own history of expansion. Further complicating Tasaki's critical reception, his novel's protagonist is a Japanese subject on Japanese soil, with Japanese compatriots. By omitting explicitly Nisei themes and characters, Tasaki was out of sync with the narratives that dominated in the postwar and Cold War era, such as Nisei "Americanism" as representing the ability of Japanese subjects to assimilate to democratic ideals. Based on the imagined preferences of their audience, Tasaki and his critics framed his identity as selectively Japanese, American, and

Hawaiian, depending on the story they wanted to tell about democratization, militarism, and even racial prejudice.[57]

Nisei in postwar Japan were aware—as they had been throughout the war and before the war began—that their actions, expressions, and appearance were to be tailored to the demands of their audience. As they had performed Japanese-ness during the war in order to survive, many Nisei in the postwar gravitated toward Americanness, propelled to do so by social expectations and by the realities of their physical environment. Nisei were thus able to reflect on their actions during the war and the postwar as merely attempting to cope with the demands placed upon them by their social and material environment.

In both wartime and postwar Japan, Nisei behavior was shaped not necessarily by conscious elaborations of changing loyalty, but by trying to make sense of the intensities and demands in the everyday environment. In wartime Japan, Nisei were compelled to regulate their bodies as Japanese in action, speech, and appearance; to stifle their American mannerisms and ways of thought; and to keep quiet about their opinions on the war between their two nations. In the postwar, Nisei assisting the Allied occupation with translation, interpretation, and cultural relations faced several challenges, including contempt from those Japanese citizens resentful of Nisei support for the Allied conquerors, ambivalence about siding with America after weathering the storms of war in Japan, and tension within the Nisei community itself. And in the *post*-postwar, Nisei self-representation continues to be shaped by social preferences regarding the legacy of the war as remembered. In considering Nisei performance as influenced by multiple environmental factors, Muriel Tanaka's work translating broadcasts with her fellow Nisei at a Japanese military radio reception unit and Iva Toguri's bantering with Allied prisoners of war over the airwaves of the Pacific echo the self-regulatory process of Marion Tsutekawa Kanemoto helpfully chatting with GIs, of Mary Kimoto striving to establish a library in occupied Kyoto, and even of Frank Hironobu Hirata appealing to the rhetoric of brainwashing as he shared his story with Densho interviewers in 2010.

To appreciate identity as ever malleable is to pay homage to the rhizomic power of soft propaganda in the everyday environment. Action is never directly correlated to unambiguous convictions. Memory colors emotion and personal narratives. Identity is a process of self-representation and self-understanding, a performance that is constantly in flux. Individuals engage in self-representation, but only through that which the authority of significations has postulated as possible subject positions for these individuals. In wartime Japan, those paradigms for Nisei included the compliant subject volunteering for the war effort, the brave soldier training for his final fight, the young woman attentively toiling away at the weapons factory, and the student reciting the virtues of self-sacrifice. In occupied Japan, the idealized subject positions shifted, and Nisei could survive and thrive by performing as the working woman emerging from centuries of patriarchy into a new era of gender equality, the hidden patriot finally able to "act American" again, and the *kakehashi* fulfilling the two-way passage by effortlessly bridging two opposite cultures. Even decades after defeat, Nisei who weathered the years of war and occupation in Japan continued to regulate themselves and their stories in the context of roles posited by social discourse: the brainwashed subject, the pragmatic son or daughter struggling to survive, or the ensnared pawn of fate who laments, "*shikata ga nai*."

Collaboration, analyzed here through the example of Nisei cooperation with and mimicry of shifting hegemons across nearly a century, is inspired by an individual's assessments of her own goals and her audience's preferences. To be sure, there were Nisei in wartime Japan who whole-heartedly committed to the Japanese war cause and killed Allied soldiers, tormented POWs, and translated intelligence to ensure a Japanese victory in battle, fully aware that their actions were contributing to a war effort against the United States. But to dismiss collaborators with a moral judgment of "treason" is to fail to appreciate the factors of behavior regulation that shape collaborative action in the moment—and the narration of collaboration years later. By paralleling the process of collaboration of American Nisei in wartime and occupied Japan, it becomes clear that collaboration is a performance embedded in its historical moment. This more nuanced understanding of the complexities of collaboration, and of the role of emotions and identity in behavior, is useful not only in considering World War II as lived by Nisei and their families, but more broadly—as the concluding chapter will explore—in understanding the process of racial and cultural assimilation, and the conceptualization of loyalty and treason. A consideration of collaboration as assimilation offers a lens through which to consider those accused of treason, to appreciate the factors that guided their behavior and kindled in them an aspiration to act in a way that could later be judged as traitorous.

Conclusion

Loyalty in Practice

In the late summer of 1932, nearly one year after the Manchurian Incident and the start of Japan's belligerent expansion in Asia, United States Rear Admiral Yates Stirling, Jr., addressed the Conference of Japanese American Citizens in Honolulu, declaring himself "on record in an official report published by Congress in which I question the pronouncement that you [Japanese Americans] have adopted without reserve citizenship in a nation different in many fundamental respects from the nation of your forefathers." Stirling substantiated his dubiousness of Japanese American loyalty by citing "the virility, pride, efficiency, and determination of the Japanese nation." He asserted that the proud heritage of the Japanese people—in particular their devotion to their emperor and the warrior code of *bushidō*—would make it "very difficult for those in Hawai'i of Japanese ancestry to truly efface their allegiance to Japan and accept full loyalty to a nation so different in historical background." The audience of Nisei youths responded vehemently to Stirling's assertions, pointing out that they had to be even *more* loyal to America than the average citizen to counterbalance their kinship with the militaristic, ambitious Japanese empire. They insisted that they and their fellow Japanese Americans were indeed loyal to the United States and would fight for the American cause in the event of a war with Japan.[1]

This exchange typifies the struggles of the Japanese American community in America in the first half of the twentieth century. No matter how enthusiastically Japanese American voices responded to similar suspicions of disloyalty throughout Hawai'i and the American mainland, racial prejudice and ultra-Americanism fostered a social environment in which race was understood as an external indicator of an individual's convictions of loyalty. Across the United States, fears about economic competition from Asian immigrants willing to live on lower wages compounded with chatter predicting a Pacific Age in which "the Orient" would ascend as a legitimate player on the international stage. Rising awareness of tensions between the US and Japan resulted in a maelstrom of electric racial friction that placed significant stress on the Japanese American community—in particular Nisei, whose ethnic ambiguity complicated distinct racial divisions.

As the chapters of this book have demonstrated, Admiral Stirling was far from alone in his facile conflation of race and loyalty. On both sides of the Pacific in the early twentieth century, many politicians, educators, and intellectuals broadly equated membership in the Japanese ethno-nation with innate allegiance to Japan and her causes. In America during the years of World War II, assumptions about racial loyalty trumping national allegiance notoriously resulted in the forced internment of all persons of Japanese ancestry living on the West Coast under Executive Order 9066, including US citizens of Japanese descent. And as discussed in Part Two, Nisei living in Japanese-held territory were spared internment and incarceration due to their Japanese racial heritage, regardless of the details of their citizenship. The Japanese government could not afford to intern all enemy nationals, and authorities in wartime Japan calculated that the Japanese blood in Nisei veins made Nisei a less-threatening security risk than non-Japanese residents. Indeed, phenotypically Japanese features granted Nisei the opportunity to "pass" as fully Japanese members of the imperial populace, provided that they mastered mimicry of Japanese behavior, expression, and dress.

Loyalty is the refrain that echoes throughout the history of transwar Japanese America. It colors inescapably the delivery of Nisei wartime narratives. It thematically frames the legacy of Nisei soldiers who served in the US 442nd Infantry Regiment, the 100th Infantry Battalion, and in military intelligence—American citizens who in many cases went against the wishes of their relatives and volunteered for service to demonstrate that Japanese Americans were indeed loyal to the United States. Internees in the War Relocation Authority camps in the US interior lived alongside the shadow of questioned loyalty and its implications every day: prevention of traitorous action was the rationale for their confinement.

In early 1943, motivated by a need for manpower and the demand of streamlined spending, the US War Relocation Authority administered a questionnaire to every adult internee in the Japanese American camps as a means to determine which of the internees they might release. The so-called Loyalty Questionnaire is best remembered for its 27th and 28th questions, which asked respondents whether they were willing to enlist in the US military if found qualified (Question 27) and if they would "swear unqualified allegiance to the United States of America" (Question 28).[2] Stirling's speech, the various versions of the Loyalty Questionnaire, the trial of Iva Toguri, and Nisei postwar battles for citizenship restoration serve as benchmarks through which to trace the changing shape of loyalty—how it "looked" to the American public or to the Japanese public, and how it was imagined and even tested by authorities in the government and the court system. These public reference points give form to the intangible force called "loyalty."

The history of Japanese Americans in the first half of the twentieth century demonstrates that government officials and public opinion in Japan and America broadly considered race to be a likely indicator of loyalty. But to press the question further, why was the effort to diagnose loyalty so strikingly salient on both sides of the confrontation? It is because loyalty has long been understood as the primary force governing an individual's behavior in times of conflict. Admiral Stirling believed that his racially Japanese Nisei listeners would naturally possess some measure of loyalty to the Japanese race—a loyalty which, whether they admitted it or not, would influence them to act in support of the Japanese nation. Accordingly, in the eyes of Stirling and his contemporaries, Nisei who indeed intended to fight for the United States in a war against Japan would first need to cultivate proper loyalty to the United States—and erase any vestiges of loyalty to Japan. Should a citizen act against her nation, it must be because she was compelled by the force of misplaced loyalties. In this line of thinking, California-born Iva Toguri delivered the "Tokyo Rose" propaganda broadcasts on behalf of the Japanese nation because she was loyal to Japan and disloyal to the United States, making her a traitor to the country of her birth.

However, as the examples of Nisei experiences throughout this book have shown, loyalty (whether to race, to nation, to ideology, or to religion) should not be considered the dominant force inspiring human behavior. Loyalty—which is discussed across nations and time as internal, as deeply emotional, and as a force that regulates human actions—is instead the frame we use to rationalize an individual's behavior in a moment of decision. Human behavior is guided not only by personal convictions, but also by the physical environment, by discourse, by disciplinary forces, and by economic and interpersonal circumstances—all of which constrict and determine an individual's actions. The aim of this book has been to clarify the power of the physical environment and of social discourse—informed by the propaganda of Japanese institutions and of the Allied occupation—to inspire self-regulation of the body and thereby to shape racial, cultural, and gender identities. Loyalty as a conscious emotion is just one factor that influences action, and loyalty can be conflicted and divided. It is therefore necessary to understand loyalty not as the sole force determining an individual's actions, but as just one element that can influence the path through which that individual navigates her environment.

Just as discourse crystallizes values, the everyday material environment echoes these values in tangible form. Individuals regulate their behavior and appearance according to values promulgated by discourse and by their physical surroundings in a process of assimilation. Thus, the actions of Nisei in transwar Japan should not be assessed as proof of loyalty or disloyalty to the United States. Rather, these actions should be utilized as access points that viscerally connect us (the contemporary audience) to the opportunities, preferences, anxieties, liabilities, and ambitions of a historical moment—that is, to the everyday experience of being an American Nisei woman or youth on the Japanese home front, or an American Nisei soldier in the uniform of imperial Japan.

In the self-representation of American Nisei in transwar Japan—as lived and as remembered—we see that an individual's behavior is guided consciously and subconsciously by norms and ideals in her environment. Therefore, when analyzing an individual's actions and expressions in a historical moment, we should consider that individual's agency—her options, goals, and the path she takes—as shaped by the opportunities available to her in her physical and discursive reality. Yes, American Nisei in Japan did indeed participate in a war effort that envisioned America as the enemy. However, their actions were the manifestation of millions of moments of individual decisions, of affectively guided behaviors only conglomerated as "treason" by the backward-glancing telescopic lens of Allied victory.

Collaboration is a conscious and subconscious performance embedded in the exigencies of a moment. Treason—the story told about collaboration with one's presumed enemy—is colored inescapably by legacy, by the way the public collectively remembers the act itself. Iva Toguri misread the tenor of new anxieties in her immediate postwar surroundings and became a political pawn through whom President Truman could demonstrate that he was tough on treason. By reenacting her broadcasts for the cameras and retelling her story to journalists after Japan's defeat, Iva stridently, publicly, jarringly dislodged her wartime performance from its cage of time and displaced it into a new social and discursive environment with which that performance was out of sync. Muriel Tanaka, on the other hand, was flexible in her performance—as were Mary Kimoto, Peter Sano, and the other Nisei in the pages of this book who did not face treason trials. They altered their behavior and appearance in harmony with the shifting hegemonic preferences of their historical moment.

Environmental codes and discursive values have established goals for these individuals and set into motion behaviors designed to achieve those goals. The emotional energy directing those actions is only cognitively assessed as loyalty. Thus, American Nisei living on the Japanese home front who contributed first to the war effort and then to the occupation agenda were not just "switching" their loyalties. They were instead regulating their behaviors according to the ideals established by the hegemon of their historical moment. Perhaps a thorough transformation of loyalty followed in some cases, but that loyalty must be considered as something deeply entangled with the other situational factors that influence behavior.

In this sense, collaboration in wartime Japan and collaboration in postwar Japan are parallel processes. Institutions and intellectuals establish preferences that infuse the everyday environment with those preferences. Organizations and individuals tasked with oversight police the populace to reinforce these preferences through various modes of surveillance. The institutions and organizations change—for example, from the Ministry of Education to a SCAP-directed Textbook Authorization Committee, and from the Kempeitai to the Civil Censorship Detachment—but the process through which individuals consciously and subconsciously regulate themselves in conversation with these preferences and prohibitions remains the same.

To rationalize an individual's past actions or predict her future actions through a diagnosis of "loyalty" is to flatten even subconscious behaviors into a conscious and intelligible narrative. But as reiterated throughout the chapters of this book, human behavior is not wholly the result of cognitive choices. It is the manifestation of the affective experience of a physical environment. Our actions are the product of an unceasing quest to quell anxieties, to make sense of the unfamiliar. Hegemonic preferences in the environment hold sway over human behavior. Norms in the environment draft the "social stories" about what we aspire to feel, generating the aspiration to emote and behave in ways reinforced (and even glorified) by those norms.[3] This concept of the ways in which society—through propaganda, for example—can generate subconscious aspirations in individuals helps to clarify the process through which American-born Nisei in wartime Japan performed the work of war.

Loyalty, Reinstatement, and Return

Nisei battles for restoration of American citizenship in the postwar era demonstrate precisely this mode of collaboration: individual preferences and behaviors that shift in tandem with the shift in hegemony. In the early days of the occupation, as discussed in Chapter Six, there had been such an overwhelming need for English-language assistance that staff were hired quickly and, in many cases, without extensive background checks. Nisei who had weathered the years of war on the Japanese home front were readily sought in rural and urban Japan to assist SCAP in achieving the occupation's missions. For their efforts, they enjoyed tangible benefits such as food, clothing, and warm shelter, as well as intangible benefits such as psychological penance for years of non-resistance. Nisei who proved American citizenship could earn higher pay in SCAP jobs, better bene-fits, and could seek employment opportunities unavailable to non-US citizens. They could even begin the process of securing passage to the United States, where many had family members—or dreams of a brighter future in a country un-marred by bombing and starvation.

But as the one-year anniversary of Japan's surrender approached, the occupa-tion apparatus had found its operating rhythm, and the frenzied months of scrambling a sufficient workforce were fading into memory. In the early days, SCAP had been focused on the immediately pressing concerns of disarmament, catching war criminals, releasing POWs, and preventing starvation. As time passed, though, SCAP concerns shifted to more intricate questions of citizen-ship, relocation, and the day-to-day operations that would prepare Japan for a democratic, capitalist future. Turning to the questions of citizenship, for exam-ple, on Saturday, May 18, 1946, SCAP ordered the Japanese government to sub-mit lists of the names of all American nationals who had applied for Japanese citizenship, served in the Japanese armed forces, or who had "accepted or per-formed the duties of any office, post, or employment under the Japanese Govern-ment or any political subdivision thereof" since January 13, 1941.[4] According to the US Nationality Act of 1940, all of these American citizens who served in the Japanese military or in governmental positions during the war had, through those actions, effectively forfeited their American citizenship.

The occupation's efforts to delve into questions of citizenship were cause for anxiety among Nisei who had lived in Japan during the war, as many of them had either renounced American citizenship or registered for Japanese citizenship during their years in Japan. Nisei like Iva Toguri, who had maintained only American citizenship during the war, were exceedingly rare. Most Nisei in war-time Japan who were not yet registered by their parents as Japanese citizens in the United States had registered (or had been registered) for Japanese citizenship after moving to Japan, for reasons such as school enrollment or to receive ra-tions.[5] Some had renounced their American citizenship during the war years to avoid suspicion or harassment by special police. Others had surrendered it (knowingly or unknowingly) by serving in Japan's armed forces, in government positions, or by voting in elections. Having lost or renounced American citizen-ship, many Nisei wavered in the postwar about whether or not to undertake the application process to regain it.

The citizenship narrative of California-born Nisei Yayoi Cooke demonstrates that the citizenship reversals of Nisei in transwar Japan were governed by the complexities of everyday concerns such as salary, deadlines, and family con-straints—as well as cognitive reflections on wartime actions and emotions. In a

1978 interview with historian Marlene Mayo, Yayoi recalled that at her family home in Yamanashi just before the attack on Pearl Harbor, she and her siblings received a letter from the American Consulate in Yokohama informing them that they faced a choice: sail home to America or lose their US citizenship. They ignored the letter. During the years of war, Yayoi sided with the Japanese and earnestly hoped Japan would win the war against the United States. She had no intention of returning to America, where, she said, she and her siblings had faced and would surely continue to face discrimination.

When the war ended, Yayoi was warned that if she ever hoped to return to the United States, she should petition to regain her American citizenship by registering with the consulate in Yokohama. As a further enticement, American citizenship would guarantee Yayoi, who was an occupation employee, higher pay and access to transportation privileges unavailable to non-US citizens. Reinstatement as a US citizen would ensure for Yayoi shopping privileges at the commissary and Post Exchange (PX), as well as a "branch civilian" job available to Allied citizens only. Drawn by these practical benefits, Yayoi undertook the process of reinstatement, formally re-establishing herself as a dual citizen. For Yayoi, the reinstatement process lasted for a relatively short two months. Even her brother who had served in the Japanese army was able to regain his citizenship by demonstrating that he had not volunteered but had rather been drafted into service. A few years later, when SCAP was downsizing on staffing, Yayoi found a different job as a typist with the Decorations and Awards Division of GHQ. By that time, in the wake of the San Francisco Peace Treaty, the Japanese government "didn't like the Niseis having dual citizenship." When they required that Yayoi make a choice between her two nations, Yayoi opted for American citizenship.[6]

Despite her distaste for American GI indulgence in the face of abject poverty of the Japanese population, and despite her professed wartime loyalty to Japan, Yayoi chose American citizenship over Japanese citizenship. She framed her decision to reinstate citizenship—and eventually to move back to the United States—as a decision not based on race, nor on a sense of loyalty or cultural identity, but rather on the practical input factors of economic considerations and shifting hegemonic preferences in occupied Japan. Her citizenship decisions—which many might assess as establishing and affirming the dominant direction of her allegiance to a nation-state—were in reality the result of practical life concerns and the force of administrative policies. Yayoi's self-representational shift from collaborating with the Japanese war effort to collaborating with SCAP is evidence of the unchangingly performative character of allegiance.

Many Nisei in postwar Japan who sought reinstatement recognized, like Yayoi, that American citizenship provided access to significant advantages in the era of the Allied occupation. The postwar letters of Mary Kimoto are full of anxieties over citizenship reinstatement, attesting to the draw of tangible benefits implicated in Nisei citizenship battles in postwar Japan. For example, in a letter to her friend Kay Oka dated July 20, 1946, Mary raved covetously about the reinstatement successes of her Nisei coworkers, fretting over the urgency of her own reinstatement:

> Both Peggy and Amy have their citizenship papers now! I'm happy for them, but very envious too. Amy got hers a month ago, and she didn't say a word to me about it! I asked them why didn't they get civil service jobs, and Amy says, "Things don't come as quickly as that!" So, they are no better off than we are. Except that they can write to the States. Just think, Kay, by the time we get our papers, there will be so many applicants for civil service jobs that we won't get any. Listen, if you see any opportunities to put in an application or get any pull, please let's get in on it. I'll be darned if I'll continue to work as a foreign national after I get my papers! Just think of all the privileges we are missing out on— pay in dollars, PX supplies, commissary, mail, and the rights of an American citizen. But by the time we get our papers, if I can go back, I'll take the first boat home. I'm sick and tired of this place.[7]

Subsequent letters reveal that Mary successfully regained her citizenship through a lengthy application process in Yokohama. She gushed to her California-based friend Miye Yamasaki in California in a letter on August 30, 1946:

> I must tell you the good news—my registration is over with, and my papers will come through in two or three months, and I can go home anytime after that. That is, if everything goes as it should. Look, Miye, I can hardly believe that my dreams are about to come true! And sooner than I dared expect, too! They asked me if I wanted to go back next month, can you imagine! It took my breath away. I do want to go as soon as I can, yet common sense tells me I should stay for at least half a year after I get my papers in order to not go back broke. O, the whole country will be mine after I have a War Department civil service job! And as soon as I get my papers, I can write as much as I want! So it won't be long now.[8]

Mary's enthusiasm over her reinstatement affirms what she values most about American citizenship in her current situation: the prospect of sailing home to her family in California, access to a civil service job, and freedom to use the APO mail service to her heart's content. Despite the language she might have used to appeal to the officials at the consulate, nowhere in her letters do we see expressions of loyalty or patriotism as directing the action she took to regain American citizenship. Mary's performance of Americanness, including her decision to don the mantle of American citizenship, is evidence of assimilation inspired by American hegemony in postwar Japan.

Many Nisei who had renounced or lost their American citizenship during the war scrambled to regain it in the postwar for fear that if they did not reestablish US citizenship quickly, they may forever lose their chance of returning to America. Muriel Chiyo Tanaka of Hawai'i, for example, who had served as a monitor for Japan during the war, was working as a liaison between the Japanese government and the occupation when she received notice from the US government. It said, "all of us working for the government, Japanese government . . . who wanted to reestablish American citizenship should leave this country, Japan, by October 15 or something. They gave us a deadline. So we all got on the *General Gordon* ship to come home."[9] Muriel had lost her citizenship during the war, and the process of investigating the details of her eligibility for reinstatement took two years. After a lengthy effort, though, she was able to return to the United States on the troop ship *General Gordon,* along with nineteen other Nisei who had regained their citizenship at the same time.

For many Nisei petitioning for reinstatement of citizenship, a voyage back to America held the promise of a better life. Bombing had leveled the landscape of postwar Japan, obliterating houses, buildings, and factories in all major cities save Kyoto. Unemployment was soaring, and food shortages necessitated that the government extend the wartime rationing system, which granted each person one-third of the calories served as a minimum to American soldiers.[10] Many practical-minded Nisei endeavored to reclaim the American citizenship that would provide access to a higher standard of living in America, regardless of when (if ever) they intended to return to the United States.

The factors influencing Nisei who decided not to return to the United States are equally complicated and situational. For these Nisei, too, environmental and situational elements in everyday life charted this decision. Benefits of American citizenship or of returning to America were outweighed by situational factors that made life in Japan the more practical choice. Morio Morishima, for example, who had sailed from Washington to Hiroshima at the age of five and had been drafted into the Japanese army, wanted to return to the United States, but he had married a Japanese woman and started a family in Japan, so he never took the steps necessary to regain citizenship (although as a draftee, he would have been eligible).[11] Kay Nishimura, who had also been conscripted into the Japanese military, regained his US citizenship in 1952, but by then, he had a good job in Japan and was in love with a Japanese woman, so he chose to live in Japan rather than return to the United States.[12] Just as Yayoi, Mary, and Muriel reinstated their US citizenship and returned to America because of certain situational factors, so, too, did Morio and Kay elect to remain in Japan because it was the practical alternative. These Nisei were making sense of their environment, goals, and options. The aspiration to survive and thrive charted the course for their behavior in the postwar as it had during the war years.

And yet, in the social milieu of transwar Japan, loyalty was considered a conviction, a dominant force guiding a person's behavior. In struggles for reclamation of citizenship, Nisei highlighted their steady loyalty by emphasizing a lack of volition in matters of wartime participation and renunciation. They insisted that their actions should not be understood as demonstrations of strayed loyalty but rather as evidence of coercion. In addition to Nisei who navigated paper trails and red tape to regain citizenship at the American Consulate in Yokohama, hundreds of other postwar Nisei citizenship battles were waged through lengthy court proceedings, often on a case-by-case basis, such as this example reported in the *Pacific Citizen:*

> The U.S. citizenship of Mrs. Kikuyo Ichiki, 46, of Aiea, Oahu, was restored by a Federal Court ruling of Judge Delbert E. Metzger last week. Mrs. Ichiki in 1949 was denied a passport by consular authorities in Japan because she had voted in the 1946 general elections. Judge Metzger found the Oahu-born Nisei woman was coerced into voting through fear of losing her rations if she did not cast a ballot.[13]

As this report suggests, coercion had to be the chief alibi of Nisei collaborators, simply because coercion was the only viable exoneration posited by the American authorities in administrative policies and legal proceedings. If they could sufficiently depict themselves as victims of Japan's wartime systems of conscription, forced labor, and fear mongering, Nisei renunciants could succeed in regaining lost citizenship. In so arguing, Nisei were attempting to convince the legal authorities that their loyalty had never been misplaced, despite what their actions might have been. The Japanese American Citizens League (JACL) even established an office in Tokyo to assist Nisei who desired to nullify citizenship registrations made under duress, helping with paperwork and with bringing suits in Japanese courts.[14] Nisei could achieve reinstatement by proving that they had been forced unwillingly into service, government jobs, or voting in elections. Even former imperial soldiers were able to reinstate citizenship and return to the United States by demonstrating that they had not volunteered but had instead been conscripted.

Iwao Peter Sano, a US-born Nisei soldier in the imperial Japanese army, first concealed the truth of his American birth from Russian captors during his three-year stint as a POW in Siberia. Eventually, though, Peter was able to regain his American citizenship by demonstrating that he had been conscripted into the army—that he had no choice in the matter. When he was finally interviewed in order to reestablish American citizenship, the Nisei interpreter conducting his interview sought evidence of volition amid coercion: "[They asked,] Did you re-sist? Did you try to escape?"[15] Peter could supply them with no examples of resis-tance. Instead, his defense rested on demonstration of coercion. His examiners sought indication of steady allegiance to America: proof of loyalty despite his coerced military service. This emphasis on volition and coercion in matters of citizenship demonstrates the prevalent belief that an individual's actions are de-termined by a sense of loyalty—in this case, to his race or to his birth nation. By demonstrating coercion, Peter could prove that despite his Japanese race, his loy-alty to the United States had never been misplaced.

For adult Nisei men, the question of citizenship reinstatement was straight-forward: had they been drafted, or had they volunteered? By proving coercion, these Nisei soldiers could make a case that they had never sought to engage in the fight against America, and that their true allegiance to the United States had not wavered. For Nisei women, who had not been forcibly drafted into service, evi-dence of coercion was less distinct. And yet, because the women of imperial Ja-pan were broadly painted by occupation propaganda as victims of centuries of feudalistic patriarchy, wartime collaboration of all Japanese women was essen-tially deemed coerced—until proven volitional. In this sense, the smiling gusto with which Iva Toguri reenacted her propaganda broadcasting before the cam-eras of American journalists (rather than her US citizenship) was her downfall. She demonstrated intentionality, enthusiasm, and satisfaction in her work as a pro-Japan propagandist. In the eyes of the American public, she was not the weak woman acquiescing to distasteful work in order to survive the horrors of war. She was instead the wily, disloyal seductress whose convictions of allegiance to Japan had set the course for her traitorous behavior.

According to Iva Toguri biographer Masayo Duus, by the end of the consul-ate applications and the court battles, about half of the "stranded Nisei" in Japan were ultimately able to return to America.[16] These Nisei were granted reinstate-ment and return to America, because they could prove that they had never of their own volition acted disloyally to the United States. Underage Nisei school-children pledging self-sacrifice to the Japanese emperor, female Nisei "victims of the patriarchy" forced to work in weapons factories and intelligence offices, and even Nisei soldiers conscripted to die in a war against America—never had the light of their true loyalty wavered. Vilified instead was "Tokyo Rose" Iva Toguri, who had maintained her US citizenship throughout the war, but had (it was argued) wantonly misled and demoralized American soldiers on the airwaves of Radio Tokyo for "traitor's pay" of one hundred *yen* a month.[17] Her actions were judged as proof of her disloyalty to the United States. No thought was given to the prospect that her actions, too, were also shaped by factors beyond her control—by the forces of economic necessity, by incessant agitation by the special police, and even by the regulatory power of the physical environment.

Tokyo Rose is the American "traitor" who typically comes to mind in conversations about World War II collaborators against the United States. But as this book has described in detail, there were thousands of other American Nisei who worked for the Japanese war effort against America during the war. The circumstances of their nationality differ—some were dual citizens, some (like Iva) had only American citizenship, and some renounced their American citizenship—but they were nevertheless mobilized against the country of their birth, or less abstractly, against their friends and even blood relatives still living in the United States. As the stories of this garden of Nisei "Roses" represent, in matters of collaboration, there is no distinct and primary "volition" as opposed to coercion. Rather, Nisei collaborative actions—in support of Japan during the war and in support of the United States during the occupation—demonstrate that individual actions and behaviors are not necessarily first checked against convictions such as loyalty. Instead, so much of behavior is precognitive, regulated by situational realities and preferences reinforced by soft propaganda in the environment.

Accusations of treason—of disloyalty to a certain cause—hinge too heavily on an assumption that an individual precalculates her every action. We wrongly seek a process of conscious decision-making assumed to underlie and even precede collaboration. We vilify an individual for her treasonous *choices,* and we exonerate her if she can demonstrate that coercion rendered her unable to act the way she *wished* to act. The presumed connection between intention and collaboration during World War II continues to pollute the stories we tell about the war as lived. For example, administrative officials, military figures, artists, and leading intellectuals in Japanese-occupied Korea whose wartime actions are deemed "pro-Japanese" (*shin-nichi*) are pariahs—their statues desecrated, their names erased from public buildings, and their actions denigrated in Korean national textbooks.[18] Scholars paint the pro-Japanese actions of colonized Koreans, Manchurians, and Chinese as a sort of calculated ruse. Eric C. Han, for example, scans the history of Chinese residents in wartime Yokohama for evidence of "hidden resistance," suggesting that Chinese in Yokohama participated in pro-Japanese war demonstrations only as a knowing pretense, as a means of self-defense.[19] Collaborative action is automatically implicated in a moral judgment because of the assumption that human action is the result of calculated intention to act in a certain way. When we reconsider collaborative action as the process of an individual subconsciously navigating her environment and quelling affective anxieties, we distance ourselves from moral judgment, and we gain a better understanding of the power of propaganda—and of the haze through which collective memory can distort historical fact.

Volition and Coercion

Nisei who had spent the years of war "stranded" in Japan were prompted by media and social discourse to distance themselves from their wartime activities as much as possible by obfuscating and compensating for their wartime actions, and by demonstrating the victimhood that aligned with SCAP's narrative of the oppressed people of feudal Japan. They were provided with the script of coercion as the primary avenue for regaining their citizenship or their self-worth in the years after Japan's defeat. Coercion is the opposite of volition, and volition points to a willing intention to be disloyal to the United States—unredeemable and even punishable in the eyes of the U.S courts reviewing treason and renunciation cases in the postwar era. But as the chapters in this book have emphasized, there are situational and environmental factors that influence actions in a moment, and a very small percentage of human behavior is inspired by conscious elaboration.

Claims of coercion "saved" many Nisei who battled to regain citizenship lost either by renunciation, by serving Japan's war effort, or by voting in Japanese elections. Obvious volition, on the other hand, could be a Nisei's downfall. Such was the case for Iva Toguri: she volunteered herself as "the one and original 'Tokyo Rose,'" she smiled for publicity shots by a Radio Tokyo microphone just weeks after Japan's surrender, and even throughout her trial, her defense team (led by famed civil rights attorney Wayne Collins) attempted to exonerate her by arguing that her broadcasts were not damaging to morale, that she and her POW co-hosts worked together subversively to render the broadcasts ineffective, that she was one of many female broadcasters on Radio Tokyo, and that she remained loyal and refused to renounce her US citizenship despite pressure from Japanese authorities to do so. Perhaps a resounding through-line of coercion would have saved Tokyo Rose from conviction. Instead, coercion was just one of the defense's many arguments, fading into the background among the other attempts to exonerate her, and contradictory statements from the government's prosecution witnesses emphasized that Iva had not been coerced but had delivered the broadcasts willingly.

Amid the postwar rhetoric of the Japanese populace as victims of a militaristic, feudalistic imperial government, those who had spent the years of war in Japan—including Nisei who could have presented potential targets for treason trials—were presumed "coerced" until bared as having acted of their own volition. Such was the fate of Iva, and such, too, was the fate of Tomoya Kawakita, the only other Nisei tried for treason after World War II. Tomoya, a dual citizen, had spent the war years as an interpreter at a mining and metals company in Japan that used POWs from an adjoining camp as laborers. After Japan's surrender, he served the Americans as an interpreter at the same mining plant for a short period, and in December 1945 he applied at the US Consulate in Tokyo to renew his American passport, explaining that he had registered as a Japanese citizen under duress during the war. He received his passport the following year and sailed home to California, where a former POW later randomly sighted him at a department store, leading to his indictment for thirteen counts of treason, with each count representing a separate incident of brutality toward POWs.

At the trial, Tomoya's defense team focused on the status of Tomoya's citizenship during the war, emphasizing that he was acting as a Japanese citizen during the war and not as an American, and also that his actions lacked the "element of secrecy and cunning" that would qualify as treachery.[20] The prosecution team countered that American citizenship could not be turned off and on like "a faucet," and that the defendant had misled the US Consulate when applying for a passport renewal in 1945—he had not been coerced but had voluntarily registered as Japanese during the war.[21] Testimony from POWs painted a picture of Tomoya as embittered, as taking advantage of his position of authority to engage in gratuitous acts of violence, taking satisfaction while doing so. However Tomoya may have tried to blend in with the rest of the population in postwar California, these former POWs saw him only for who he was in their memory: the cruel, pro-Japan interrogator who had voluntarily gone overboard in committing gratuitous violence against Americans. Indeed, presiding judge William C. Mathes speculated that Tomoya would have "willingly blown up our Pacific Fleet and disclosed to the Japanese the secrets of our atomic bomb." In his decision, Judge Mathes pointed out that by contrast, there were also hundreds of "good" Japanese Americans, including the members of the 442nd Regimental Combat Team and the 100th Infantry Battalion and who died for their nation.[22] Tomoya, depicted in depositions by former POWs as particularly cruel, was convicted of treason in 1952 and sentenced to death. President Eisenhower later commuted the sentence to life imprisonment, and by an order by President Kennedy in 1963,

Tomoya Kawakita was released on the condition that he never return to the United States.[23]

Surely, thousands of other Nisei who had spent the years of war in Japan might have been targeted for their efforts against the United States, if coercion had not served as the negation of treason. Instead, their legacy faded into the narrative of the Japanese people forced to cooperate with an overbearing, militaristic, hyper-suspicious government. Their fates were further shaped by the flavor of growing national embarrassment over Japanese internment in America during the war, and by the triumphant legacy of patriotic Japanese Americans who had supported America's cause despite internment and discrimination, such as Judge Mathes's "good" Nisei who served in the US Army. The thousands of other Nisei who did collaborate with the war effort were not put on trial for treason; whatever public disdain they may have faced, they were not rounded up by occupation authorities as treason suspects with a burden to prove coercion and disprove volition. Instead, as the chapters in Part Three described, SCAP relied on many such Nisei to help the transition into Allied occupation go as smoothly as possible.

Over the years, the legacies of Nisei collaborators in Japan (Tokyo Rose and Tomoya Kawakita aside) have melted into the history of the total war mobilization of all Japanese people. As Japan remembers important anniversaries of the end of the war, there have been a handful of television specials and museum exhibitions that share the history of Nisei in wartime Japan. There have also been a few casual gatherings organized by Nisei who had lived in Japan during the war, such as "The Gathering for Nikkei Niseis Residing in Wartime Japan," held in Shibuya in October 2004. However, such reunions were scarce and did not materialize until several decades after Japan's defeat.[24] Ask the average Japanese person today about Japanese Americans living in Japan during World War II, and you are likely to be met with confusion and denial.

The enduring legend of Tokyo Rose suggests that in questions of treason, determining whether the individual acted of her own volition is of paramount concern. Did her loyalty waver, or was she coerced?—these are the two options, posited as polar opposites. As it took shape in the postwar treason trials of Japanese Americans, voluntarily pursuing disloyal action constituted a crime of treason. What should be made of volition when assessing an individual's actions as treason? The factors that subconsciously shape action—soft propaganda in the physical and discursive environment, modes of discipline, economic and physical realities, and the demands of human relationships—are tempered, surely, by the cognitive will of the individual as she moves through the world. As humans navigating our environments, we are not solely propelled

「戦時下、滞日・日系二世の集い」2004年10月、東京渋谷にて

Figure C.1. "The Gathering for Nikkei Niseis Residing in Wartime Japan,"
October 2004 Reunion in Shibuya. Courtesy Kadoike Hiroshi.

by soft propaganda and modes of discipline; we do make cognitive choices, and
we do identify those choices as tied to our own free will. But as the chapters of
Unthinking Collaboration have emphasized, volition and coercion in wartime
and postwar Japan were not so black and white. Propaganda, rituals, and mnemonic sites that influence preferences and taboos; segregation, surveillance,
and physical mobilization that discipline the body; threats of physical violence
that cow a human struggling to survive; and situational and economic realities
that shape behavior—these are additional forces that must be considered when
understanding collaborative actions, when considering the texture of coercion
and volition. The goal of this more nuanced understanding of collaboration is
not to absolve Iva Toguri or Tomoya Kawakita of their crimes—nor to con-
demn them of those crimes. It is likewise not to cast suspicion on the thousands
of Nisei in wartime Japan who did contribute to a war effort that targeted the
country of their birth as an enemy. The goal is instead an updated method of
history, one that takes into account the power of the subconscious brain to navigate the environment and propel a historical subject to action, one that considers volition as merely the deceptive tip of the iceberg—a neat story told about a
decision that masks depths of additional forces shaping behavior. To see collaboration as solely voluntary is to sail blindly past myriad access points to a

historical milieu lurking below the surface of a seemingly simple story. A more nuanced understanding of collaborative behavior as deeply implicated in a web of complicated concerns and psychological forces emphasizes that a historical subject's actions are shaped not just by free will, but also by the power of his physical and discursive surroundings.

In practice, loyalty is the story told *about* behavior rather than the sole driving force that directs behavior. In collaboration, the performance of loyalty itself has a tendency toward charade: it continues even when both sides seem cognizant of the farce. To collaborate is to participate in the performance of assimilation. This may be either quite obviously coerced or seemingly volitional. Either way, multiple input factors (and not simple loyalty convictions) inspire the collaboration and draft the script of the performance. Factors in the environment and in social discourse compel individuals on conscious and subconscious levels to edit their behavior. In considering all of the layers that inspire collaborative actions, it is possible to see human behavior as embedded in the realities of a historical moment. This reimagining of collaboration offers a more thorough understanding of treason and loyalty—to race, to nation, to religion, and even to ideology.

The discursive projections of Nisei considered in *Unthinking Collaboration* demonstrate that the propaganda shaping Nisei behavior during World War II and the occupation period spans more than just the eleven years of 1941–1952. The self-representation of Nisei as alternately "Japanese" or "American" is the product of several environmental factors: the exclusionary flavor of Japanese American networks in pre-World War II America; the pointed connectedness to both Japan and America in Nisei daily life; the pressures of cultural ambassadorship expectations; the struggles of confronting daily life as a member of a problematized category of society; methods of discipline; and the legacy of Nisei loyalty or duplicity as remembered in the postwar period. Nisei were told by some authority figures that they could (and should) play the part of the Japanese and the American. They were also told that they could (and should) hide or stifle certain characteristics. Therefore, life as a Nisei in the years leading up to, during, and after World War II was an exercise in cultural performance—of complicated formulas of costume changes, scripted lines, and choreography designed to approximate "Japaneseness" or "Americanness," according to the circumstances of the setting and the audience.

A reconceptualization of collaboration—as a performance subconsciously and consciously cultivated by multiple layers of discipline and self-regulation—provides a method through which to unpack complicated concepts too often imagined as monolithic: loyalty and treason, coercion and volition, and even identity. This rethinking extends to the assimilative self-regulation by members of colonized races, religions, nation-states, and ideologies. It also extends to include loyalty or treason to a subaltern culture, as seen in contemporary exercises of multi-ethnic nation-building in countries like China, with its diverse ethnic minority cultures.

Because society imagines behavior as a manifestation of loyalty and morality rather than a performance inspired by subconscious assessments of the environment, the source of collaboration is misunderstood. Contemporary efforts to prevent extinction of minor cultures at the hand of mainstream assimilation are ineffective. Until we cleave action from direct elision with volition in our understanding of assimilation, until we disentangle treason from its connotation of loyalty negotiated via race or the nation-state form, and until we strip "collaboration" of its inherent moral judgment, we join the conversation a step too late. We become modern-day Admiral Stirlings, blustering about innate loyalties that will, if merely recognized, predict which options an individual will choose to pursue. To understand collaboration, we should focus instead on the everyday realities an individual faces: the environmental and social preferences in the environment that, like magnets, draw human beings toward certain actions and self-representations. This sharper historical focus suggests that we should not seek any bedrock of true loyalty that inspired the collaborative behavior of American Nisei in transwar Japan. Their moments of collaboration are, rather, access points through which we may track changing preferences in transwar Japanese and American society.

This book was originally a quest to understand the wartime experiences of American Nisei who were mobilized for the Japanese war effort against the country of their birth. Which face of Iva Toguri was the charlatan: the ever-loyal American citizen silently sabotaging imperial Japan's propaganda efforts, or the diminutive Tokyo resident willing to use her fluent American English to demoralize the Yankee troops in the Pacific, or neither—or both? What were the factors that motivated Nisei to cooperate so flexibly with the Japanese war effort during World War II and with the Allied occupation after Japan's defeat? And how could strikingly similar wartime actions on behalf of the Empire of Japan land Iva Toguri languishing in prison and Nisei like Muriel Tanaka smiling at Hawaiian shores from the deck of the homebound *General Gordon?* The answer to these questions must be sought in a reunderstanding of collaboration, one that takes into consideration the other psychological and situational factors that influence behavior. The history of Nisei in Japan during World War II does tell a story about loyalty—a story not of shifting loyalties in given moments of action or inaction, but rather of the shifting definition of loyalty, ever defined in the moment of *judgment,* and not in the moment of action.

Epilogue

I remember a conversation I shared on a train platform in 2015 with a Japanese scholar who also works on the history of Nisei in wartime Japan. We could not seem to agree on a term I was using in Japanese to describe the people we were both researching. I called Nisei in wartime Japan *tekikokujin* (敵国人), meaning "enemy alien." It was proving difficult to move on to deeper conversations about Nisei life during the war, because this scholar was so hung up on my usage of the term. "They were Japanese," he insisted. "Maybe they were American, too, but they were also Japanese, so they could not possibly be called *tekikokujin*."

"But what about Nisei who only held American citizenship?" I protested. "They were *only* American citizens. After Pearl Harbor, Americans became enemy aliens. These Nisei became enemy aliens, too, just like the white Americans who were interned or put on house arrest."

He looked at me incredulously. "But they were Japanese. They were not enemy aliens." His train came, and I was traveling in the opposite direction.

To be sure, many of the Nisei who spent the years of World War II in Japan were dual citizens whose status as enemy nationals could easily be disputed. And thousands of those Nisei were the children of *dekasegi* immigrant families who had long before moved home to Japan. Though they had a stint of American experience in their personal backgrounds, they were fully assimilated to Japanese culture, not as a result of the sustained performance like those of the Nisei youths I discuss in *Unthinking Collaboration* but because they had moved back early enough or had lived in America for such a short time or in such household environments that they had not fully developed a dual identity.

But as the stories of Nisei whose narratives fill the pages of this book reflect, many Nisei *did* struggle with dual cultural identities. And many Nisei in wartime Japan had never been registered officially as Japanese. At the time of the attack on Pearl Harbor, they were only American citizens, at least according to their passports. But to the Japanese authorities in wartime Japan—and evidently, even to some Japanese people today—the Japanese blood in their veins granted them membership in the Japanese citizenry, whether that membership was real (official citizenship) or imagined ("no, they could not possibly be called enemy aliens").

In Japan, the emphasis on Japanese heritage as extending to members of the Japanese diaspora with Japanese blood—especially though the patrilineal bloodline, and especially if that blood is 100 percent Japanese—has complicated the legacy of Nisei who supported the war effort in Japan during World War II. Perhaps it is one of the reasons that the complicated history of this group of individuals is so little-known, in both Japan and America. Puck Brecher's history of foreign civilians in wartime Japan (*Honored and Dishonored Guests*) is a welcome step in the direction of English-language scholarship that draws attention to the ways questions of race and citizenship were conflated in Japan during the war. But scouring the Japanese-language tourist guidebooks and signposts in Karuizawa—my favorite Japanese town and a major hub for foreigners during World War II—produces only a few phrases mentioning the history of any enemy nationals (or even stateless or Axis nationals) who found themselves in Karuizawa on or after December 8, 1941. In Hakone, another hub, I found no traces of this history at all.

Prisoners of war. Nisei soldiers fighting for America. The scourge of the forced internment of persons of Japanese ancestry in the US. And Tokyo Rose. These are the threads of history that constitute the dominant story of Nisei and other foreigners in Japan during World War II, as that story is known today. *Unthinking Collaboration* is an effort to approach collaboration in a more nuanced way, to question methods of history that place primary emphasis on free will, and to reimagine loyalty and treason. But it is also an effort to draw attention to the sheer existence of this thread of history in the Nisei story—to the poignant stories of Nisei who, for whatever reason, found themselves on Japanese soil when war broke out between their two nations. It is my hope that others will be inspired by the experiences of these Nisei—the way they navigated their environment, and the way they framed their experiences as time wore on—to investigate the formation of loyalty and identity in multicultural individuals, and to dig further into the remarkable history of individuals trapped on one side of a conflict that implicated their birth nation and the nation of their ancestors.

Notes

Introduction

1 Historian Paul Spickard estimates that 35,420 Nisei were living in Japan in 1942. "Twice Immigrants: Kibei in America and Japan and America, 1910–1950" (paper presented to Japanese American Experience conference, Williamette University, Salem, Oregon, September 18, 1998). Spickard's calculations are based on research and statistics appearing in D. S. Thomas, C. Kikuchi, and J. Sakoda, *Japanese American Evacuation and Resettlement*, vol. 2, *The Salvage* (Berkeley: University of California Press, 1952), 580–591. Historian W. Puck Brecher's estimates are a more modest 20,000. See W. Puck Brecher, *Honored and Dishonored Guests: Westerners in Wartime Japan* (Cambridge, Massachusetts: The Harvard University Asia Center, 2017).

2 Notable works focusing on Nisei military contributions include: Brenda L. Moore, *Serving Our Country: Japanese American Women in the Military during World War II* (New Brunswick, New Jersey: Rutgers University Press, 2003), James C. McNaughton, *Nisei Linguists: Japanese Americans in the Military Intelligence Service during World War II* (Washington, DC: Department of the Army, 2006), and Masayo Duus, *Unlikely Liberators: The Men of the 100th and 442nd* (Honolulu: University of Hawai'i Press, 2006).

3 For studies of journalists, see Yuji Ichioka, "The Meaning of Loyalty: The Case of Kazumaro Buddy Uno," in *Before Internment: Essays in Prewar Japanese American History,* ed. Gordon H. Chang and Eiichiro Azuma (Stanford: Stanford University (Press, 2006), Greg Robinson, "Nisei Journalists and the Occupation of China: Buddy Uno and Bill Hosokawa Compared—Part 3 of 3," Discover Nikkei, May 4, 2012, http://www.discovernikkei.org/en /journal/2012/5/4/4401/. For scholarship on postwar Nisei, see Edward Tang, *From Confinement to Containment: Japanese/American Arts during the Early Cold War* (Philadelphia: Temple University Press, 2019), Caroline Chung Simpson, *An Absent Presence: Japanese Americans in Postwar American Culture, 1945–1960* (Durham, North Carolina: Duke University Press, 2001), Greg Robinson, *After Camp: Portraits in Midcentury Japanese American Life and Politics.* (Berkeley: University of California Press, 2012), Christine Reiko Yano, *Crowning the Nice Girl: Gender, Ethnicity, and Culture in Hawai'i's Cherry Blossom Festival* (Honolulu: University of Hawai'i Press, 2006), and Christine Reiko Yano, *Airborne Dreams: "Nisei" Stewardesses and Pan American World Airways* (Durham: Duke University Press, 2011).

4 For biographies of Iva Toguri, see Masayo Duus, *Tokyo Rose, Orphan of the Pacific* (Tokyo: Kodansha International, 1983), Frederick Phelps Close, *Tokyo Rose/An American Patriot: A Dual Biography* (Maryland: Scarecrow, 2010), Russell Warren Howe, *The Hunt for Tokyo Rose* (Lanham, Maryland: Madison Books, 1990), and a study from a legal perspective: Yasuhide Kawashima, *The Tokyo Rose Case: Treason on Trial* (Lawrence, Kansas: University Press of Kansas, 2013).

5 Masayo Duus, *Tokyo Rose: Orphan of the Pacific* (Tokyo: Kodansha International, 1979), 46–47, 51.

6 Frederick Phelps Close, *Tokyo Rose/An American Patriot: A Dual Biography* (Lanham, Maryland: Scarecrow, 2010), 90.

7 Iva and Felipe wed in April of 1945. Felipe was three-quarters Japanese, but because of patrilineal citizenship policies in Japan at the time, his nationality was based on that of his (half-Japanese) father, a Portuguese national. Felipe was raised in Yokohama, spoke fluent English, and was also proficient in spoken Japanese. Iva took Felipe's surname (d'Aquino), but the couple divorced in 1980 after decades of estrangement (Duus, *Tokyo Rose*, 61). I have chosen to use Iva's maiden name (Toguri) throughout this book.

8 Michael Jin, "Beyond Two Homelands: Migration and Transnationalism of Japanese Americans in the Pacific, 1930–1955" (PhD diss., University of California, Santa Cruz, 2013), 215.

9 "Tokyo Rose: Victim of Propaganda," *Biography*, A & E Networks, first aired August 9, 1995, 44 minutes.

10 Naoko Shibusawa, "Femininity, Race and Treachery: How 'Tokyo Rose' Became a Traitor to the United States after the Second World War," *Gender & History* 22, no. 1 (2010): 178.

11 Yuji Ichioka, "The Meaning of Loyalty: The Case of Kazumaro Buddy Uno."

12 Brad Hunter, "Kamloops Kid: Treason Treated with a Rope," *Toronto Sun*, 4 November 2018.

13 "Four Torturers of POW's Given Prison Sentences," *Nippon Times*, 5 March 1948, "More War Suspects Received at Sugamo," *Nippon Times*, 22 April 1946.

14 Close, *Tokyo Rose/An American Patriot*, 461, cf. *Opinion*, U.S. Court of Appeals for the Ninth Circuit, *Iva Ikuko Toguri D'Aquino v. United States of America*, No. 12,383, October 10, 1951, 11.

15 Suk-Jung Han, "On the Question of Collaboration in South Korea," *The Asia-Pacific Journal* 6, no. 7 (July 2008).

16 Timothy Brook, *Collaboration: Japanese Agents and Local Elites in Wartime China* (Cambridge, Massachusetts: Harvard University Press, 2005), 2, 7, 125, 245.

17 David Franks, "The Neuroscience of Emotions," in *Handbook of the Sociology of Emotions*, ed. Jan Stets and Jonathan H. Turner (Boston: Springer US, 2006), 51.

18 David Joel Steinberg, *Philippine Collaboration in World War II* (Ann Arbor: University of Michigan Press, 1967), vii.

19 Marc Bloch, *The Historian's Craft*, Peter Putnam, trans. (New York: Random House, 1953).

20 The video interviews of the Densho Digital Repository were conducted by Densho volunteers and staff members in the 1990s and early 2000s and are indexed by topic, location, and chronology. I focused on the interviews of fifty-two Japanese American individuals who had lived in Japan either before, during, or after World War II. Historian Marlene J. Mayo's oral histories were conducted in the late 1970s and focus on SCAP organization and policies. Similar themes emerge in the interviews of Columbia's Occupation of Japan Project, which were conducted mostly in the early 1960s. Tomi Knaefler's interviews were conducted in 1966 for a commemorative edition of the Honolulu Star-Bulletin. The interviews I conducted myself (some in person, some by phone) took place in both Japan and the United States between August 2013 and July 2015.

21 Jonathan E. Abel, *Redacted: The Archives of Censorship in Transwar Japan* (Berkeley: University of California Press, 2012), 18. See also the work of Andrew Gordon, most notably

"Consumption, Leisure and the Middle Class in Transwar Japan," *Social Science Japan Journal* 10, no. 1 (April 2007): 1–21.

22 For deeper discussions of cultural assimilation in the context of colonization, immigration, and race studies, see for example: Bill Ashcroft, Gareth Griffiths, and Helen Tiffin, *Post-Colonial Studies: The Key Concepts*, 2nd ed. (London: Routledge, 2007) and its references. See also Mark Caprio, *Japanese Assimilation Policies in Colonial Korea, 1910–1945* (Seattle: University of Washington Press, 2009), 6–48.

Chapter 1. Sojourner, Alien, Ambassador

1 Muriel Chiyo Tanaka Onishi, interview by Tom Ikeda, June 2, 2009, *Densho: The Japanese American Legacy Project*.

2 This understanding of the internalization and reproduction of norms is informed in particular by the work on gender norms by Julia C. Bullock, *The Other Women's Lib: Gender and Body in Japanese Women's Fiction* (Honolulu: University of Hawai'i Press, 2010) and Judith Butler, *Bodies That Matter: On the Discursive Limits of "Sex"* (New York: Routledge, 1993).

3 Monica Sone, *Nisei Daughter* (Boston: Little, Brown and Company, 1953), 40.

4 Paul Spickard, *Japanese Americans: The Formation and Transformations of an Ethnic Group* (New Brunswick, New Jersey: Rutgers University Press, 1996), 30–31.

5 Yuji Ichioka, *The Issei: The World of the First Generation Japanese Immigrants, 1885–1924* (New York: The Free Press, 1988), 207.

6 Spickard, *Japanese Americans*, 22.

7 Suzuki Jōji, *Nihonjin dekasegi imin* (Toyko: Heibonsha, 1992), 64.

8 For a deeper introduction to the history of Japanese immigration from the perspective of Asian American Studies, see these key works: Eiichiro Azuma, *Between Two Empires: Race, History, and Transnationalism in Japanese America* (New York: Oxford University Press, 2005), Yuji Ichioka, *The Issei: The World of the First Generation Japanese Immigrants, 1885–1924* (New York, 1990), Yuji Ichioka, *Before Internment: Essays in Prewar Japanese American History* (Stanford: Stanford University Press, 2006), and Paul Spickard, *Japanese Americans: The Formation and Transformations of an Ethnic Group* (New Brunswick, New Jersey: Rutgers University Press, 2009).

9 Brenda L. Moore, *Serving Our Country: Japanese American Women in the Military during World War II* (New Brunswick, New Jersey: Rutgers University Press, 2003), 35, cf. Joe R. Feagin and Clairece Booher Feagin, *Racial and Ethnic Relations,* 6th ed. (Upper Saddle River, New Jersey: Prentice Hall, 1999), 383.

10 Yamazaki Shunichi, *Hawai dekasegi jinmeibo shimatsuki: Nikkei imin no hyakunen* (Tokyo: Nihon Hōsō Shuppan Kyōkai, 1985), 79.

11 James A. Hirabayashi, "Four Hirabayashi Cousins: A Question of Identity," in *Nikkei in the Pacific Northwest: Japanese Americans and Japanese Canadians in the Twentieth Century,* ed. Louis Fiset and Gail M. Nomura (Seattle: University of Washington Press, 2005), 148.

12 Spickard, *Japanese Americans*, 54. As Spickard notes, connections were less strong (or even virtually non-existent) in other parts of the country where the population of Japanese immigrants was lower and more scattered, such as Texas, Arizona, Alaska, and the East Coast.

13 Sakaguchi Mitsuhiro, *Nihon Amerika iminshi* (Tokyo: Fuji Shuppan, 2001), 127.

14 Rudy Tokiwa, interview by Tom Ikeda and Judy Niizawa, July 2–3, 1998, *Densho: The Japanese American Legacy Project*.

15 Yoshida Ryō, *Amerika Nihonjin imin to Kirisutokyō shakai: Kariforunia Nihonjin imin no haiseki, dōka to E. A. Sutōji* (Tokyo: Nihon Tosho Sentā, 1995), 9–10.

16 Frank Miyamoto, interview by Stephen Fugita, February 26, 1998, *Densho: The Japanese American Legacy Project*.

17 Ibid.

18 Gail Lee Dubrow, Donna Graves, and Karen Cheng, *Sento at Sixth and Main: Preserving Landmarks of Japanese American Heritage* (Seattle: Seattle Arts Commission, 2002), 110–111.

19 Teruko Kumei, "'The Twain Shall Meet' in the Nisei?" in *New Worlds, New Lives: Globalization and People of Japanese Descent in the Americas and from Latin America in Japan,* ed. Lane Ryo Hirabayashi, Akemi Kimura-Yano, and James A. Hirabayashi (Stanford: Stanford University Press, 2002), 111.

20 Noriko Asato, "Americanization vs. Japanese Cultural Maintenance: Analyzing Seattle's Nihongo Tokuhon, 1920," in *Nikkei in the Pacific Northwest: Japanese Americans and Japanese Canadians in the Twentieth Century,* ed. Louis Fiset and Gail M. Nomura (Seattle: University of Washington Press, 2005), 101–108.

21 For further reading on Nisei life in early twentieth-century America, see for example: Bill Hosokawa, *Nisei: The Quiet Americans* (Boulder: University Press of Colorado, 2002), David Yoo, *Growing Up Nisei: Race, Generation, and Culture among Japanese Americans of California, 1924–49* (Urbana: University of Illinois Press, 2000), and Valerie Matsumoto, *City Girls: The Nisei Social World in Los Angeles, 1920–1950* (New York: Oxford University Press, 2014).

22 According to a 1910 census, some four hundred plus Japanese had received naturalization papers in lower federal courts. Ichioka, *The Issei*, 211.

23 Fears of stripped citizenship among Nisei were further supported by the 1928 case of California native Toshiko Inaba, who after sixteen years in Japan was denied reentry to the country of her birth, due to her marriage to a Japanese national. The San Francisco immigration authorities reasoned that her marriage represented a voluntary withdrawal of the young woman's US citizenship in light of the Cable Act of 1922. Anxiety about continued citizenship status among Nisei was further heightened by the actions of anti-immigration activist V. S. McClatchy, who wrote widely that the Japanese government planned to dispatch an army of indoctrinated Nisei living in Japan back to the US to expand Japanese influence there. See Michael Jin, "A Transnational Generation: Japanese Americans in the Pacific before World War II," in *Ritsumeikan Studies in Language and Culture* 21:4 (March 2010), 188–192.

24 Roger Daniels, *The Politics of Prejudice: The Anti-Japanese Movement in California and the Struggle for Japanese Exclusion* (Gloucester, Massachusetts: Peter Smith, 1966), 1.

25 Literally "white person," this term was broadly used in Japanese American communities to refer to all white Americans.

26 Rose Ito Tsunekawa, interview by Tom Ikeda and Steve Fugita, January 26, 2011, *Densho: The Japanese American Legacy Project*.

27 Ichioka, *The Issei*, 176–180.

28 Aiko Herzig-Yoshinaga, interview by Tom Ikeda, July 7, 2009, *Densho: The Japanese American Legacy Project*.

29 David Yoo, *Growing Up Nisei: Race, Generation, and Culture among Japanese Americans of California, 1924–49* (Urbana: University of Illinois Press, 2000), 31.

30 Yuji Ichioka, Gordon H. Chang, and Eiichiro Azuma, *Before Internment: Essays in Prewar Japanese American History* (Stanford: Stanford University Press, 2006), 102, cf. *Japanese American Courier*, April 7, 1928.

31 For more context on changes to Japanese schools, particularly Issei and Japanese efforts to build Japanese spirit and combat perceived delinquency among Nisei, see Eiichiro Azuma, *Between Two Empires*, 122–129, 145–146.

32 For an overview of the discrimination of Japanese language schools in the United States, see Noriko Asato, *Teaching Mikadoism: The Attack on Japanese Language Schools in Hawaii, California, and Washington, 1919–1927* (Honolulu: University of Hawai'i Press, 2006).

33 "Various Measures Planned by Gaimusho to Further American-Japanese Amity," *Japan Times and Mail*, April 8, 1934.

34 Ichioka, *Before Internment*, 101, cf. *Japanese American Courier*, June 3, 1933.

35 At the 1932 Summer Olympics in Los Angeles, Japan won a total of 18 medals (7 gold, 7 silver, and 4 bronze). They boasted a particularly strong showing in swimming events. This unexpected display of athletic prowess was a point of pride for Japanese Americans.

36 Yamashita Sōen, *Nichibei wo tsunagu mono* (Tokyo: Bunseisha, 1938), 266.

37 "Boy Scout Party Reaches Japan: Includes 27 Americans of Nippon Descent," *Japan Times and Mail*, June 20, 1933; "Two US-Born Japanese Boys Help Delegates to Education Parley," *Japan Times and Mail*, August 5, 1935; "Women Lead Japan-America Societies on Pacific Coast," *Japan Times and Mail*, July 27, 1936.

38 Carey McWilliams, *Prejudice: Japanese-Americans: Symbol of Racial Intolerance.* (Boston: Little, Brown, 1944), 314, cf. *Great Northern Daily News*, January 1, 1940.

39 "Pictures for U.S.-Born Japanese to See," *Japan Times and Mail*, May 9, 1939.

Chapter 2. Nisei Child, Problem Child

1 Edward K. Strong, Jr., *The Second-Generation Japanese Problem* (Stanford: Stanford University Press, 1934), 229.

2 "Picnic Shows There Are Many Japanese: South Park Residents Wonder Where All of the 2,000 Brown Men Who Met There Sunday Came From," *Seattle Times*, March 17, 1908, 12.

3 Tsunekawa, interview by Ikeda and Fugita, January 26, 2011, Densho.

4 Marion Tsutakawa Kanemoto, interview by Alice Ito, August 3–4, 2003, *Densho: The Japanese American Legacy Project; John Aiso Oral History*, Marlene J. Mayo Oral Histories, held in the Gordon W. Prange Collection, University of Maryland Libraries.

5 Herzig-Yoshinaga, interview by Ikeda, July 7, 2009, Densho.

6 Kumei, "'The Twain Shall Meet' in the Nisei?" 118.

7 Yamada Tatsumi, *Kaigai dai Nisei mondai* (Tokyo: Kibundō, 1936).

8 Roy Hidemichi Akagi, *The Second Generation Problem: Some Suggestions Toward Its Solution*, Japanese Students' Christian Association Pamphlets No. 1, (New York: J.S.C.A., 1926), 7–9, 13.

9 V. Benet-Martinez, J. Leu, F. Lee, and M. W. Morris, "Negotiating Biculturalism: Cultural Frame Switching in Biculturals with Oppositional Versus Compatible Cultural Identities," *Journal of Cross-Cultural Psychology* 33, no. 5 (2002): 495. See also Jean S. Phinney and Mona Devich-Navarro, "Variations in Bicultural Identification Among African American and Mexican American Adolescents," *Journal of Research on Adolescence* 7, no. 1 (1997): 7.

10 Ichioka, *Before Internment*, 26, cf. *Nichibei Shinbun*, September 6, 13, 1924, cf. *Shin Sekai*, September 13, 1924.

11 Ibid., 57–58, cf. editorial, *Nichibei Shinbun*, February 18, 1925.

12 Ibid., 64, cf. *Nichibei Shinbun*, June 26, 1925.

13 Azuma Eiichirō, "1930 nendai no Tōkyō ni okeru Nikkei Amerikajin Nisei ryūgaku jigyō to Nihon shokuminchi shugi," in *Amerika Nikkei Nisei to ekkyō kyōiku: 1930 nendai wo omo ni shite*, ed. Yoshida Ryō (Kyoto: Dōshisha Daigaku Jinbunkagaku Kenkyūjo, 2012), 36.

14 Ibid., 37, cf. *Kaigai kyōiku kyōkai: Zaidan hōjin kaigai kyōiku yōran*, 1937, 22.

15 Michael Jin, "The Japanese American Transnational Generation: Rethinking the Spatial and Conceptual Boundaries of Asian America," in *The Routledge Handbook of Asian American Studies*, ed. Cindy I-Fen Cheng (New York: Routledge, 2016), 246–259.

16 *Nisei Stories of Wartime Japan*. Thomas Mazawa and Mary McDonald, 2010. 76 minutes.

17 Eiichiro Azuma, *Between Two Empires: Race, History, and Transnationalism in Japanese America* (Oxford: Oxford University Press, 2005), 141.

18 Takemoto Hideo, "Tōkyō YMCA no Nikkei Nisei kyōiku," in *Amerika Nikkei Nisei to ekkyō kyōiku*, 62, cf. *Nichigo Bunka Gakkō Nikkei beijinbu hōkoku* (February–September, 1933).

19 Ichioka, *Before Internment*, 33–34.

20 Kawai Michi, *My Lantern*. Ginza, Tokyo: Kyo Bun Kwan, 1939.

21 *Keisen Jogakuen gojūnen no ayumi* (Tokyo: Keisen Jogakuen, 1979), 115.

22 Mary Kimoto Tomita, *Dear Miye: Letters Home from Japan, 1939–1946*, ed. Robert G. Lee (Stanford: Stanford University Press, 1995), 34.

23 Azuma, "1930 nendai no Tōkyō ni okeru Nikkei Amerikajin Nisei ryūgaku jigyō to Nihon shokuminchi shugi," 38.

24 Azuma, *Between Two Empires*, 136–137.

25 Yamashita Sōen, *Nikkei shimin no Nihon ryūgaku jijō* (Tokyo: Bunseisha, 1935), 227.

26 Tomita, *Dear Miye*, 48, 74.

27 Yamashita, *Nikkei shimin no Nihon ryūgaku jijō*, 239.

28 The Imperial Rescript on Education, a proclamation signed on October 30, 1890, by Emperor Meiji, detailed the principles of education in the Empire of Japan. Students and school faculty were required to memorize the text, and a single slip-up could result in severe punishment.

29 Archie Miyatake, interview by Martha Nakagawa, August 31–September 1, 2010, *Densho: The Japanese American Legacy Project*.

30 Shigenobu Imai, interview by Linda Tamura, October 30, 2013, *Densho: The Japanese American Legacy Project*.

31 Sumiko M. Yamamoto, interview by Tom Ikeda and Barbara Takei, December 8, 2009, *Densho: The Japanese American Legacy Project*.

32 Kanemoto, interview by Ito, August 3–4, 2003, Densho.

33 Tomita, *Dear Miye*, 78.

34 *Yayoi Cooke Oral History*, Marlene J. Mayo Oral Histories, held in the Gordon W. Prange Collection, University of Maryland Libraries.

35 Hiroko Nakashima, interview by Tracy Lai, October 15, 1999, *Densho: The Japanese American Legacy Project*.

36 Nisei Survey Committee, Keisen Girls' School, *The Nisei: A Survey of Their Educational, Vocational, and Social Problems* (Tokyo: Keisen Girls' School, 1939), 29.

37 Yamashita, *Nikkei shimin no Nihon ryūgaku jijō*, 173.
38 Kazuko Uno Bill, interview by Megan Asaka, May 7, 2008, *Densho: The Japanese American Legacy Project*.
39 Sone, *Nisei Daughter*, 99.
40 Bruce T. Kaji, interview by Martha Nakagawa, July 28, 2010, *Densho: The Japanese American Legacy Project*.
41 Herzig-Yoshinaga, interview by Ikeda, July 7, 2009, Densho.
42 Sone, *Nisei Daughter*, 123.
43 Nisei Survey Committee, *The Nisei*, 19–20.
44 Ichioka, *Before Internment*, 26, cf. Miya Sannomiya interview, June 1, 1980, cf. Miya S. Kikuchi to Robert A. Wilson, Jan. 13, 1968, in Kikuchi Papers, JARP; Miya Sannomiya, interview, tapes no. 83 and 84, JARP.
45 McWilliams, *Prejudice*, 315.
46 Nisei Survey Committee, *The Nisei*, 50–53.
47 Yamashita, *Nikkei shimin no Nihon ryūgaku jijō*, 150–156, 226–227, 266–273.
48 Tomita, *Dear Miye*, 43.
49 For a deeper discussion of "passing," see María Carla Sánchez and Linda Schlossberg, *Passing: Identity and Interpretation in Sexuality, Race, and Religion* (New York: New York University Press, 2001).
50 Frances Ota, interview by Jane Comerford, April 2, 2003, *Densho: The Japanese American Legacy Project*.
51 Peggy S. Furukawa, interview by Tom Ikeda, March 20, 2012, *Densho: The Japanese American Legacy Project*.
52 Mitsue May Yamada, Joe Yasutake, and Tosh Yasutake, interview by Alice Ito and Jeni Yamada, October 8–9, 2002, *Densho: The Japanese American Legacy Project*.
53 Yoneko Dozono, interview by Margaret Barton Ross, June 7, 2003, Oregon Nikkei Endowment Collection, *Densho: The Japanese American Legacy Project*.
54 Yamada and Yasutake siblings, interview by Ito and Yamada, October 8–9, 2002, Densho.
55 Frank Hirata, interview by Martha Nakagawa and Tom Ikeda, February 23, 2010, *Densho: The Japanese American Legacy Project*.
56 Frank Fukuhara, interview by Gayle K. Yamada, February 9, 2000, *Densho: The Japanese American Legacy Project*.
57 Kazue Murakami Tanimoto, interview by Tom Ikeda, June 10, 2010, *Densho: The Japanese American Legacy Project*.
58 Iwao Peter Sano, interview by Tom Ikeda and Steve Fugita, November 30, 2010, *Densho: The Japanese American Legacy Project*.
59 Grant Hirabayashi, interview by Tom Ikeda, January 11, 2006, *Densho: The Japanese American Legacy Project*.
60 Minoru Tonai, interview by Tom Ikeda, September 2, 2010, *Densho: The Japanese American Legacy Project*.
61 Letter from Kawasaki Shizuko, Yamashita, *Nikkei shimin no Nihon ryūgaku jijō*, 245.
62 Nakashima, interview by Lai, October 15, 1999, Densho.
63 Jack Dairiki, interview by Martha Nakagawa, March 15, 2011, *Densho: The Japanese American Legacy Project*.
64 Dozono, interview by Ross, June 7, 2003, Densho.
65 Nisei Survey Committee, *The Nisei*, 39.

Chapter 3. Liminal, Subliminal, Sublime

1 Tomita, *Dear Miye*, 141–143.

2 For a rich discussion on the power of culture to fashion identity through the materiality of objects designed to display power, see Leora Auslander, *Cultural Revolutions: Everyday Life and Politics in England, North America, and France* (Berkeley and Los Angeles: University of California Press, 2009).

3 W. Puck Brecher, *Honored and Dishonored Guests: Westerners in Wartime Japan* (Harvard University Asia Center: Cambridge, Massachusetts, 2017), 287–302.

4 Leonard Mlodinow, *Subliminal: How Your Unconscious Mind Rules Your Behavior*, New York: Vintage Books, 2012.

5 Tomita, *Dear Miye*, 46, 123–124.

6 Mary Tomita, "Coming of Age in Japan," *Amerasia Journal* 23, no. 3 (1997): 170.

7 John Morris, *Traveller from Tokyo* (London: Cresset Press, 1944), 89.

8 P. Scott Corbett, *Quiet Passages: The Exchange of Civilians between the United States and Japan during the Second World War* (Kent, Ohio: Kent State University Press, 1987), 20.

9 *Nisei Stories of Wartime Japan*. Thomas Mazawa and Mary McDonald, 2010. 76 minutes.

10 Duus, *Tokyo Rose*, 54.

11 Harry Harootunian, *Overcome by Modernity: History, Culture, and Community in Interwar Japan* (Princeton, New Jersey: Princeton University Press, 2000), 19–20, 27–33.

12 Oikawa Yoshinobu and Maeda Kazuo, *Misshon sukūru to sensō: Rikkyō Gakuin no direnma* (Tokyo: Tōshindō, 2008), 185.

13 Ōishi Itsuo, *Eigo wo kinshi seyo: Shirarezaru senjika no Nihon to Amerika* (Tokyo: Goma Shobo, 2007), 12.

14 Ibid., 68, cf. *Asahi Shinbun* July 7, 1942.

15 Ōishi, *Eigo wo kinshi seyo*, 68.

16 Ibid. 68, cf. *Tokyo Nichi Nichi Shinbun* July 7, 1942.

17 Ōishi, *Eigo wo kinshi seyo*, 69.

18 Dairiki, interview by Nakagawa, March 15, 2011, Densho.

19 *Yayoi Cooke Oral History*, Marlene J. Mayo Oral Histories.

20 Ōishi, *Eigo wo kinshi seyo*, 23.

21 *Yayoi Cooke Oral History*, Marlene J. Mayo Oral Histories.

22 Ōishi, *Eigo wo kinshi seyo*, 27.

23 Kanemoto, interview by Ito, August 3–4, 2003, Densho.

24 Nobuko Gerth, interview by the author, August 9, 2013.

25 Ōishi, *Eigo wo kinshi seyo*, 96–103.

26 Takaaki Aikawa, *Unwilling Patriot* (Tokyo: Jordan, 1960), 7–8.

27 Robert G. Lee, "Introduction," Tomita, *Dear Miye*, 15.

28 Tomita, *Dear Miye*, 148.

29 Furukawa, interview by Ikeda, March 20, 2012, Densho.

30 Ōishi, *Eigo wo kinshi seyo*, 50–59.

31 Ben-Ami Shillony, *Politics and Culture in Wartime Japan* (Oxford: Clarendon Press, 1981), 144.

32 Michiko Usui Kornhauser, interview by Stephen Gilchrist, September 23, 2003, *Densho: The Japanese American Legacy Project*.

33 *Nippon Times*, October 14, 1942.

34 George Yoshida, *Reminiscing in Swingtime: Japanese Americans in American Popular Music: 1925–1960* (Japanese National Historical Society, 1997), 90–97.

35 Ōishi, *Eigo wo kinshi seyo*, 70–71.

36 Dollase, "Girls on the Home Front," 326–329.

37 For a fuller consideration of *kōminka* campaigns, see Leo T. S. Ching, *Becoming Japanese: Colonial Taiwan and the Politics of Identity Formation* (Berkeley: University of California Press, 2001) and Takashi Fujitani, *Race for Empire: Koreans as Japanese and Japanese as Americans during World War II* (Berkeley: University of California Press, 2011).

38 Charles Nelson Spinks, "Indoctrination and Re-Education of Japan's Youth," *Pacific Affairs* 17, no. 1 (March 1944): 64.

39 Komurasaki Toshio, "Senjika no gakkō kyōiku to gakudō sokai," in *Kataritsugu Shōwa shi: Utsusareta kiroku*, vol. 2 (Tokyo: Shinjinbutsu Ōraisha, 1993), 88.

40 Sakuma Kunisaburō, interview by the author, November 4, 2014.

41 Hamazaki Shigenobu, interview by the author, March 24, 2015.

42 Hirata, interview by Nakagawa and Ikeda, February 23, 2010, Densho. Frank Hirata here was likely referring to the *ichioku*, the "one hundred million."

43 Haruko Taya Cook, "Women's Deaths as Weapons of War in Japan's 'Final Battle,'" in *Gendering Modern Japanese History*, eds. Barbara Molony and Katherine Uno (Cambridge, Massachusetts: Harvard University Press, 2005), 338.

44 Hiromi Tsuchiya Dollase, "Girls on the Home Front: An Examination of *Shōjo no tomo* Magazine, 1937–1945," *Asian Studies Review* 32, no. 3 (2008): 324.

45 Harootunian, *Overcome by Modernity*, 13.

46 Jimmie S. Matsuda, interview by Tom Ikeda and Steve Fugita, January 25, 2011, *Densho: The Japanese American Legacy Project*.

47 Edward Toru Horikiri, interview by John Esaki and Yoko Nishimura, January 31, 2012, *Discover Nikkei*, Japanese American National Museum.

48 *Kaigun ni akogareta gunkoku shōnen: Minoru Teruya*, Yokohama: JICA, February 2015, exhibition material for "Nikkei Nisei ga mita senchū, sengo: Bokoku to sokoku no hazama de."

49 Kadota Ryūshō, *Sōkai ni kiyu: Sokoku Amerika e tokkō shita kaigun shōi Matsufuji Ōji no shōgai* (Tokyo: Shūeisha, 2011), 171–172.

50 Brecher, *Honored and Dishonored Guests*, 234–235.

51 Henry Ueno, interview by Stephan Gilchrist, May 1, 2003, *Densho: The Japanese American Legacy Project*.

52 Michael Hirsch, "Pride, Pain Linger for Japanese-Americans Caught on Wrong Side of War," *Los Angeles Times*, September 9, 1990.

53 Kadoike Hiroshi, *Nihon gunheishi ni natta Amerikajin tachi: Bokoku to tatakatta Nikkei Nisei* (Tokyo: Genshu Shuppansha, 2010), 35.

54 *Gakuto tachi no senjō*, Aizu Yaichi Memorial Museum, Waseda University, April 18, 2015.

55 Fukuhara, interview by Yamada, February 9, 2000, Densho.

56 Hiroshi Morishima, interview by the author, March 20, 2015.

57 Kadoike, *Nihon gunheishi ni natta Amerikajin tachi*, 58–61.

58 Kadota Ryūshō, *Sōkai ni kiyu*, 14, 135.

59 Kay Nishimura, interview with the author. 26 June, 2015.

60 Sheldon Garon, *Molding Japanese Minds: The State in Everyday Life* (Princeton, New Jersey: Princeton University Press, 1997), 122.

61 Ibid., 124–126.

62 Cook, "Women's Deaths as Weapons of War in Japan's 'Final Battle,'" 338.

63 Thomas R. H. Havens, *Valley of Darkness: The Japanese People and World War Two* (New York: W.W. Norton and Company, Inc., 1978), 92.

64 Ibid., 108.

65 Ibid., 108, cf. Yoneda Sayoko, *Kindai Nihon joseishi* vol. 2 (Tokyo: Shin Nihon Shuppansha, 1972), 66.

66 Sandra Wilson, "Family or State?: Nation, War, and Gender in Japan, 1937–45," *Critical Asian Studies* 38, no. 2 (2006): 210.

67 Yoshiko Miyake, "Doubling Expectations: Motherhood and Women's Factory Work Under State Management in Japan in the 1930s and 1940s," in *Recreating Japanese Women, 1600–1945*, ed. Gail L. Bernstein (Berkeley: University of California Press, 1991), 288.

68 Ibid., 288, cf. Mitsui, *Gendai fujin undōshi nenpyō*, 173.

69 Takashi Fujitani, *Splendid Monarchy: Power and Pageantry in Modern Japan* (Berkeley: University of California Press, 1996), 9–18.

70 Thomas R. H. Havens, "Women and War in Japan, 1937–45," *The American Historical Review* 80, no. 4 (1975): 932.

71 Inoue Masahito, *Yōfuku to Nihonjin: Kokuminfuku to iu mōdo* (Tōkyō: Kosaidō, 2001), 23.

72 Minami Hiroshi, *Kindai shōmin seikatsushi* (Tōkyō: Sanichi Shobō, 1984), 533.

73 Inoue, *Yōfuku to Nihonjin*, 53

74 Takaaki Aikawa, *Unwilling Patriot* (Tokyo: Jordan, 1960), 62.

75 Utsunomiya Fumiko, "Watashi mo jūgo wo mamoru otome datta." in *Kataritsugu Shōwa shi: Utsusareta kiroku* (Tokyo: Shinjinbutsu Ōraisha, 1993), 183.

76 Sharalyn Orbaugh, *Japanese Fiction of the Allied Occupation: Vision, Embodiment, Identity* (Leiden: Brill, 2007), 219.

Chapter 4. Visible and Invisible Discipline

1 The modes of discipline discussed in this chapter are rooted in the work of Michel Foucault in *Discipline and Punish: The Birth of the Prison* (New York: Pantheon, 1977).

2 Tomita, *Dear Miye*, 145.

3 Komiya Mayumi, *Tekikokujin yokuryū: Senjika no gaikoku minkanjin* (Tokyo: Yoshikawa Kōbunkan, 2003), 47.

4 Tomita, *Dear Miye*, 138.

5 *Yayoi Cooke Oral History*, Marlene J. Mayo Oral Histories.

6 Komiya, *Tekikokujin yokuryū*, 19, cf. Interior Ministry, *Gaiji keisatsu gaikyō*.

7 Brecher, *Honored and Dishonored Guests*, 124, cf. Interior Ministry, *Tekikokujin yokuryū kankei*.

8 Morris, *Traveller from Tokyo*, 98–101.

9 Komiya, *Tekikokujin Yokuryū*, 25.

10 Ibid., 23–24 cf. *"Gaiji geppō" 1941 nen 12 getsubun, Naimushō keihokyoku* (Fuji Shuppan, 1994).

11 Komiya, *Tekikokujin yokuryū*, 55.

12 Ibid., 11.

13 Robert Harrison Crowder, *My Lost Japan* (self-pub., 2006), ix–x.

14 Max Hill, *Exchange Ship* (New York: Farrar & Rinehart, 1942), 20.

15 Duus, *Tokyo Rose*, 56.

16 In an article for a law journal, Mark K. Hanasono stated that none of the Japanese Americans stranded in Japan found passage on the exchange ships that went out during the war. See Mark K. Hanasono, "Stranded in Japan and the Civil Liberties Act of 1988 Recognition for an Excluded Group of Japanese Americans," *Asian American Law Journal* 6 (January 1999), 153. This statement has been cited by historians, but comments made by exchange ship passenger Max Hill and the Crew Lists preserved at the National Archives contradict this. At least six US citizens of Japanese descent are listed as arriving at the port of New York on the 1942 *Gripsholm* exchange ship: Chikao Hamasaki, Yuki ("Clara") Hamasaki, and James Hamasaki of California; Mitsuko Hirata and Tamaya Hirata of Seattle; and Mary Osawa of Idaho. Despite their US citizenship, they were pulled aside in New York City and marked as aliens subject to further questioning. See Max Hill, *Exchange Ship*. See also *Passenger and Crew Lists of Vessels Arriving at New York, New York, 1897–1957*, Microfilm Publication T715, Roll 6649. NAI: 300346, Records of the Immigration and Naturalization Service, National Archives at Washington, DC. See also the Japanese records of this passenger list, as recorded in the *Foreign Affairs Monthly Report* by the Ministry of Internal Affairs and Police Department, June 1942.

17 Robert Harrison Crowder, *My Lost Japan*, xi.

18 George Sidline, *Somehow, We'll Survive: A Memoir: Life in Japan during World War II through the Eyes of a Young Caucasian Boy* (Portland, Oregon: Vera Vista, 2007), 166.

19 See Heinz Altschul, *As I Record These Memories . . . : Erinnerungen eines deutschen Kaufmanns in Kobe, 1926–29, 1934–46* [Memories of a German Merchant in Kobe], eds. Nikola Herweg, Thomas Pekar, Christian W. Spang (Munich: Iudicium, 2014).

20 Lucille Apcar, *Shibaraku: Memories of Japan, 1926–1946* (Denver: Outskirts Press, 2011), 95.

21 Ibid., 100–101.

22 Beate Sirota Gordon, *The Only Woman in the Room* (Tokyo: Kodansha, 1997).

23 Sidline, *Somehow, We'll Survive*, 162.

24 Komiya, *Tekikokujin yokuryū*, 216.

25 Gwen Terasaki, *Bridge to the Sun* (Chapel Hill: University of North Carolina Press, 1957), 152–153; Komiya, *Tekikokujin yokuryū*, 184.

26 For a thorough analysis of the "mixed nation theory" and its impact on the concept of Japaneseness, see Oguma Eiji, *A Genealogy of "Japanese" Self-Images* (Melbourne: Trans Pacific Press, 2002).

27 As David Howell points out, however, although the category of "Japanese subject" expanded to be inclusive of other Asian peoples during Japan's quest for a multi-national empire, "Contemporary Japan is ethnically 'homogeneous' not because there is only one ethnic group within its borders, but because the state, having incorporated Japanese ethnicity into the category of national identity, recognizes only one ethnicity as having political meaning." David Howell, *Geographies of Identity in Nineteenth-Century Japan* (Berkeley: University of California Press, 2005), 203.

28 Brecher, *Honored and Dishonored Guests*, 9.

29 Duus, *Tokyo Rose*, 55, cf. Iva Toguri testimony, Sept 7, 1949.

30 McWilliams, *Prejudice*, 317, cf. *Gila News-Courier,* December 16, 1943.

31 Komiya Mayumi, email message to the author, June 24, 2015.

32 Mark Felton, *Japan's Gestapo: Murder, Mayhem, and Torture in Wartime Asia* (Barnsley: Pen and Sword Military, 2009), 17.

33 Koketsu Atsushi, *Kanshi to dōkatsu no jidai* (Tokyo: Shin Nihon Shuppansha, 2008), 30–31.

34 Raymond Lamont-Brown, *Kempeitai: Japan's Dreaded Military Police* (Phoenix Mill, Stroud, United Kingdom: Sutton Publishing, 1998), 16.

35 Benjamin Uchiyama's *Japan's Carnival War: Mass Culture on the Home Front, 1937–1945* (Cambridge: Cambridge University Press, 2019) provides an important counterpoint to this assessment. Uchiyama's study focuses on the "carnivalesque" ways average citizens in wartime Japan balked against official cultural practices of austerity and reconstituted their fractured daily lives as consumer-subjects. The book adds texture to the blanket story of mass cooperation with state authority, but it should be noted that Uchiyama explores the mainstream Japanese populace rather than minorities or those whose position as imperial subjects was at all ambiguous. He also does not dive into the interiority of his historical subjects, such as how they coped with the stress of "cheating" on the official narrative, of paying lip service to the wartime mood while playing a different game entirely.

36 Koketsu, *Kanshi to dōkatsu no jidai*, 52.

37 Lamont-Brown, *Kempeitai*, vii, cf. R. H. Whitecross, *Slaves of the Son of Heaven* (Sydney: Dymock's Book Arcade, 1952).

38 Lamont-Brown, *Kempeitai,* 16.

39 Tomita, *Dear Miye,* 149.

40 Hirata, interview by Nakagawa and Ikeda, February 23, 2010, Densho.

41 Bill Hashizume, interview by Norm Ibuki, *Sedai: The Japanese Canadian Legacy Project*, Toronto, Canada, October 29, 2005, http://www.discovernikkei.org/en/interviews/profiles/51/.

42 Matsuda, interview by Ikeda and Fugita, January 25, 2011, Densho.

43 Tsunekawa, interview by Ikeda and Fugita, January 26, 2011, Densho.

44 Dairiki, interview by Nakagawa, March 15, 2011, Densho.

45 Abe Teruo, interview by the author, November 4, 2014.

46 Lamont-Brown, *Kempeitai*, 75.

47 Kornhauser, interview by Gilchrist, September 23, 2003, Densho.

48 Havens, *Valley of Darkness,* 53–54.

49 Morris, *Traveller from Tokyo,* 88.

50 Aikawa, *Unwilling Patriot*, 48, 9.

51 *Yayoi Cooke Oral History,* Marlene J. Mayo Oral Histories.

52 Paul Yempuku, interview by Tom Ikeda, June 4, 2009, *Densho: The Japanese American Legacy Project.*

53 Tomi Kaizawa Knaefler, *Our House Divided: Seven Japanese American Families in World War II* (Honolulu: University of Hawai'i Press, 1981), 76.

54 Duus, *Tokyo Rose,* 55.

55 Morris, *Traveller from Tokyo*, 41.

56 Dairiki, interview by Nakagawa, March 15, 2011, Densho.

57 Henry Ueno, interview by Gilchrist, May 1, 2003, Densho.

58 Kanemoto, interview by Ito, August 3–4, 2003, Densho.

59 "Senjika no seishun," Narusei Memorial Hall, Japan Women's University, Tokyo, Japan, November 11, 2014.

60 Oikawa and Maeda, *Misshon sukūru to sensō*, 348.

61 *Yayoi Cooke Oral History,* Marlene J. Mayo Oral Histories.

62 Tomita, "Coming of Age in Japan," 174–175.

63 Kanemoto, interview by Ito, August 3–4, 2003, Densho.

64 Nakashima, interview by Lai, October 15, 1999, Densho.

65 Rose Ito Tsunekawa, phone interview by the author, April 24, 2015.

66 Furukawa, interview by Ikeda, March 20, 2012, Densho.

67 Atami Ueno, interview by Stephan Gilchrist, May 1, 2003, *Densho: The Japanese American Legacy Project.*

68 Izumi Hirano, interview by Tom Ikeda, March 1, 2011, *Densho: The Japanese American Legacy Project.*

69 Dairiki, interview by Nakagawa, March 15, 2011, Densho.

70 Yempuku, interview by Ikeda, June 4, 2009, Densho.

71 Tomita, "Coming of Age in Japan," 176–177.

72 Onishi, interview by Ikeda, June 2, 2009, Densho.

73 Tomita, *Dear Miye,* 148.

74 Fukuhara, interview by Yamada, February 9, 2000, Densho.

75 Yamasaki Toyoko, *Two Homelands*, translated by V. Dixon Morris (Honolulu: University of Hawai'i Press, 2008).

76 Literally "returned to America," *kibei* (帰米) was the appellation given to Nisei who returned to the United States after spending a significant time in Japan (usually several years) for education or employment.

77 Toyoko Yamasaki, *Two Homelands,* 286.

78 For a more thorough understanding of hegemony understood rhizomically, see Bill Ashcroft, Gareth Griffiths, and Helen Tiffin, *Post-Colonial Studies: The Key Concepts.* 2nd ed. (London: Routledge, 2007), 191.

Chapter 5. Where Loyalties Lie

1 Knaefler, *Our House Divided,* 86–87.

2 Dan Ariely, *Predictably Irrational: The Hidden Forces That Shape Our Decisions* (New York: HarperCollins, 2008), 243.

3 Ibid., 97.

4 Mlodinow, *Subliminal,* 77–78.

5 Kahneman, Daniel, *Thinking, Fast and Slow* (New York: Farrar, Straus and Giroux, 2011), 202.

6 Furukawa, interview by Ikeda, March 20, 2012, Densho.

7 Leonard Mlodinow, *Subliminal: How Your Unconscious Mind Rules Your Behavior* (New York: Vintage, 2012). 190–191.

8 Hirata, interview by Nakagawa and Ikeda, February 23, 2010, Densho.

9 Knaefler, *Our House Divided,* 99.

10 Sano, interview by Ikeda and Fugita, November 30, 2010, Densho.

11 Iwao Peter Sano, phone interview by the author, May 14, 2015.

12 Iwao Peter Sano, *One Thousand Days in Siberia: The Odyssey of a Japanese-American POW* (Lincoln: University of Nebraska Press, 1997), 25.

13 Ibid., 33.

14 Knaefler, *Our House Divided,* 31–37.

15 Tomita, *Dear Miye,* 147–154.

16 John Dower, *War without Mercy: Race and Power in the Pacific War* (New York: Pantheon Books, 1986), 303, cf. US Senate, Committee on Armed Services and the Committee on Foreign Relations, 82nd Cong., 1st sess., *Hearings to Conduct an Inquiry into the Military Situation in the Far East and the Facts Surrounding the Relief of General of the Army Douglas MacArthur from His Assignments in That Area,* 1951, pt. 1: 312–313.

17 Mire Koikari, "Exporting Democracy? American Women, 'Feminist Reforms,' and Politics of Imperialism in the U.S. Occupation of Japan, 1945–1952," *Frontiers* 23, no. 1 (2002): 24.

18 Onishi, interview by Ikeda, June 2, 2009, Densho.

19 Azuma, "1930 nendai no Tōkyō ni okeru Nikkei Amerikajin Nisei ryūgaku jigyō to Nihon shokuminchi shugi," 21, cf. "Sensen fukoku no hi" (*Gakusei sakubunshū dai san shū*), (Waseda Kokisai Gakuin, 1942), 124.

20 Hirsch, "Pride, Pain Linger for Japanese-Americans Caught on Wrong Side of War."

21 Kadoike, *Nihon gunheishi ni natta Amerikajin tachi,* 171.

22 Jin, "Beyond Two Homelands," 219–220.

23 Knaefler, *Our House Divided,* 100.

24 Spickard, "Twice Immigrants," cf. Thomas et al., *The Salvage,* 580–591.

25 Yempuku, interview by Ikeda, June 4, 2009, Densho.

26 Matsuda, interview by Ikeda and Fugita, January 25, 2011, Densho.

27 Knaefler, *Our House Divided,* 79.

28 Fukuhara, interview by Yamada, February 9, 2000, Densho.

29 Hirsch, "Pride, Pain Linger for Japanese-Americans Caught on Wrong Side of War."

30 Dairiki, interview by Nakagawa, March 15, 2011, Densho.

31 Tomita, *Dear Miye,* 152.

32 Tomita, "Coming of Age in Japan," 176.

33 Kanemoto, interview by Ito, August 3–4, 2003, Densho.

34 Matsuda, interview by Ikeda and Fugita, January 25, 2011, Densho.

35 Knaefler, *Our House Divided,* 79.

36 Fukuhara, interview by Yamada, February 9, 2000, Densho.

37 G. L. Clore and A. Ortony, "Appraisal Theories: How Cognition Shapes Affect into Emotion," in *Handbook of Emotions,* 3rd edition, eds. M. Lewis, J. M. Haviland-Jones, and L. F. Barnett (New York: Guilford Press, 2008), 629; Roy F. Baumeister, Kathleen D. Vohs, C. Nathan DeWall, and Liqing Zhang, "How Emotion Shapes Behavior: Feedback, Anticipation, and Reflection, Rather than Direct Causation," *Personality and Social Psychology Review* 11, no. 2 (May 2007): 168.

38 Richard S. Lazarus, "Thoughts on the Relations Between Emotion and Cognition," *American Psychologist* 37, no. 9 (September 1982): 1019.

39 In behavioral psychology, the constructionist approach to emotions emphasizes culturally rooted "feeling rules" as determining emotions by setting the standards by which intensities are assessed. See Arlie Hochschild, *The Managed Heart: Commercialization of Human Feeling* (Berkeley: University of California Press, 1983).

Chapter 6. The Passage Home

1 *Yayoi Cooke Oral History,* Marlene J. Mayo Oral Histories.

2 Louis Adamic, *Two-Way Passage* (New York: Harper & Brothers, 1941), 268.

3 "Use of Nisei GIs in Army's Occupation of Japan Follows 'Two-Way Passage' Proposal," *Pacific Citizen,* December 14, 1946.

4 McWilliams, "The Nisei in Japan," 72.

5 Kayoko Takeda, "The Role of Nisei (Second-Generation Japanese Americans) Linguists during World War II and the Allied Occupation of Japan," *Studies of Translation and Interpretation* 17 (2014): 165.

6 Gladys Ishida, "The Japanese American Renunciants of Okayama Prefecture: Their Accommodation and Assimilation into Japanese Culture" (PhD diss., University of Michigan, 1955), 166.

7 Rose Tsunekawa, phone interview by the author, April 24, 2015.

8 Tomita, *Dear Miye,* 164.

9 *Beate Gordon Oral History,* Marlene J. Mayo Oral Histories, held in the Gordon W. Prange Collection, University of Maryland Libraries.

10 Kayoko Takeda, "The Visibility of Collaborators: Snapshots of Wartime and Postwar Interpreters," in *Framing the Interpreter: Towards a Visual Perspective,* eds. Anxo Fernández Ocampo and Michaela Wolf (New York: Routledge, 2014), 155.

11 Kelly Y. Nakamura, "'They Are Our Human Secret Weapons': The Military Intelligence Service and the Role of Japanese-Americans in the Pacific War and in the Occupation of Japan," *Historian* 70, no. 1 (Spring 2008): 71.

12 Yamamoto Taketoshi, "Nihonjin ken'etsusha meibo kaisetsu," Website for Historical Studies of Censorship in Japan and the World, accessed June 17, 2014. http://www.waseda.jp/prj-Kennetsu/explain.html.

13 "Shirarezaru 'dōhō kanshi': GHQ, Nihonjin ken'etsukan tachi no kokuhaku," NHK, accessed November 5, 2013. www.nhk.or.jp/gendai/kiroku/detail_3425.html.

14 Yamamoto, "Nihonjin ken'etsusha meibo kaisetsu."

15 Takemae Eiji, *Inside GHQ: The Allied Occupation of Japan and Its Legacy,* Sebastian Swann, trans. (Atlantic Highlands, New Jersey: Humanities Press International, 2002), 182.

16 Ibid., xxix.

17 Nakamura, "They Are Our Human Secret Weapons," 62–63.

18 Matsuda, interview by Ikeda and Fugita, January 25, 2011, Densho.

19 Rose Ito Tsunekawa, phone interview by the author, April 24, 2015.

20 Yujin Yaguchi, "Japanese Reinvention of Self through Hawai'i's Japanese Americans," *Pacific Historical Review* 83, no. 2 (November 2012): 335–336.

21 Tomita, *Dear Miye,* 369–370. Mary's letter to the *Nippon Times* was published in that paper on October 25, 1946.

22 Dairiki, interview by Nakagawa, March 15, 2011, Densho.

23 Tomita, "Coming of Age in Japan," 177.

24 Michael Jin, "The Japanese American Transnational Generation," in *The Routledge Handbook of Asian American Studies,* ed. Cindy I-Fen Cheng (New York: Routledge, 2016), 256, cf. *Heishikan Newsletter,* November 2006.

25 Naoko Shibusawa, "Femininity, Race and Treachery: How 'Tokyo Rose' Became a Traitor to the United States after the Second World War," *Gender & History* 22, no. 1 (April 2010):

170, cf. Ronald Yates, "Tokyo Rose's Accusers Claim US Forced them to Lie," *Chicago Tribune*, 22 March 1976, 15.

26 "Give the Veterans Priority," *Pacific Stars and Stripes*, October 13, 1946, 3.

27 "A View of Citizenship," *Pacific Stars and Stripes*, October 17, 1936, 3.

28 Tomita, *Dear Miye*, 363–364.

29 Mary Kimoto, "A Statement to Charges," *Pacific Stars and Stripes* (October 25, 1946), 3.

30 Kayoko Takeda, *Interpreting the Tokyo War Crimes Tribunal: A Sociopolitical Analysis* (Ottawa: University of Ottawa Press, 2010), 32.

31 "Shirarezaru 'dōhō kanshi.' "

32 Okinawa Peace Memorial Museum, Okinawa, Japan, January 28, 2015.

33 Yoneko Dozono, interview by Ross, June 7, 2003, Densho.

34 Tomita, "Coming of Age in Japan," 179.

35 Tomita, *Dear Miye*, 160–167, 178 185, 242–252, 348.

36 Atami Ueno, interview by Gilchrist, May 1, 2003, Densho.

37 Fukuhara, interview by Yamada, February 9, 2000, Densho.

38 Matsuda, interview by Ikeda and Fugita, January 25, 2011, Densho.

39 "Soft Life for Occupation Workers," *U.S. News & World Report* 26, no. 3 (1949): 27.

40 *Yayoi Cooke Oral History,* Marlene J. Mayo Oral Histories.

41 Tomita, "Coming of Age in Japan," 178.

42 Takemae, *Inside GHQ,* 73.

43 Tomita, *Dear Miye,* 223.

44 Ibid., 244, 164, 233, 270.

45 Donald E. Collins, *Native American Aliens: Disloyalty and the Renunciation of Citizenship by Japanese Americans during World War II* (Westport, Connecticut: Greenwood Press, 1985), 121, cf. War Relocation Authority, Evacuated People, 196.

46 Jonathan van Harmelen, "Infamy's Legacy: Tule Lake and Repatriation Remembered," Discover Nikkei, 10 April 2020, http://www.discovernikkei.org/en/journal/2020/4/10/infamys-legacy/.

47 George Kikuta, interview by Richard Potashin, July 18, 2008, *Densho: The Japanese American Legacy Project.*

48 "Shirarezaru 'dōhō kanshi.' "

49 Takemae, *Inside GHQ,* 79–80.

50 Aikawa, *Unwilling Patriot,* 130–131.

51 Kanemoto, interview by Ito, August 3–4, 2003, Densho.

52 Tomita, *Dear Miye,* 268.

53 Ibid., 176.

54 *Reminiscences of Burton Crane (1961),* Occupation of Japan Project, Columbia Center for Oral History Archives, Rare Book & Manuscript Library, Columbia University in the City of New York, 50.

55 Kanemoto, interview by Ito, August 3–4, 2003, Densho.

56 Edward Tang, *From Confinement to Containment: Japanese/American Arts during the Early Cold War* (Philadelphia: Temple University Press, 2019), 19.

57 Ibid., 16–36.

Conclusion

1 "Japanese in Hawaii Ready to Fight for U.S. in Event of War with This Country," *Japan Times and Mail,* September 5, 1932.

2 Takashi Fujitani, *Race for Empire: Koreans as Japanese and Japanese as Americans during World War II* (Berkeley: University of California Press, 2011), 133, cf. War Relocation Authority, Community Analysis Section, "Army and Leave Clearance Registration at War Relocation Centers," June 1943, Appendix A, 52.

3 Hochschild, *The Managed Heart,* 39.

4 "SCAP Orders Listing of U.S. Nationals Who Applied for Japanese Citizenship," *Nippon Times,* May 20, 1946.

5 Japanese citizenship was granted automatically to Japanese-heritage babies born in the United States until 1924. Beginning in 1924, their parents had to register American-born babies with the consulate for dual citizenship.

6 *Yayoi Cooke Oral History,* Marlene J. Mayo Oral Histories.

7 Tomita, *Dear Miye,* 267–268.

8 Ibid., 313.

9 Onishi, interview by Ikeda, June 2, 2009, Densho.

10 Moore, *Serving Our Country,* 81–82.

11 Morishima Hiroshi, interview by the author, March 20, 2015.

12 Nishimura Kay, interview by the author and Kadoike Hiroshi, Tokyo, Japan, June 26, 2015.

13 "Citizenship Restored," *Pacific Citizen,* Jan 12, 1952.

14 Duus, *Tokyo Rose,* 108.

15 "Nagai tabiji: Nihon hei ni natta Amerikajin (II)," NHK, first aired August 16, 2013, 50 minutes.

16 Duus, *Tokyo Rose,* 108.

17 Ibid., 25, cf. Clark Lee, "Traitor's Pay: Tokyo Rose Got 100 a Month—$6.60," *Los Angeles Examiner,* September 3, 1945.

18 See, for example, controversy over the memory of Kim Hwal-lan, the founder of Korea's elite Ewha Women's University.

19 Eric C. Han, "A True Sino-Japanese Amity? Collaborationism and the Yokohama Chinese (1937–1945)," *The Journal of Asian Studies* 72, no. 3 (August 2013): 587–609.

20 "Tomoya Kawakita," *Densho Encyclopedia,* accessed 24 September 2019, http://encyclopedia.densho.org/Tomoya_Kawakita/, cf. *Reporter's Transcript of Proceedings United States vs. Tomoya Kawakita,* criminal case 19665, RG 21 Records of the District Court of the United States, Southern District of California, NARA-Laguna Nigel (hereafter Kawakita transcript), 5041.

21 Ibid., cf. Kawakita transcript 5418, 5003, 5028.

22 Ibid., cf. *United States v Tomoya Kawakita,* 96 F. Supp. 824, 860.

23 "POW Camp Atrocities Led to Treason Trial," *Los Angeles Times,* September 20, 2002.

24 Kadoike, *Nihon gunheishi ni natta Amerikajin tachi,* 176–177.

Bibliography

Primary Sources

Abe Teruo. Interview by the author. Tokyo, Japan. November 4, 2014.

Adamic, Louis. *Two-Way Passage*. New York: Harper & Brothers, 1941.

Aikawa, Takaaki. *Unwilling Patriot*. Tokyo: Jordan, 1960.

Altschul, Heinz. *As I Record These Memories . . . : Erinnerungen eines deutschen Kaufmanns in Kobe, 1926–29, 1934–46*. Nikola Herweg, Thomas Pekar, and Christian W. Spang, eds. Munich: Iudicium, 2014.

Apcar, Lucille. *Shibaraku: Memories of Japan, 1926–1946*. Denver: Outskirts Press, 2011.

Beate Gordon Oral History. Marlene J. Mayo Oral Histories, held in the Gordon W. Prange Collection, University of Maryland Libraries.

Bill, Kazuko Uno. Interview by Megan Asaka. *Densho: The Japanese American Legacy Project*. Seattle, May 7, 2008. Video.

Crowder, Robert Harrison. *My Lost Japan*. Self-published, 2006.

Dairiki, Jack. Interview by Martha Nakagawa. *Densho: The Japanese American Legacy Project*. Emeryville, California, March 15, 2011. Video.

Dozono, Yoneko. Interview by Margaret Barton Ross. Oregon Nikkei Endowment Collection. *Densho: The Japanese American Legacy Project*. June 7, 2003. Video.

Esaki, Alice. Testimony to the Commission on Wartime Relocation and Internment of Civilians. 1981. Personal files of Bill Yoshino, Japanese American Citizens League, Chicago.

Fukuhara, Frank. Interview by Gayle K. Yamada. *Densho: The Japanese American Legacy Project*. Hawai'i, February 9, 2000. Video.

Furukawa, Peggy S. Interview by Tom Ikeda. *Densho: The Japanese American Legacy Project*. San Jose, California, March 20, 2012. Video.

Gaither, Sarah. Interview by the author. Chicago, Illinois. November 2, 2015.

Gerth, Nobuko. Interview by the author. Ann Arbor, Michigan. August 9, 2013.

———. *Seven Downs and Eight Ups: An Autobiography*. Bloomington, Indiana: AuthorHouse, 2013.

Gordon, Beate Sirota. *The Only Woman in the Room*. Tokyo: Kodansha, 1997.

Hamazaki Shigenobu. Interview by the author. Tsuruma, Japan. March 24, 2015.

Hashizume, Bill. Interview by Norm Ibuki, *Sedai: The Japanese Canadian Legacy Project,* Toronto, Canada, October 29, 2005. Discover Nikkei. Video. http://www.discovernikkei.org/en/interviews/profiles/51/.

Herzig-Yoshinaga, Aiko. Interview by Tom Ikeda. *Densho: The Japanese American Legacy Project.* Torrance, California, July 7, 2009. Video.

Hill, Max. *Exchange Ship.* New York: Farrar & Rinehart, 1942.

Hirabayashi, Grant. Interview by Tom Ikeda. *Densho: The Japanese American Legacy Project.* Seattle, Washington, January 11, 2006. Video.

Hirano, Izumi. Interview by Tom Ikeda. *Densho: The Japanese American Legacy Project.* Honolulu, Hawai'i, March 1, 2011. Video.

Hirata, Frank. Interview by Martha Nakagawa and Tom Ikeda. *Densho: The Japanese American Legacy Project.* Culver City, California, February 23, 2010. Video.

Horikiri, Edward Toru. Interview by John Esaki and Yoko Nishimura. *Discover Nikkei,* Japanese American National Museum. Los Angeles, California, January 31, 2012. Video.

Imai, Shigenobu. Interview by Linda Tamura. *Densho: The Japanese American Legacy Project.* Hood River, Oregon, October 30, 2013. Video.

Ishigaki, Ayako. *Restless Wave: My Life in Two Worlds, a Memoir.* New York: Feminist Press at the City University of New York, 2004.

Itō Bunkichi VIII. Interview by the author. Niigata, Japan. November 28, 2013.

John Aiso Oral History. Marlene J. Mayo Oral Histories, held in the Gordon W. Prange Collection, University of Maryland Libraries.

John M. Maki Oral History. Marlene J. Mayo Oral Histories, held in the Gordon W. Prange Collection, University of Maryland Libraries.

Kaji, Bruce T. Interview by Martha Nakagawa. *Densho: The Japanese American Legacy Project.* Los Angeles, July 28, 2010. Video.

Kanemoto, Marion Tsutakawa. Interview by Alice Ito. *Densho: The Japanese American Legacy Project.* SeaTac and Seattle, Washington, August 3–4, 2003. Video.

Kawai Michi. *My Lantern.* Tokyo: Kyo Bun Kwan, 1939.

Keisen Jogakuen gojūnen no ayumi. Tokyo: Keisen Jogakuen, 1979.

Key Kobayashi Oral History. Marlene J. Mayo Oral Histories, held in the Gordon W. Prange Collection, University of Maryland Libraries.

Kikuta, George. Interview by Richard Potashin. *Densho: The Japanese American Legacy Project.* Los Angeles: July 18, 2008. Video.

Kornhauser, Michiko Usui. Interview by Stephen Gilchrist. *Densho: The Japanese American Legacy Project.* Honolulu, Hawai'i, September 23, 2003. Video.

Matsuda, Jimmie S. Interview by Tom Ikeda and Steve Fugita, *Densho: The Japanese American Legacy Project.* San Jose, California, January 25, 2011. Video.

Miyamoto, Frank. Interview by Stephen Fugita. *Densho: The Japanese American Legacy Project.* Seattle, Washington: February 26, 1998. Video.

Miyatake, Archie. Interview by Martha Nakagawa. *Densho: The Japanese American Legacy Project.* Los Angeles, California, August 31–September 1, 2010. Video.

Morishima, Hiroshi. Interview by the author. Hiroshima, Japan. March 20, 2015.

Morris, John. *Traveller from Tokyo.* London: Cresset Press, 1944.

Nakamoto, Hiroko, and Mildred Mastin Pace. *My Japan 1930–1951.* New York: McGraw-Hill, 1970.

Nakashima, Hiroko. Interview by Tracy Lai. *Densho: The Japanese American Legacy Project*. Seattle, October 15, 1999. Video.

Nisei Survey Committee, Keisen Girls' School. *The Nisei: A Survey of Their Educational, Vocational, and Social Problems*. Tokyo: Keisen Girls' School, 1939.

Nishimura Kay. Interview by the author and Kadoike Hiroshi. Tokyo, Japan. June 26, 2015.

Okada, John. *No-No Boy*. San Francisco: Combined Asian American Resources Project, 1976.

Onishi, Muriel Chiyo Tanaka. Interview by Tom Ikeda. *Densho: The Japanese American Legacy Project*. Honolulu, Hawai'i, June 2, 2009. Video.

Ota, Frances. Interview by Jane Comerford. *Densho: The Japanese American Legacy Project*. Portland, Oregon, April 2, 2003. Video.

Passenger and Crew Lists of Vessels Arriving at New York, New York, 1897–1957. Microfilm Publication T715, Roll 6649. NAI: 300346. Records of the Immigration and Naturalization Service; National Archives at Washington, DC.

Reminiscences of Burton Crane (1961). Occupation of Japan Project. Columbia Center for Oral History Archives, Rare Book & Manuscript Library, Columbia University in the City of New York.

Reminiscences of Faubion Bowers (1960). Occupation of Japan Project. Columbia Center for Oral History Archives, Rare Book & Manuscript Library, Columbia University in the City of New York.

Sakuma Kunisaburō. Interview by the author. Tokyo, Japan. November 4, 2014.

Sakurada, Jane. Phone interview by the author. May 14, 2015.

Sano, Iwao Peter. Interview by Tom Ikeda and Steve Fugita. *Densho: The Japanese American Legacy Project*. San Jose, California, November 30, 2010. Video.

———. *One Thousand Days in Siberia: The Odyssey of a Japanese-American POW*. Lincoln: University of Nebraska, 1997.

———. Phone interview by the author. May 5, 2015.

Sawada, Emiko. E-mail correspondence with the author. October 24–December 5, 2014.

Sidline, George. *Somehow, We'll Survive: A Memoir: Life in Japan during World War II through the Eyes of a Young Caucasian Boy*. Portland, Oregon: Vera Vista, 2007.

Soeda Kiomi. Interview by the author. Kōya, Japan. April 3, 2015.

Sone, Monica. *Nisei Daughter*. Boston: Little, Brown and Company, 1953.

Strong, Jr., Edward K. *The Second-Generation Japanese Problem*. Stanford: Stanford University Press, 1934.

Tanimoto, Kazue Murakami. Interview by Tom Ikeda. *Densho: The Japanese American Legacy Project*. Hilo, Hawai'i, June 10, 2010. Video.

Terasaki, Gwen. *Bridge to the Sun*. Chapel Hill: University North Carolina Press, 1957.

Tokiwa, Rudy. Interview by Tom Ikeda and Judy Niizawa. *Densho: The Japanese American Legacy Project*. Honolulu, Hawai'i, July 2–3, 1998. Video.

Tomita, Mary. "Coming of Age in Japan." *Amerasia Journal* 23, no. 3 (1997): 165–180.

———. *Dear Miye: Letters Home from Japan, 1939–1946*. Edited by Robert G. Lee. Stanford: Stanford University Press, 1995.

Tonai, Minoru. Interview by Tom Ikeda. *Densho: The Japanese American Legacy Project.* Los Angeles, September 2, 2010. Video.

Tsunekawa, Rose Ito. Interview by Tom Ikeda and Steve Fugita. *Densho: The Japanese American Legacy Project.* San Jose, California, January 26, 2011. Video.

———. Phone interview by the author. April 24, 2015.

Ueno, Atami. Interview by Stephan Gilchrist. *Densho: The Japanese American Legacy Project.* May 1, 2003. Video.

Ueno, Henry. Interview by Stephan Gilchrist. *Densho: The Japanese American Legacy Project.* May 1, 2003. Video.

Utsunomiya Fumiko. "Watashi mo jūgo wo mamoru otome datta. In *Kataritsugu Shōwa: Utsusareta kiroku.* Vol. 2. Tokyo: Shinjinbutsu Ōraisha, 1993, 182–183.

Yamada, Mitsue May, Joe Yasutake, and Tosh Yasutake. Interview by Alice Ito and Jeni Yamada. *Densho: The Japanese American Legacy Project.* Seattle, Washington, October 8–9, 2002. Video.

Yamada Tatsumi. *Kaigai dai Nisei mondai.* Tokyo: Kibundō, 1936.

Yamamoto, Sumiko M. Interview by Tom Ikeda and Barbara Takei. *Densho: The Japanese American Legacy Project.* Sacramento, California, December 8, 2009. Video.

Yamasaki Toyoko. *Two Homelands.* Translated by V. Dixon Morris. Honolulu: University of Hawai'i Press, 2008.

Yayoi Cooke Oral History. Marlene J. Mayo Oral Histories, held in the Gordon W. Prange Collection, University of Maryland Libraries.

Yempuku, Paul. Interview by Tom Ikeda. *Densho: The Japanese American Legacy Project.* Honolulu, Hawai'i, June 4, 2009. Video.

Secondary Sources

1942 Nichibei kōkansen to sono jidai. Yokohama: Nihon Yūsen Rekishi Hakubutsukan, 2012.

Abel, Jonathan E. *Redacted: The Archives of Censorship in Transwar Japan.* Berkeley: University of California Press, 2012.

Akagi, Roy Hidemichi. *The Second Generation Problem: Some Suggestions Toward Its Solution.* New York: Japanese Students' Christian Association in North America, 1926.

Ariely, Dan. *Predictably Irrational: The Hidden Forces That Shape Our Decisions.* New York: HarperCollins, 2008.

Asato, Noriko. "Americanization vs. Japanese Cultural Maintenance: Analyzing Seattle's Nihongo Tokuhon, 1920." In *Nikkei in the Pacific Northwest: Japanese Americans and Japanese Canadians in the Twentieth Century,* edited by Louis Fiset and Gail M. Nomura, 95–119. Seattle: University of Washington Press, 2005.

———. *Teaching Mikadoism: The Attack on Japanese Language Schools in Hawaii, California, and Washington, 1919–1927.* Honolulu: University of Hawai'i Press, 2006.

Ashcroft, Bill, Gareth Griffiths, and Helen Tiffin. *Post-Colonial Studies: The Key Concepts.* 2nd ed. London: Routledge, 2007.

Auslander, Leora. *Cultural Revolutions: Everyday Life and Politics in England, North America, and France.* Berkeley and Los Angeles: University of California Press, 2009.

Azuma Eiichiro. "1930 nendai no Tōkyō ni okeru Nikkei Amerikajin Nisei ryūgaku jigyō to Nihon shokuminchi shugi." In *Amerika Nikkei Nisei to ekkyō kyōiku: 1930 nendai wo omo ni shite,* edited by Yoshida Ryō, 21–56. Tokyo: Fuji Shuppan, 2012.

———. *Between Two Empires: Race, History, and Transnationalism in Japanese America.* Oxford: Oxford University Press, 2005.

Benet-Martinez, V., J. Leu, F. Lee, and M. W. Morris. "Negotiating Biculturalism: Cultural Frame Switching in Biculturals with Oppositional Versus Compatible Cultural Identities." *Journal of Cross-Cultural Psychology* 33, no. 5 (2002): 492–516.

Braw, Monica. *The Atomic Bomb Suppressed: American Censorship in Occupied Japan.* Armonk, New York: M. E. Sharpe, Inc., 1991.

Brecher, W. Puck. *Honored and Dishonored Guests: Westerners in Wartime Japan.* Cambridge, Massachusetts: Harvard University Asia Center, 2017.

Brecher, W. Puck and Michael W. Myers, eds. *Defamiliarizing Japan's Asia-Pacific War.* Honolulu: University of Hawai'i Press, 2019.

Brook, Timothy. "Collaboration in the History of Wartime East Asia." *The Asia-Pacific Journal* 6, no. 7 (July 2008). https://apjjf.org/-Timothy-Brook/2798/article.html.

———. "Collaboration in the Postwar." *The Asia-Pacific Journal* 6, no. 7 (July 2008). https://apjjf.org/-Timothy-Brook/2802/article.html.

———. *Collaboration: Japanese Agents and Local Elites in Wartime China.* Cambridge, Massachusetts: Harvard University Press, 2005.

Brown, Raymond. *Kempeitai: Japan's Dreaded Military Police.* Stroud, England: Sutton, 1998.

Bullock, Julia C. *The Other Women's Lib: Gender and Body in Japanese Women's Fiction.* Honolulu: University of Hawai'i Press, 2010.

Butler, Judith. *Bodies That Matter: On the Discursive Limits of "Sex."* New York: Routledge, 1993.

Caprio, Mark. *Japanese Assimilation Policies in Colonial Korea, 1910–1945.* Seattle: University of Washington Press, 2009.

"Caught Between Countries." NHK World. First aired December 8, 2011. 5 minutes.

Chin, Frank. *Born in the USA: A Story of Japanese America, 1889–1947.* Lanham, Maryland: Rowman & Littlefield Publishers, 2002.

Ching, Leo T. S. *Becoming Japanese: Colonial Taiwan and the Politics of Identity Formation.* Berkeley: University of California Press, 2001.

Christgau, John. "Collins Versus the World: The Fight to Restore Citizenship to Japanese American Renunciants of World War II." *The Pacific Historical Review* 54 (1985): 1–31.

Christy, A. S. "The Making of Imperial Subjects in Okinawa." *Positions: East Asia Cultures Critique* 1, no. 3 (1993): 607–639.

Clore, G. L., and A. Ortony. "Appraisal Theories: How Cognition Shapes Affect into Emotion." In *Handbook of Emotions,* 3rd edition, edited by M. Lewis, J. M. Haviland-Jones, and L. F. Barnett, 628–642. New York: Guilford Press, 2008.

Close, Frederick Phelps. *Tokyo Rose/An American Patriot: A Dual Biography.* Lanham, Maryland: Scarecrow, 2010.

Collins, Donald E. *Native American Aliens: Disloyalty and the Renunciation of Citizenship by Japanese Americans during World War II.* Westport, Connecticut: Greenwood, 1985.

Cook, Haruko Taya. "Women's Deaths as Weapons of War in Japan's 'Final Battle.'" In *Gendering Modern Japanese History,* edited by Barbara Molony and Katherine Uno, 326–356. Cambridge, Massachusetts: Harvard University Press, 2005.

Corbett, P. Scott. *Quiet Passages: The Exchange of Civilians between the United States and Japan during the Second World War.* Kent, Ohio: Kent State University Press, 1987.

Daniels, Roger. *The Politics of Prejudice: The Anti-Japanese Movement in California and the Struggle for Japanese Exclusion.* Gloucester, Massachusetts: Peter Smith, 1966.

Dollase, Hiromi Tsuchiya. "Girls on the Home Front: An Examination of *Shōjo no tomo* Magazine 1937–1945." *Asian Studies Review* 32, no. 3 (2008): 323–339.

Dower, John W. *War without Mercy: Race and Power in the Pacific War.* New York: Pantheon Books, 1986.

Duara, Prasenjit. *Sovereignty and Authenticity: Manchukuo and the East Asian Modern.* Lanham, Maryland: Rowman & Littlefield Publishers, 2003.

Dubrow, Gail Lee, Donna Graves, and Karen Cheng. *Sento at Sixth and Main: Preserving Landmarks of Japanese American Heritage.* Seattle: Seattle Arts Commission, 2002.

Duus, Masayo. *Tokyo Rose: Orphan of the Pacific.* Tokyo: Kodansha International, 1979.

———. *Unlikely Liberators: The Men of the 100th and 442nd.* Honolulu: University of Hawai'i Press, 2006.

Felton, Mark. *Japan's Gestapo: Murder, Mayhem, and Torture in Wartime Asia.* Barnsley: Pen and Sword Military, 2009.

Foucault, Michel. *Discipline and Punish: The Birth of the Prison.* New York: Pantheon, 1977.

Franks, David. "The Neuroscience of Emotions." In *Handbook of the Sociology of Emotions,* edited by Jan Stets and Jonathan H. Turner, 38–62. New York: Springer, 2006.

Fujitani, Takashi. *Race for Empire: Koreans as Japanese and Japanese as Americans during World War II.* Berkeley: University of California Press, 2011.

———. *Splendid Monarchy: Power and Pageantry in Modern Japan.* Berkeley: University of California Press, 1996.

"Gakuto tachi no senjō." Aizu Yaichi Memorial Museum. Waseda University. Tokyo, Japan. April 18, 2015.

Garon, Sheldon M. *Molding Japanese Minds: The State in Everyday Life.* Princeton, New Jersey: Princeton University Press, 1997.

Gleich-Anthony, Jeanne M. "Democratizing Women: American Women and the U.S. Occupation of Japan, 1945–1951." PhD diss., Ohio University, 2007.

Goffman, Erving. *The Presentation of Self in Everyday Life.* Garden City, New York: Doubleday, 1959.

———. *Stigma: Notes on the Management of Spoiled Identity.* Englewood Cliffs, New Jersey: Prentice-Hall, 1963.

Han, Eric C. "A True Sino-Japanese Amity? Collaborationism and the Yokohama Chinese (1937–1945)." *The Journal of Asian Studies* 72, no. 3 (August 2013): 587–609.

Han, Suk-Jung. "On the Question of Collaboration in South Korea." *The Asia-Pacific Journal* 6, no. 7 (July 2008). https://apjjf.org/-Suk-Jung-Han/2800/article.html.

Hanasono, Mark K. "Stranded in Japan and the Civil Liberties Act of 1988 Recognition for an Excluded Group of Japanese Americans." *Asian American Law Journal* 6 (January 1999): 151–186.

Harootunian, Harry. *Overcome by Modernity: History, Culture, and Community in Interwar Japan*. Princeton, New Jersey: Princeton University Press, 2000.

Havens, Thomas R. H. "Women and War in Japan, 1937–45." *The American Historical Review* 80, no. 4 (1975): 913–934.

———. *Valley of Darkness: The Japanese People and World War Two*. New York: W. W. Norton and Company, Inc., 1978.

"The Heritage and Future of Rikkyō." Mather Library Memorial Hall. Rikkyō University. November 26, 2014.

Higonnet, Margaret R. *Behind the Lines: Gender and the Two World Wars*. New Haven, Connecticut: Yale University Press, 1987.

Hirabayashi, James A. "Four Hirabayashi Cousins: A Question of Identity." In *Nikkei in the Pacific Northwest: Japanese Americans and Japanese Canadians in the Twentieth Century*, edited by Louis Fiset and Gail M. Nomura, 146–170. Seattle: University of Washington Press, 2005.

Hirabayashi, Lane Ryo, Akemi Kimura-Yano, and James A. Hirabayashi, eds. *New Worlds, New Lives: Globalization and People of Japanese Descent in the Americas and from Latin America in Japan*. Stanford: Stanford University Press, 2002.

Hirsch, Michael. "Pride, Pain Linger for Japanese-Americans Caught on Wrong Side of War." *Los Angeles Times*, September 9, 1990. Accessed February 13, 2015. http://articles.latimes.com/1990-09-09/news/mn-417_1_american-citizenship.

Hochschild, Arlie Russell. *The Managed Heart: Commercialization of Human Feeling*. Berkeley: University of California Press, 1983.

Hosokawa, Bill. *Nisei: The Quiet Americans*. Boulder, Colorado: University Press of Colorado, 2002.

Howe, Russell Warren. *The Hunt for "Tokyo Rose."* Lanham, Maryland: Madison Books, 1990.

Howell, David L. *Geographies of Identity in Nineteenth-Century Japan*. Berkeley: University of California Press, 2005.

Ichioka, Yuji. *The Issei: The World of the First Generation Japanese Immigrants, 1885–1924*. New York: The Free Press, 1988.

Ichioka, Yuji, Gordon H. Chang, and Eiichiro Azuma. *Before Internment: Essays in Prewar Japanese American History*. Stanford: Stanford University Press, 2006.

Inoue, Masahito. *Yōfuku to Nihonjin: Kokuminfuku to iu mōdo*. Tokyo: Kosaidō Shuppan, 2001.

Ishida, Gladys. "The Japanese American Renunciants of Okayama Prefecture: Their Accommodation and Assimilation into Japanese Culture." PhD diss., University of Michigan, Ann Arbor, 1955.

Jin, Michael. "Beyond Two Homelands: Migration and Transnationalism of Japanese Americans in the Pacific, 1930–1955." PhD diss., University of California, Santa Cruz, 2013.

———. "A Transnational Generation: Japanese Americans in the Pacific before World War II." *Ritsumeikan Studies in Language and Culture* 21, no. 4 (March 2010): 185–196.

———. "The Japanese American Transnational Generation: Rethinking the Spatial and Conceptual Boundaries of Asian America." In *The Routledge Handbook of Asian American Studies*, edited by Cindy I-Fen Cheng, 246–259. New York: Routledge, 2016.

Kadoike Hiroshi. *Nihon gunheishi ni natta Amerikajin tachi: Bokoku to tatakatta Nikkei Nisei.* Tokyo: Genshu Shuppansha, 2010.

Kadota Ryūshō. *Sōkai ni kiyu: Sokoku Amerika e tokkō shita kaigun shōi Matsufuji Ōji no shōgai.* Tokyo: Shūeisha, 2011.

Kahneman, Daniel. *Thinking, Fast and Slow.* New York: Farrar, Straus and Giroux, 2011.

Kaigun ni akogareta gunkoku shōnen: Minoru Teruya. Yokohama: JICA, February 2015. Exhibition material for "Nikkei Nisei ga mita senchū, sengo: Bokoku to sokoku no hazama de."

Kawashima, Yasuhide. *The Tokyo Rose Case: Treason on Trial.* Lawrence: University Press of Kansas, 2013.

Keys, Scott Matthew. "Shades of Gray: Japanese American Citizenship Renunciation During World War II." MA thesis, California State University, Fullerton, 2008.

Kiyota, Minoru. *Beyond Loyalty: The Story of a Kibei.* Translated by Linda Klepinger Keenan. Honolulu: University of Hawai'i Press, 1997.

Knaefler, Tomi Kaizawa. *Our House Divided: Seven Japanese American Families in World War II.* Honolulu: University of Hawai'i Press, 1991.

Koikari, Mire. "Exporting Democracy? American Women, 'Feminist Reforms,' and Politics of Imperialism in the U.S. Occupation of Japan, 1945–1952." *Frontiers* 23, no. 1 (2002): 23–45.

Koketsu Atsushi. *Kanshi to dōkatsu no jidai.* Tokyo: Shin Nihon Shuppansha, 2008.

Komiya Mayumi. *Tekikokujin yokuryū: Senjika no gaikoku minkanjin.* Tokyo: Yoshikawa Kōbunkan, 2003.

Komurasaki Toshio. "Senjika no gakkō kyōiku to gakudō sokai." In *Kataritsugu Shōwa shi: Utsusareta kiroku.* Vol. 2. Tokyo: Shinjinbutsu Ōraisha, 1993, 88–90.

Kumei, Teruko. "'The Twain Shall Meet' in the Nisei? Japanese Language Education and U.S.-Japan Relations, 1900–1940." In *New Worlds, New Lives: Globalization and People of Japanese Descent in the Americas and from Latin America in Japan*, edited by Lane Ryo Hirabayashi, Akemi Kimura-Yano, and James A. Hirabayashi, 108–125. Stanford: Stanford University Press, 2002.

Kushner, Barak. *The Thought War: Japanese Imperial Propaganda.* Honolulu: University of Hawai'i Press, 2006.

Kwon, Nayoung Aimee. "Collaboration, Coproduction, and Code-Switching: Colonial Cinema and Postcolonial Archaeology." *Cross-Currents: East Asian History and Culture Review* 5 (December 2012). E-Journal. http://cross-currents.berkeley.edu/e-journal/issue-5.

Lamont-Brown, Raymond. *Kempeitai: Japan's Dreaded Military Police.* Phoenix Mill Stroud, United Kingdom: Sutton Publishing, 1998.

Lazarus, Richard S. "Thoughts on the Relations Between Emotion and Cognition." *American Psychologist* 37, no. 9 (September 1982): 1019–1024.

McAndrew, Malia. "Beauty, Soft Power, and the Politics of Womanhood During the U.S. Occupation of Japan, 1945–1952." *Journal of Women's History* 23, no. 4 (2014): 83–107.

McDonald, Mary, and Thomas Mazawa, directors. *Nisei Stories of Wartime Japan.* 2012. 76 minutes.

McNaughton, James C. *Nisei Linguists: Japanese Americans in the Military Intelligence Service during World War II.* Washington, DC.: Department of the Army, 2006.

McVeigh, Brian. "Wearing Ideology: How Uniforms Discipline Minds and Bodies in Japan." *Fashion Theory: The Journal of Dress, Body & Culture* 1, no. 2 (1997): 189–214.

McWilliams, Carey. "The Nisei in Japan." *Far Eastern Survey* 13, no. 8 (April 1944): 70–72.

———. *Prejudice: Japanese-Americans: Symbol of Racial Intolerance.* Boston: Little, Brown, 1944.

Matsumoto, Valerie. *City Girls: The Nisei Social World in Los Angeles, 1920–1950.* New York: Oxford University Press, 2014.

Minami Hiroshi. *Kindai shomin seikatsushi.* Tōkyō: San'ichi Shobō, 1984.

Minamikawa Fuminori. *"Nikkei Amerikajin" no rekishi shakaigaku: Esunishiti, jinshu, nashonarizumu.* Tokyo: Sairyūsha, 2007.

Mitchell, Richard H. *Thought Control in Prewar Japan.* Ithaca, New York: Cornell University Press, 1976.

Miyake, Yoshiko. "Doubling Expectations: Motherhood and Women's Factory Work Under State Management in Japan in the 1930s and 1940s." In *Recreating Japanese Women, 1600–1945,* edited by Gail L. Bernstein, 267–295. Berkeley: University of California, 1991.

Mlodinow, Leonard. *Subliminal: How Your Unconscious Mind Rules Your Behavior.* New York: Vintage, 2012.

Moore, Brenda L. *Serving Our Country: Japanese American Women in the Military during World War II.* New Brunswick, New Jersey: Rutgers University Press, 2003.

Morris-Suzuki, Tessa. *East Asia beyond the History Wars: Confronting the Ghosts of Violence.* Milton Park, United Kingdom: Routledge, 2013.

———. *Re-inventing Japan: Time, Space, Nation.* Armonk, New York: M. E. Sharpe, 1998.

Murakawa Yōko. *Nichibei senji kōkansen, sengo sōkansen "kikoku"-sha ni kansuru kisoteki kenkyū: Nikkei Amerikajin no rekishi no shiten kara.* Tokyo: Toyota Zaidan, 1992.

"Nagai tabiji: Nihon hei ni natta Amerikajin (I)." NHK. First aired August 15, 2013. 50 minutes.

"Nagai tabiji: Nihon hei ni natta Amerikajin (II)." NHK. First aired August 16, 2013. 50 minutes.

Nagy, Margit. "Middle-Class Working Women During the Interwar Years." In *Recreating Japanese Women, 1600–1945,* edited by Gail L. Bernstein, 199–216. Berkeley: University of California, 1991.

Nakamura, Kelly Y. "They Are Our Human Secret Weapons: The Military Intelligence Service and the Role of Japanese-Americans in the Pacific War and in the Occupation of Japan." *Historian* 70, no. 1 (Spring 2008): 54–74.

Niiya, Brian, ed. *Encyclopedia of Japanese American History: An A-to-Z Reference from 1868 to the Present.* New York: Checkmark Books, 2001.

"Nikkei Nisei ga mita senchū, sengo: Bokoku to sokoku no aida de." Japan Overseas Migration Museum JICA. Yokohama, Japan. February 23, 2015.

Oguma, Eiji. *A Genealogy of "Japanese" Self-Images.* Translated by David Askew. Portland, Oregon: Trans Pacific Press, 2002.

Oikawa Yoshinobu and Maeda Kazuo. *Misshon sukūru to sensō: Rikkyō Gakuin no direnma.* Tokyo: Tōshindō, 2008.

Ōishi Itsuo. *Eigo wo kinshi seyo: Shirarezaru senjika no Nihon to Amerika.* Tokyo: Goma Shobō, 2007.

Orbaugh, Sharalyn. *Japanese Fiction of the Allied Occupation: Vision, Embodiment, Identity.* Leiden: Brill, 2007.

Osuga, William M., and Teruko Suga. *Aru Nikkei Nisei ga mita BC kyū senpan no saiban.* Tokyo: Sōshisha, 1991.

Phinney, Jean S., and Mona Devich-Navarro. "Variations in Bicultural Identification Among African American and Mexican American Adolescents." *Journal of Research on Adolescence* 7, no. 1 (1997): 3–32.

Randau, Carl, and Leane Zugsmith. *The Setting Sun of Japan.* New York: Random House, 1942.

Reddy, William. *The Navigation of Feeling: A Framework for the History of Emotions.* Cambridge, United Kingdom: Cambridge University Press, 2001.

Sakaguchi Mitsuhiro. *Nihon Amerika iminshi.* Tokyo: Fuji Shuppan, 2001.

Sánchez, María Carla, and Linda Schlossberg. *Passing: Identity and Interpretation in Sexuality, Race, and Religion.* New York: New York University Press, 2001.

Sanders, Holly. "Panpan: Streetwalking in Occupied Japan." *Pacific Historical Review* 81, no. 3 (August 2012): 404–431.

Sato, Barbara Hamill. *The New Japanese Woman: Modernity, Media, and Women in Interwar Japan.* Durham, North Carolina: Duke University Press, 2003.

Schonberger, Howard B. *Aftermath of War: Americans and the Remaking of Japan, 1945–1952.* Kent, Ohio: The Kent State University Press, 1989.

Seaton, Philip A. *Japan's Contested War Memories: The "Memory Rifts" in Historical Consciousness of World War II.* New York: Routledge, 2007.

"Senjika no seishun." Narusei Memorial Hall. Japan Women's University. Tokyo, Japan. November 11, 2014.

Shibusawa, Naoko. "Femininity, Race and Treachery: How 'Tokyo Rose' Became a Traitor to the United States after the Second World War." *Gender & History* 22, no. 1 (April 2010): 169–188.

"Shirarezaru 'dōhō kanshi': GHQ, Nihonjin ken'etsukan tachi no kokuhaku." NHK. Accessed November 5, 2013. www.nhk.or.jp/gendai/kiroku/detail_3425.html.

Shillony, Ben-Ami. *Politics and Culture in Wartime Japan.* Oxford: Clarendon Press, 1981.

Silverberg, Miriam. "Remembering Pearl Harbor, Forgetting Charlie Chaplin, and the Case of the Disappearing Western Woman: A Picture Story." *Positions* 1, no. 1 (1993): 24–76.

Siu, Paul C. P. "The Sojourner." *American Journal of Sociology* 58, no. 1 (1952): 34–44.

Smith, Bradford. *Americans from Japan*. Philadelphia: J. B. Lippincott, 1948.

Spickard, Paul R. *Japanese Americans: The Formation and Transformations of an Ethnic Group*. New York: Twayne, 1996.

———. "Twice Immigrants: Kibei in America and Japan and America, 1910–1950." Paper presented to Japanese American Experience conference, Willamette University, Salem, Oregon, September 18, 1998.

Spinks, Charles Nelson. "Indoctrination and Re-Education of Japan's Youth." *Pacific Affairs* 17, no. 1 (March 1944): 56–70.

Stephan, John J. *Hawaii Under the Rising Sun: Japan's Plans for Conquest After Pearl Harbor*. Honolulu: University of Hawai'i Press, 1984.

Steinberg, David Joel. *Philippine Collaboration in World War II*. Ann Arbor: University of Michigan Press, 1967.

Sterner, C. Douglas. *Go for Broke: The Nisei Warriors of World War II Who Conquered Germany, Japan, and American Bigotry*. Clearfield, Utah: American Legacy Historical Press, 2008.

Suzuki Jōji. *Nihonjin dekasegi imin*. Tokyo: Heibonsha, 1992.

Takeda, Kayoko. *Interpreting the Tokyo War Crimes Tribunal: A Sociopolitical Analysis*. Ottawa: University of Ottawa Press, 2010.

———. "The Role of Nisei (Second-Generation Japanese Americans) Linguists During World War II and the Allied Occupation of Japan." *Studies of Translation and Interpretation* 17 (2014): 161–174.

———. "The Visibility of Collaborators: Snapshots of Wartime and Postwar Interpreters." In *Framing the Interpreter: Towards a Visual Perspective*, edited by Anxo Fernández Ocampo and Michaela Wolf, 150–159. New York: Routledge, 2014.

Takemae Eiji. *Inside GHQ: The Allied Occupation of Japan and Its Legacy*. Translated by Sebastian Swann. Atlantic Highlands, New Jersey: Humanities Press International, 2002.

Takemoto Hideo. "Tōkyō YMCA no Nikkei Nisei kyōiku." In *Amerika Nikkei Nisei to ekkyō kyōiku*, edited by Yoshida Ryō, 57–80. Kyoto: Dōshisha Daigaku Jinbunkagaku Kenkyūjo, 2012.

Tang, Edward. *From Confinement to Containment: Japanese/American Arts during the Early Cold War*. Philadelphia: Temple University Press, 2019.

Tansman, Alan. *The Aesthetics of Japanese Fascism*. Berkeley: University of California Press, 2009.

Thomas, D. S., C. Kikuchi and J. Sakoda. *Japanese American Evacuation and Resettlement*. Vol. 2, *The Salvage*. Berkeley: University of California Press, 1952.

Toeda Hirokazu. "The Home Ministry and GHQ/SCAP as Censors of Literature: Media Regulations and the Battle Over Expression in 1920s–1940s Japan." In *Censorship, Media, and Literary Culture in Japan: From Edo to Postwar,* edited by Suzuki Tomi,

Toeda Hirokazu, Hori Hikari, and Munakata Kazushige, 96–107. Tokyo: Shin'yōsha, 2012.

"Tokyo Rose: Victim of Propaganda." *Biography*. A&E Networks. First aired August 9, 1995. 44 minutes. http://www.biography.com/people/tokyo-rose-37481.

Tsurumi Kazuko, *Social Change and the Individual: Japan before and after Defeat in World War II*. Princeton, New Jersey: Princeton University Press, 1970.

Uchiyama, Benjamin. *Japan's Carnival War: Mass Culture on the Home Front, 1937–1945*. Cambridge: Cambridge University Press, 2019.

Urata Minoru. *Senryōgun no yūbin ken'etsu to yūshu*. Tokyo: Nihon Yūshu Sābisusha, 1982.

Wilson, Sandra. "Family or State?: Nation, War, and Gender in Japan, 1937–45." *Critical Asian Studies* 38, no. 2 (2006): 209–238.

Yaguchi, Yujin. "Japanese Reinvention of Self through Hawai'i's Japanese Americans." *Pacific Historical Review* 83, no. 2 (November 2012): 333–349.

Yamaguchi, Precious. *Experiences of Japanese American Women during and after World War II: Living in Internment Camps and Rebuilding Life Afterwards*. Lanham, Maryland: Lexington Books, 2014.

Yamamoto Taketoshi. "Nihonjin ken'etsusha meibo kaisetsu." Website for Historical Studies of Censorship in Japan and the World. Accessed June 17, 2014. http://www.waseda.jp/prj-Kennetsu/explain.html.

Yamashita Sōen. *Nichibei wo tsunagu mono*. Tokyo: Bunseisha, 1938.

———. *Nikkei shimin no Nihon ryūgaku jijō*. Tokyo: Bunseisha, 1935.

Yamazaki Shunichi. *Hawai dekasegi jinmeibo shimakki: Nikkei imin no hyakunen*. Tokyo: Nihon Hōsō Shuppan Kyōkai, 1985.

Yenne, Bill. *Rising Sons: The Japanese American GIs Who Fought for the United States in World War II*. New York: Thomas Dunne, 2007.

Yoo, David. *Growing up Nisei: Race, Generation, and Culture among Japanese Americans of California, 1924–49*. Urbana: University of Illinois, 2000.

Yoshida, George. *Reminiscing in Swingtime: Japanese Americans in American Popular Music, 1925–1960*. San Francisco: National Japanese American Historical Society, 1997.

Yoshida Ryō. *Amerika Nihonjin imin to Kirisutokyō shakai: Kariforunia Nihonjin imin no haiseki, dōka to E. A. Sutōji*. Tokyo: Nihon Tosho Sentā, 1995.

Periodicals

Japan Times (Nippon Times)
Japan Times and Advertiser
Japan Times and Mail
Los Angeles Examiner
Los Angeles Times
Marin Independent Journal
The New York Times
Nichibei Shinbun

Pacific Citizen
Pacific Stars and Stripes
Seattle Times
Toronto Sun
U.S. News & World Report

Index

Page numbers in boldface type refer to illustrations.

ABOUT THE AUTHOR

A. CARLY BUXTON is a historian and user research consultant who focuses on human behavior and decision making. She earned her PhD in East Asian Languages and Civilizations at the University of Chicago, where she specialized in the history of Japan's colonial empire, assimilation policies, and propaganda. She lives in Richmond, Virginia, and can be found online at www.carlybuxton.com.